Mark Le Fanu is a well-known film critic who has contributed regular pieces to *Sight and Sound*, *Positif* and the *East – West Review*. A former Research Fellow at Downing College, Cambridge, he was Director of Studies in Film History at the European Film College in Ebeltoft, Denmark from 1993 to 2007, and now teaches at University College London. He is the author of *The Cinema of Andrei Tarkovsky* (1987) and *Mizoguchi and Japan* (2005), the latter shortlisted in its year of publication for the Kraszna-Krausz Moving Image Book of the Year.

'Mark Le Fanu's superb book offers a relaxed and urbane account of some of the great European film directors, focusing on the degree to which their work reflects a commitment to, obsession with or sometimes mere puzzlement over religion. This is writing which wears its learning lightly, and which allows a lifetime of watching and teaching films to inform descriptions that are always engaging and invariably revealing of why a film matters – why it delights or shocks (sometimes both at once), and above all why it demands our attention.'

– Gerard Loughlin, Professor of Theology, Durham University, author of *Alien Sex: The Body and Desire in Cinema and Theology*

'Mark Le Fanu addresses a fraught question here: why, in this secular era, do so many European directors draw upon religion in their feature films? This book is both erudite and engaging: newcomers to European cinema and aficionados alike will learn much from the author's analyses, which do not shy away from the personal: Le Fanu often reveals his own aesthetic judgments, and – in the Afterword – briefly and lightly situates this work in his own spiritual journey. I look forward to many hours of happy viewing, with this wonderful book as my guide.'

– Adele Reinhartz, Professor of Religious Studies, University of Ottawa, author of *The Bible and Cinema: An Introduction* and *Jesus of Hollywood*

Cinema and Society series
General Editor: Jeffrey Richards

Acting for the Silent Screen: Film Actors and Aspiration between the Wars
Chris O'Rourke

The Age of the Dream Palace: Cinema and Society in 1930s Britain
Jeffrey Richards

Banned in the USA: British Films in the United States and their Censorship, 1933–1960
Anthony Slide

Best of British: Cinema and Society from 1930 to the Present
Anthony Aldgate & Jeffrey Richards

Beyond a Joke: Parody in English Film and Television Comedy
Neil Archer

Brigadoon, Braveheart and the Scots: Distortions of Scotland in Hollywood Cinema
Colin McArthur

Britain Can Take It: British Cinema in the Second World War
Tony Aldgate & Jeffrey Richards

The British at War: Cinema, State and Propaganda, 1939–1945
James Chapman

British Children's Cinema: From the Thief of Bagdad to Wallace and Gromit
Noel Brown

British Cinema and the Cold War: The State, Propaganda and Consensus
Tony Shaw

British Film Design: A History
Laurie N. Ede

Children, Cinema and Censorship: From Dracula to the Dead End Kids
Sarah J. Smith

China and the Chinese in Popular Film: From Fu Manchu to Charlie Chan
Jeffrey Richards

Christmas at the Movies: Images of Christmas in American, British and European Cinema
Edited by Mark Connelly

The Classic French Cinema 1930–1960
Colin Crisp

The Crowded Prairie: American National Identity in the Hollywood Western
Michael Coyne

The Death Penalty in American Cinema: Criminality and Retribution in Hollywood Film
Yvonne Kozlovsky-Golan

Distorted Images: British National Identity and Film in the 1920s
Kenton Bamford

The Euro-Western: Reframing Gender, Race and the 'Other' in Film
Lee Broughton

An Everyday Magic: Cinema and Cultural Memory
Annette Kuhn

Family Films in Global Cinema: The World Beyond Disney
Edited by Noel Brown and Bruce Babington

Femininity in the Frame: Women and 1950s British Popular Cinema
Melanie Bell

Film and Community in Britain and France: From La Règle du jeu to Room at the Top
Margaret Butler

Film Propaganda: Soviet Russia and Nazi Germany
Richard Taylor

The Finest Years: British Cinema of the 1940s
Charles Drazin

Frank Capra's Eastern Horizons: American Identity and the Cinema of International Relations
Elizabeth Rawitsch

From Moscow to Madrid: European Cities, Postmodern Cinema
Ewa Mazierska & Laura Rascaroli

From Steam to Screen: Cinema, the Railways and Modernity
Rebecca Harrison

Hollywood and the Americanization of Britain: From the 1920s to the Present
Mark Glancy

The Hollywood Family Film: A History, from Shirley Temple to Harry Potter
Noel Brown

Hollywood Genres and Postwar America: Masculinity, Family and Nation in Popular Movies and Film Noir
Mike Chopra-Gant

Hollywood Riots: Violent Crowds and Progressive Politics in American Film
Doug Dibbern

Hollywood's History Films
David Eldridge

Hollywood's New Radicalism: War, Globalisation and the Movies from Reagan to George W. Bush
Ben Dickenson

Licence to Thrill: A Cultural History of the James Bond Films
James Chapman

The New Scottish Cinema
Jonathan Murray

Past and Present: National Identity and the British Historical Film
James Chapman

Powell and Pressburger: A Cinema of Magic Spaces
Andrew Moor

Projecting Tomorrow: Science Fiction and Popular Cinema
James Chapman & Nicholas J. Cull

Propaganda and the German Cinema, 1933–1945
David Welch

Shooting the Civil War: Cinema, History and American National Identity
Jenny Barrett

Spaghetti Westerns: Cowboys and Europeans from Karl May to Sergio Leone
Christopher Frayling

Spectacular Narratives: Hollywood in the Age of the Blockbuster
Geoff King

Typical Men: The Representation of Masculinity in Popular British Cinema
Andrew Spicer

The Unknown 1930s: An Alternative History of the British Cinema, 1929–1939
Edited by Jeffrey Richards

Withnail and Us: Cult Films and Film Cults in British Cinema
Justin Smith

Believing in Film: Christianity and Classic European Cinema
Mark Le Fanu

Believing in Film

Christianity and Classic European Cinema

Mark Le Fanu

BLOOMSBURY ACADEMIC
LONDON • NEW YORK • OXFORD • NEW DELHI • SYDNEY

BLOOMSBURY ACADEMIC
Bloomsbury Publishing Plc
50 Bedford Square, London, WC1B 3DP, UK
1385 Broadway, New York, NY 10018, USA

BLOOMSBURY, BLOOMSBURY ACADEMIC and the Diana logo are trademarks of
Bloomsbury Publishing Plc

First published in Great Britain by I.B.Tauris 2019
This edition published 2020

Copyright © Mark Le Fanu, 2019, 2020

Mark Le Fanu has asserted his right under the Copyright,
Designs and Patents Act, 1988, to be identified as Author of this work.

For legal purposes the Acknowledgements on pp. 256–7
constitute an extension of this copyright page.

Cover design: Chris Bromley
Cover image © Andrei Rublev, 1971, directed by Andrei Tarkovsky at Mosfilm Studios.
Actor Anatoly Solonitsyn as Andrei Rublev (Photo TASS).

All rights reserved. No part of this publication may be reproduced or transmitted in any
form or by any means, electronic or mechanical, including photocopying, recording, or
any information storage or retrieval system, without prior permission in writing from
the publishers.

Bloomsbury Publishing Plc does not have any control over, or responsibility for, any
third-party websites referred to or in this book. All internet addresses given in this book
were correct at the time of going to press. The author and publisher regret any inconvenience
caused if addresses have changed or sites have ceased to exist, but can accept no responsibility
for any such changes.

A catalogue record for this book is available from the British Library.

A catalog record for this book is available from the Library of Congress.

ISBN: HB: 978-1-7883-1144-1
PB: 978-1-350-16049-1
ePDF: 978-1-7867-3452-5
eBook: 978-1-7867-2452-6

Series: Cinema and Society

Typeset by OKS Prepress Services, Chennai, India

To find out more about our authors and books visit www.bloomsbury.com
and sign up for our newsletters

For Cristina de Gabriac

Contents

	General Editor's Introduction	xi
	Introduction	0
CHAPTER 1:	Russia: Tarkovsky, Eisenstein and Christianity	13
CHAPTER 2:	Poland: A Trio of Catholics	39
CHAPTER 3:	France: The Apostasy of Robert Bresson	67
CHAPTER 4:	Italy: Christianity and Neo-Realism	105
CHAPTER 5:	Scandinavia: Lutheran Interludes	141
CHAPTER 6:	Spain: The Heresies of Don Luis	177
CHAPTER 7:	Russia Again: Millennial Faith and Nihilism	209
	Afterword	251
	Acknowledgements	256
	List of Illustrations	258
	Bibliography	264
	Index	268

General Editor's Introduction

In this impressive and thought-provoking study, Mark Le Fanu explores the paradox that in an increasingly secular age religion remains a preoccupation of filmmakers. His focus is on the 'golden age of European art cinema', defined as the period from the 1940s to the 1980s. His analysis takes the form of a series of auteurist essays for which the cultural context is carefully established and the question of the state of belief is examined. In countries that were officially atheist like Russia or formally secular like France, that were Lutheran like Sweden or deeply Catholic like Italy and Spain, filmmakers of all shades of belief and none found themselves drawn to the theology and philosophy of belief. Le Fanu's subjects constitute a roll call of some of the most celebrated artists in cinema history: Eisenstein, Tarkovsky, Kieślowski, Bresson, Bergman, Dreyer, Buñuel, Rossellini and Pasolini among them. From Pasolini's *The Gospel According to St Matthew* and Bresson's *Diary of a Country Priest* to Buñuel's *Nazarín* and Bergman's *Winter Light*, many of the most admired and profound cinematic art works are subjected by Mark Le Fanu to close but subtle and nuanced critical scrutiny. The whole study adds up to a revealing meditation on a neglected aspect of film history, giving us a new dimension to the interface between art and belief.

Jeffrey Richards

Introduction

At some stage in European civilisation, Christianity ceased to be the paramount driving force; it ceased to be both the primary inspiration of art, and the measure of that art's true value – its final court of appeal, so to speak. It is difficult to say exactly when this happened. Dante and the great cathedrals are one thing; obviously, here we are in the presence of pure unblemished faith. But already by Shakespeare's time, space had been made for scepticism. There is a famous essay by the Hispano-American philosopher George Santayana called 'The Absence of Religion in Shakespeare', where he ponders how curious it is that, in such a purportedly religious age, the Church and Christianity are so seldom referred to explicitly across the breadth of that mighty output. Indeed Santayana detects, or says he detects, only two or three places in Shakespeare's total production where 'genuinely religious speech' may be encountered (he names these as (1) the passage commemorating the Duke of Norfolk in *Richard II*; (2) the 'unmixed piety' of Henry V after Agincourt ('Take it God, for it is none but thine'); and (3) the sonnet beginning 'Poor soul, the centre of my sinful earth'. And even here Santayana has hesitations: 'In all this depth of experience [...] there is still wanting any *religious image*. The Sonnets are spiritual [...] but they are not Christian,' he writes). Modern scholarship would tend not to go along with this assessment, as we shall see in a moment, but meanwhile it is interesting to discover no less an eminence than T.S. Eliot (a Christian himself of course – one might even say notoriously so) weighing in on Santayana's side of the argument in another classic essay, 'Shakespeare and the Stoicism of Seneca' (1927). The touchstone for 'pure' Christianity here is once again Dante; Eliot wants to show that by Shakespeare's submitting himself to the trio of powerful literary-philosophical influences made up of Montaigne ('scepticism'), Machiavelli ('cynicism') and Seneca ('pride' or 'wilfulness'), the playwright was imperceptibly moving into modern territory – at any event, distancing himself from the truth of the Gospels. The plays' *essential* allegiance, Eliot argues, is to a certain kind of 'irreligious individualism'. It is hard to know, in the last resort, how seriously Eliot is committing himself to this view of the matter (the essay starts by complaining that Shakespeare means anything to anyone – thus 'take your pick', so to speak), but we might end up agreeing that there is a basic underlying plausibility to what is being sketched here. For the piety of Dante is surely palpable (Eliot quotes the famous line 'E'n la sua volontade è nostra pace'); whereas one can't dismiss the fact that – whether one's talking about Macbeth's 'Out out, brief candle' speech or an epigram from *Lear*, such as 'As flies to wanton boys are we to the gods; they kill us for their sport' – so many of the most memorable moments in Shakespeare have a strikingly non-Christian flavour.

Shakespeare the man must not be confused with his characters; that basic orthodoxy is plainly sound wisdom. Modern scholarship, as hinted above, has tended to bring God back into Shakespeare's plays, at least at the linguistic (if not at the plot) level. Daniel Swift's recently much-praised study, *Shakespeare's Common Prayers* (2013), follows the lead of an earlier monograph, *Cranmer's Sentences* (1999) by Ian Robinson, in tracing the poet's profoundest debt to the Book of Common Prayer. Not only is Shakespeare's language saturated by Archbishop Cranmer's famous cadences, but (if we are to follow Swift's argument) so is his *mise en scène*. Again and again across the breadth of the plays, it is argued, the ceremoniousness of Shakespeare's staging decisions can be linked to one or another of the four rites of the Church of England Prayer Book: marriage, communion, baptism and burial. This is all heady stuff, in its quiet scholarly way, and needs to be thought about carefully. Certainly, it does not on the surface seem to be reconcilable with Santayana's classic take on the plays. Other recent writers have made different contributions to the debate: James Shapiro, for example, in his rather wonderful book on Shakespeare and the year 1606, points out that, following a parliamentary decree against blasphemy dating from early in King James's reign, no explicit reference was henceforth allowed to be made on stage either to God or to the Christian religion, including (and perhaps even especially) characters being allowed to make use of oaths ('zounds', 'sblood!' etc.) – a rather more technical explanation than Santayana's, if it is true, for 'the absence of religion in Shakespeare'. Meanwhile, David Scott Kastan, in *A Will to Believe: Shakespeare and Religion* (2014), praises Daniel Swift's linguistic and liturgical research but mildly disagrees with him about the importance of the plays' 'sacramental echoes'. On the contrary, Kastan is as fascinated as everyone has always been by Shakespeare's religious invisibility, his complete absence of anger and fanaticism. Was he a Catholic? Or a loyal Protestant? Or neither? There is no evidence anywhere in the plays to say what Shakespeare 'really' believed – if indeed he believed in anything at all.

Atheism was rare at the time we are talking about, but perhaps we may agree that doubt was commonplace, as it has always been – even among the clergy. Here is an extract from a sermon preached by John Donne on New Year's Day, 1625:

> So if that *infectious inquisition*, that *Quare*, (*Why* should God command this or this particular?) be entred into me, all my *humilitie* is presently infected, and I shall looke for a reason, why God made a world, or why he made a world no sooner than 6000 yeares agoe, and why he saves *some*, and why *but some*, and I shall examine God upon all the *Interrogatories* that I can frame, upon the *Creed* (why should I believe the Sonne of a Virgin without a Man, or believe the Sonne of God to descend into Hell).

Or frame upon the *Pater Noster*, (why should I worship such a God, that must be prayed to, *not to lead me into tentation?*) Or frame upon the *Ten Commandments*, why after all is done and heapt, for any sinfull action, yet I should be guilty of all, for coveting in my heart another mans horse or house. And therfore Luther pursues it farther, with words of more vehemence, *Odiosa & exitialis vocula*, *Quare*, It is an Execrable and Damnable Monosillable, *Why*; it exasperates God, it ruines us.

'A passage like this reminds us', writes Tobias Gregory (in a sympathetic review of a new collection of essays on the poet-priest edited by Janel Mueller),

> that the implausibility of Christian fundamentals was plain to see in the early 17th century, freely conceded by the respectable 52-year-old dean of St Paul's. There was no age, golden or dark, of general untroubled belief. Potentially unsettling questions might occur to anyone. Virgin birth? Really? Ministers would provide answers where they could, but it was safer to snuff out the questioning before it got started. Donne, in this passage, wasn't trying to puzzle his auditors with fresh doubts; he assumed they had doubts already.

'There was no age, golden or dark, of general untroubled belief.' I think we have to take that for granted. Christianity's powerful self-confidence survived the revival of interest in classical pagan art that is one of the defining features of the Renaissance. Almost nothing in European culture is more extraordinary than the way that artists like Caravaggio and Rubens (and other contemporaries of Shakespeare and Donne) were able to produce titanically convincing works of art in *both* idioms. Religion was still a living reality for them; it was not to be thrust aside by their delight in pagan physical exuberance. As the centuries progressed, however, that miraculous equilibrium between sacred and profane slowly disintegrated. Religion did not 'drop out of' painting, but it became, one would have to say, a much weaker field force. Goya and Delacroix are probably the last of the Old Masters whose religious paintings could be argued to exist at the same level of accomplishment and beauty as the rest of their production. The canvases in question (I am thinking of a painting like Delacroix's 1853 *Christ on the Sea of Galilee* or the various versions of the *Lamentation* that Henry James admired so much) have a genuine, not merely a nominal, intensity. Elsewhere at this time – in the work of the Pre-Raphaelites, for example – religion tends to be sentimental and illustrative, though of course it was still hugely present across society (one only has to think of those acres of Victorian stained glass). Since we are talking of painters, Van Gogh occupies an interesting place in this trend we are noting; deeply pious himself on a personal level, and the author of several explicitly figurative biblical paintings (for example, a fine *Christ and the Virgin* from 1889 based on a pietà by Delacroix), he came to feel that the depiction of the Holy Figures and their gestures was no longer possible in modern art. Those gestures didn't 'add up', they didn't communicate conviction. His solution was to fall back on bare landscape; the beautiful painting *Olive Trees* (from the same year, 1889) is essentially a synecdoche for a painting that might have been called 'Christ in the Garden of Olives'. The onlooker is supposed to intuit the meaning of the canvas by supplying, on his own accord, and out of his own religious understanding, the absent bowed figure of Our Saviour.

In the field of music, too, Christianity, though embattled, was, and is, by no means a spent force – one only has to think of the great nineteenth-century requiems. The ancient liturgy of the Mass absorbed the new musical harmonies and, through their conjoint solemnity, took care of the question of 'belief', even when the composer, like Verdi, was not known to be a friend of the Church. Wagner (who of course wrote no requiem) was also a liberal and free thinker, like Verdi – at least in the early part of his career. The mighty operas that make up the *Ring* cycle construct an heroic mythology that owes nothing, on the surface, to the Christian religion, and might even justly be called 'anti'-Christian. *Parsifal* and

Lohengrin are another matter, however. Here the emphasis on sacrifice and redemption that is such a strong feature of the *Ring*'s metaphysics (as it also is, in a different way, in an opera like *Tristan and Isolde*) takes on what has to be called a markedly Christian flavour; it is famously the reason why Nietzsche broke with the composer. Exactly *how* Christian these liturgical verse dramas are (especially in view of their erotic element) continues to be a fascinating question, but we can say at least they are 'inflected with' religion.

Out-and-out atheism, on the other hand, on the public stage, probably had to wait until a writer like Ibsen. When it arrived it must have been very shocking. It *was* shocking, we know – so shocking as to have the work of this provincial Norwegian playwright banned in several quarters. (*Ghosts* was first put on in Chicago.) If we talk about 'atheism' in Ibsen's context, it is not because the existence or non-existence of the Deity is explicitly debated in his drama (at least in the plays that I am familiar with), but rather because the very premises of the action – the way the psychology is put together – seems to place an absolute ban on metaphysical consolation. (An important contrast with opera here; until the twentieth century, music was *always* consolatory, in some degree.) Incest, divorce, euthanasia, the inheritance of venereal disease – these subjects find their place in Ibsen's drama in profoundly complicated combinations – at once highly lucid to the audience and tantalisingly mysterious and non-political – and somehow we intuit that there are no illusions left. These deviations from the norm exist in all societies, Ibsen seems to say, and if they are 'wrong' or immoral, they are not wrong because God decreed them to be. (The affinity between Ibsen's plays and Freud's writings has often been noted.)

With the arrival of Ibsen on the international scene, closely followed by the no less revolutionary impact of Chekhov, it is possible to argue that drama on the stage (the serious stage, that is; frivolity, melodrama and entertainment have always been a large part of the theatre) will henceforth be secular in spirit. That remains true for the most part. And yet it is not saying anything new, I suppose, to point out that Christianity in the twentieth century enjoyed a long and prosperous afterlife in culture; and that even in the twenty-first century its concerns can still seem to speak to us urgently. No, religion definitively hasn't 'died out', though it has had, and continues to have, influential enemies. Ibsen, since we have singled him out for discussion, looks forward to Ingmar Bergman and to the twentieth-century artform of cinema, with which this book is concerned. How strange to discover that *that* Scandinavian artist, at important stages of his career, was not merely tangling with Christian themes, but acquiescing in Christian 'solutions'. Once Bergman has been brought into the discussion, a plethora of other well-known names suggest themselves: Fellini, Eisenstein, Bresson, Dreyer, Tarkovsky, Kieślowski – even Luis Buñuel, the great atheist. All of these cineastes have been profoundly influenced by Christianity in one way or another. It will be the purpose of these pages, then, to explore this perhaps paradoxical phenomenon, and to try to make sense of it on a personal basis. The chapters that follow, I should say now, make no pretence of presenting a sociological survey of the topic. On the contrary, they are partial and partisan. They include some obvious names but not others. The approach is 'auteurist' in flavour and substance, because I happen to think that is the best way to write about cinema (as it is the best way to write about literature and music) – as long as it is *also* understood, as it surely must be nowadays, that any given film is at the same time a collective endeavour, drawing together a huge number of disparate talents.

The main criterion for inclusion in the chapters that follow is that the directors I write about should be 'insiders' – that they show sympathy towards Christianity, and a talent for understanding its inner workings, even when (or if) they are intent on being critical of its pretensions. There have been any number of films in recent years (some of them artistically excellent) which speak about Christianity from a hostile point of view, exposing its so-called hypocrisy, and lamenting its dire effect upon those caught up by its influence. I have not chosen to write about these films on the whole.[1] But the question of *how* hostile, or friendly, has given rise to some difficult choices. Readers may legitimately wonder why, if directors like Buñuel and (in the book's modern passages) Sokurov and Muratova are included, no room has been made for extended discussions of Almodóvar, or von Trier, or Haneke, or (even) Jean-Luc Godard – artists postmodernist in temperament but plainly intelligent, to a certain degree, about our topic. I can only repeat in response what I said a moment ago, that my book is an essay, not a treatise; it aims to be suggestive rather than exhaustive. Exhaustive is 'exhausting', I find; my inclusions are perhaps long enough already. The main cut-off point is taken care of, I hope, by recourse to the word 'European' in the book's subtitle; a deliberate choice has been made *not* to extend my enquiry to the Americans. Classic Hollywood cinema grew out of two great traditions, those of comedy and melodrama; and melodrama, in the American context, most certainly does contain important Christian elements. It would have been challenging as well as enjoyable to have examined the Christian bona fides (as well as the pathos and sentimentality) of directors as various as D.W. Griffith, King Vidor, Frank Borzage and Cecil B. de Mille – as well as more recent artists like Schrader, Malick and Scorsese. But that is for another book, not the current one. 'Classic' in the subtitle (next to 'European') has already been granted, the reader

---

[1] Having alluded to this body of work I should perhaps at least name a few of the more recent examples. There is, for instance, a subgenre of modern filmmaking that explores (often sensitively and with psychological finesse) the way that the feelings of adolescents may be hijacked by the demands of family church circles. Among the best of these: *Corpo Celeste* (Alice Rohrwacher, 2011), *Stations of the Cross* (Dietrich Brüggemann, 2014), *Worldly Girl/La Ragazza del Mondo* (Marco Daniel, 2016), *Thelma* (Joachim Trier, 2017) and *Apostasy* (Daniel Kokotajlo, 2018). *Ida* (Pawel Pawlikowski, 2013) belongs residually to this group, though perhaps, on reflection, it is not really so hostile to Catholicism. Much more scathing about the Church's catastrophic moral failings in the sphere of caring for the young and the vulnerable is a group of Irish-based movies: *The Magdalene Sisters* (Peter Mullen, 2002), *Philomena* (Stephen Frears, 2013) and *Calvary* (John Michael MacDonagh, 2014). (Yet in the latter case, too, we should note that the lone priest at the centre of the drama, played by Brendan Gleeson, is treated on the whole sympathetically.)

will soon surmise, latitudinarian privileges. Thus, the main focus of the book is on directors who were operating in what may loosely be called the golden age of European art cinema, from the time of World War II up to and including the 1980s. Films that appeared in this period were made long enough ago to have *become* classics. Yet cinema is a vibrant, living artform, so I have found it important at times, for example in my thoughts about Russia, to extend the discussion forward, up to the millennium and beyond. Readers, especially younger ones, may wish I had done this more often. I have my own regrets about omissions, in addition to those European modernists already mentioned (Godard, von Trier etc.). In the chapter on Lutheran Scandinavia it would have been apposite to have included at least some words on that beautiful Christian parable *Babette's Feast*, for example. My extensive discussion of *Le journal d'un curé de campagne* in the chapter on Bresson could, perhaps, have been extended even further to consider other French films about priests such as (both magnificent in their own way) Jean-Pierre Melville's *Léon Morin Prêtre* (1961) and Maurice Pialat's *Sous le soleil de Satan* (1987). In general, my meditation on Bresson's Catholicism could profitably have been brought up to date (if up-to-dateness were the primary criterion) by a reflection not only on Eric Rohmer's films (the 'next' interesting Catholic director, so to speak), but on the work of more equivocal French commentators on religion like Bruno Dumont. Some readers will think Germany has been short-changed; Werner Herzog might have been looked at, with his grand idea of Ecstatic Truth, along with Wim Wenders, whose *Wings of Desire/Himmel über Berlin* (1988) handles with delicacy the conceit of the whispering of angels. Edgar Reitz's *Heimat*, in its three majestic *volets* the greatest German film in the latter part of the twentieth century, has no Christianity in it at all, alas, though I would be the first to agree that in scope and depth it represents a profoundly spiritual endeavour. Finally, there is a whole recent strand of Romanian filmmaking to think about, which, like the cinemas of other countries emerging from communism, has many fresh pertinent things to say about our topic. An old Chinese expression, 'following the brush', accounts for the way a writer makes decisions on such matters. He or she has to be sensitive to where the brush leads him – and to where it doesn't!

Christianity is a belief system as well as an allegiance. When someone claims to be a 'believer', what does it actually mean? It is salutary to bear in mind how exigent are the demands of faith, traditionally. The Kingdom of Heaven, we are reminded by the Gospels, is a 'pearl of great price', as also, in another parable, a 'hidden treasure'; and to find that hidden treasure the would-be inductee into Christ's mysteries must be ready to sacrifice all his or her worldly possessions. 'Those who do not believe in the kingdom of heaven enough to stake their whole future on it are unworthy of the kingdom,' so the Book says. Christ's teaching is not always 'nice' or 'liberal'. In the parables there is a lot of railing against the wicked who, making the *wrong* choice, are condemned to the suffering characterised as 'wailing and gnashing of teeth'. Such sentiments occupy a place on the 'spectrum of belief' at whose opposite ends one finds emphasised a more forgiving and inclusive understanding of the Gospels' tremendous invitation. 'Suffer the little children to come unto me,' Christ said. At the heart of the Christian system of belief is a vision of radical innocence, an intuition that we are all in some way salvageable, and maybe this is more important than anything else. And yet ... If Christianity is going to be more than mere spiritualised liberalism, there are a few other things that one has to take seriously, chief of which, surely: a sense of the existence of the Almighty, and of His approachability through submission and prayer. The Christian feels that he (she) can speak to God; the atheist finds the idea meaningless. (The distinction seems to be simple, though it isn't of course. My late wife – an atheist – used to say she wasn't sure she believed in God, but she was certain she believed in Bach. And yet, is it not the case that to believe in Bach is to believe in God? At least, that is what I told her, cleaving to the argument which asks, what are the great Masses and Cantatas if they are not *also* worship and prayer?)[2] Resurrection and, with it, the sublime promise of Eternal Life are further items in the Christian belief system that one might think of as non-negotiable, unless one is of the mind that, in the end, *everything* that has to do with religion must be – can only be – understood poetically. Perhaps there are Christians who don't believe in Heaven literally; indeed, I'm sure there are. (But then again, what does 'literally' mean in that last sentence?) As to where, on the spectrum between the 'literal' and the 'metaphorical', lie the beliefs of the film directors studied in this book, that must finally be, in each case, a matter of speculation, I think, not of certainty. At any event, it surely varies greatly. Nonetheless, in order to keep some self-discipline in the matter, I have tried, at intervals, to remind myself that not all films about redemption are necessarily, and for that very reason, Christian.

Nineteenth-century opera in Wagner's hands (to go back to that controversial giant for a moment) was to be nothing less than a 'total work of art'. In the theatre he had built for him in Bayreuth, he and his producers were theoretically able to control all aspects of the *mise en scène* towards the final goal of making the experience numinous. Thus the orchestra pit was sunk below floor level so that there should be as small a gap as possible between audience and singers; both parties would commune, immersively, over the heads of the musicians. Light too was to be carefully calibrated so that the stage, when necessary, could be made to replicate the dimness of old cathedral interiors. And so on. All this was part of Wagner's plan to reintroduce the sacred into the experience of theatre-going. As such, it had enormous influence on later experiments in the staging of drama, from Gordon Craig to Max Reinhardt and beyond. It was not part of Wagner's goal – how could it be? – that an artform named 'cinema' should be the culmination of this radical enterprise; but that, in a way, was what happened. Cinema began very modestly; but the advent of the epic in the early years of the twentieth century, first in Italy

---

[2] G.F. Handel too. I have often thought that all that anyone needs of practical Christianity, Old Testament and New, is contained within the scope of the *Messiah*.

and then in the United States, soon enough brought a grandeur to spectacle that Wagner, had he lived, could only have envied. Crucially, light and darkness could be controlled far more subtly than in the theatre. Also, there was the strange fact that, for the first 30 years or so of cinema's existence, this new form of drama was silent; communication from screen to audience took place without words (though not, of course, without intertitles or music). It would be wrong to say that cinema became, through these means, a *substitute* for ordinary pious church-going; but the communal, ritualistic, trance-like and, as it were, non-rational aspects of the experience of film provide suggestive parallels between the two activities – parallels that are relevant, I hope, to the ongoing concerns of our enquiry.

Meanwhile, the twenty-first century has brought many innovations to the artform. In particular, the advent of the long-running television series has altered the ways that it is necessary to think about, and to practise, the art of writing about film. Television, of course, is experienced in the home, not the picture palace – with a consequent falling off in 'numinosity', grandeur, sublimity, *presence*. The substitution of digital for celluloid-based technologies, in both the shooting of movies and their screening, introduces further complications that one might be tempted to call profound: the light is not the same any more. Where celluloid was a living medium, capable of registering the subtlest of nuances, digital reproduction, in all its fierce brightness, brings with it a sort of deadness and artificiality which, it could be argued, is not conducive to the spirit. Doubtless, new ways will be found to come to terms with the phenomenological changes taking place in our vast weekly consumption of visual material. For the time being, however, the one-off feature film – of on average between one-and-a-half and two hours' duration (and traditionally crafted with a certain amount of care and production value, whether celluloid-based or digitally reproduced) – survives as a viable art form. It has a noble history! How lucky we are that we can still see films in the cinema, and (if they are 'classics') in our various national cinematheques.

FIGURE 1 A modern Christian epic: Tarkovsky's *Andrei Roublev*.

1

Russia: Tarkovsky, Eisenstein and Christianity

The epic quality of cinema spectacle has been a defining aspect of its identity since the experiments of Griffith and the Italians in the early teens of the twentieth century. Like everything else in art, the genre finds itself, every so often, in need of renewal. Perhaps no modern example of this renovating imperative in epic made a greater impact than Tarkovsky's *Andrei Roublev*, shot during the period 1965–6 but only released in Russia in 1971 after bitter spats with the Soviet authorities. The ostensible concern of the censors was with the film's explicit violence and sexuality, but the secret (yet in retrospect obvious) reason for official displeasure can more plausibly be traced to the fact of its contours being unmistakably Christian. Christian in subject matter of course – the movie deals with the life of the monk/icon-painter Roublev as he travels round Russia in the early years of the fifteenth century – but Christian also, more importantly, in sympathy and allegiance.

I am assuming here that it was the latter aspect that really caused all the trouble, for after all it is theoretically possible to tell such a tale in a manner that subordinates the historical and contingent practices of religious belief to the supposedly deeper truth of dialectical materialism. There is indeed a lot of 'talk' in *Andrei Roublev* – too much for some people – yet insofar as the viewer manages to decipher the sometimes obscure and rambling dialogues that take place at intervals in the action between Andrei and his priest-companions, rather little of it is subsumable to the categories of orthodox Marxism. On the contrary, both the language and the spirit are theological. Shocking in the Soviet Union, where atheism had been inscribed as official state ideology for nigh on half-a-century, this state of affairs was perhaps no less shocking to filmgoers in the West, where (following a bungled attempt at repression by the Soviet film agency Gosfilmofond) the film was released in 1969 and received wide contemporary exposure. The shock, if one can call it that, may be described in two ways. It was an aesthetic shock first of all; the film's extraordinary energy and formal inventiveness made a deep impression on everyone who saw it. But beyond this first level of technical grandeur lay a deeper wonder for people inclined to think about such things, which was: how on earth, in a country like the Soviet Union, did the filmmakers think they could get away with it?

In the years that have unfolded since the movie's release, a number of studies have delved into the cultural background of Tarkovsky and his co-scenarist Konchalovsky (the latter still alive as I write, a frequent and articulate visitor to the West). Conferences, documentaries and informal cultural exchanges across borders in the decades since the collapse of communism have allowed researchers to investigate the private beliefs of intellectuals and artists in the Soviet period in some detail, and to document soundly what had merely once been an intuition, namely that the proscription placed by the State on religious observance never succeeded in banishing *the habit of thought about religion* from ordinary cultural life at all levels.

Tarkovsky and Konchalovsky belonged to the generation of Soviet (or, as I would prefer to call them, Russian) filmmakers who came to maturity at the time of Khrushchev's 'thaw', and it is clear that other filmmakers besides them benefited from the relative intellectual freedom of the time to write and direct movies that challenged materialist ideology. The Georgian-born Armenian director Sergei Parajanov (1924–90) springs to mind as an obvious example to place beside Tarkovsky and Konchalovsky, though in his case there were indeed repercussions in the legal sphere; his outspokenness led to periods of imprisonment. Such films by Parajanov as *Shadows of Our Forgotten Ancestors* (1964) (made in Ukraine) and *The Colour of Pomegranates* (1968) are among the most beautiful works of art of this period, in any medium. Each of them, though very different in form and content, has immense spiritual power, as well as being visually and musically gorgeous. Their outspokenness lay not so much in any direct call to religious belief – religion, as such, plays little part in the narrative development of *Shadows of Our Forgotten Ancestors* – as in the unmistakable feeling communicated to viewers of the irrelevance of atheistic communism in defining the values and traditions that the movies are interested in honouring. Religion is 'invisibly' there, so to speak, built into their texture, beauty and historical accuracy – even into the way the characters talk to each other.

Now it is true that a lofty and pious humanism had always been part – perhaps indeed a defining part – of a certain strand of Soviet

FIGURE 2 'Among the most beautiful works of art of this period, in any medium'. Sergei Parajanov's *The Colour of Pomegranates* (1968).

filmmaking (I am thinking of a director like Tarkovsky's friend Vassily Shukshin, but also others I like such as Khutsiev, Klimov, Panfilov and even Mikhalkov); yet these films by Parajanov pushed the issue a crucial step further in the direction of saying, or implying, 'No, there is nothing wrong with religion after all.' In fact he was not alone in this endeavour. A comparable, though differently expressed, boldness may be found in certain other directors of the time; Larissa Shepitko, for example, whose brief career, cut short by a fatal motor accident, occupies a significant landmark in late Soviet filmmaking. Thus, while the Western filmgoer was free (eventually) to admire the audacity, in the pre-Gorbachev era, of a movie like *Andrei Roublev*, he or she could *also* see and wonder about a movie like Shepitko's *The Ascent*, released in the following decade, though still many years before the collapse of the system.

Adapted from a novel by Vassily Bykov, the film, which came out in 1977, follows the inner spiritual journey of two contrasted partisans, Sotnikov and Rybak, seeking to evade capture in Nazi-occupied western Russia during the war. Rybak seems much the stronger, both physically

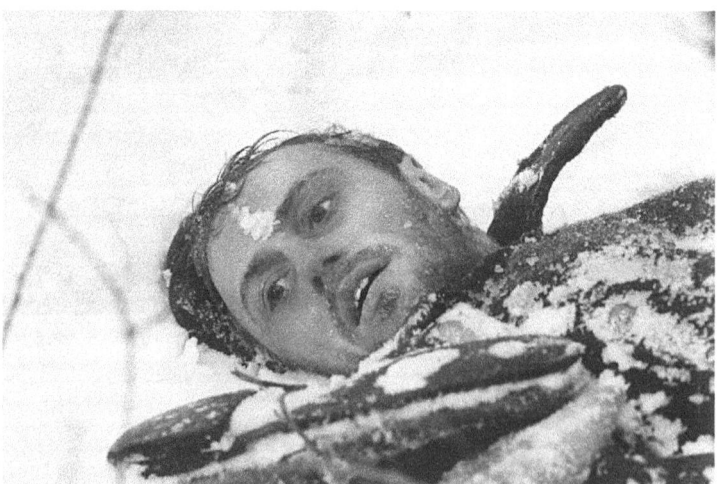

FIGURE 3   'Finding [...] the moral strength to face what is going to happen to him'. Boris Plotnikov as the Christ-like partisan Sotnikov in Larissa Shepitko's *The Ascent* (1977).

and mentally, of the two, and indeed constantly gives his companion succour; but when they are finally captured it is Sotnikov, the weakling, who shows truest fortitude in the face of the trials that await them. For fate has delivered them into the hands of a truly terrifying adversary, a nihilistic Russian interrogator in the pay of the Nazis, played with Dostoevskian brilliance by one of Tarkovsky's favourite actors, Anatoly Solonitsyn. With deft and subtle precision the film mines the complexities of conscience. The weak man, Sotnikov, finds the strength to face whatever it is that is going to happen to him, up to and including the inevitable end: a grisly death by hanging, which we witness. By contrast, Rybak's initially admirable life force (he at any event will do anything to escape his captors, in order to carry on the anti-Nazi struggle) is shown at a certain crucial moment to become corrupted into its opposite: a craven fear of personal extinction that allows him to bargain with the enemy and to betray the trust of his comrade in adversity. The important point to make, for criticism, is not, here, that the film is explicitly 'Christian' – though in a sense that is true; the interrogator is the devil, Rybak is Judas, the scenes leading up to the execution, along with the title of the film itself, make plain reference to the Christian Passion – but that its moral vocabulary, transcending Kantian humanism, belongs in the deepest sense to the traditions of world religion. The film is not able to be understood *unless* such concepts as sin, redemption and witness – notions that also belong to Judaism, of course, and to other religions – are allowed to be still-living categories.

Tarkovsky's later films take up this notion of sacrifice. A believer himself on a personal basis (as his diaries, full of plangent invocations to the Almighty, make clear), he was plainly, I would think, during his tragically abbreviated life, the most important modern *Christian* filmmaker. More than almost any other contemporary film artist, he tells us what he thinks without coquetry; he is absolutely *not* a postmodernist. Yet his Christianity is not without mystery; it is sometimes hard to say exactly and precisely *how* he is a Christian. His autobiographical film *The Mirror* (1974) manages to avoid the topic, or else broaches it only obliquely, through cultural reference to previous Christian artists (Leonardo, Pushkin, Bach etc.) None of the main characters is specifically glimpsed at prayer, though an iconography of hands (above all, hands held up so that light glimmers through them) forms an important visual motif of the movie. *Stalker* (1979), meanwhile, his next film (and the last that he made in Russia), is underpinned by an idea that is more psychoanalytical than religious: that we must be careful about the purity of our wishes (or else they will come back and bite us). This puzzling maxim is in any case borrowed from *Roadside Picnic*, the tale by the Strugatsky brothers upon which the movie is based, and is not necessarily one that Tarkovsky swore by. Nonetheless, there is a 'sort of detectable Christian undercurrent to the film, connected to humility and sacrifice and patience, qualities that are also at the heart of *Nostalghia* (1983), this time with a more recognisable Christian iconography of candles, churches and grandly beautiful images of the Madonna.

And yet *Nostalghia* is detectably pagan too! At least, the scenes set in Rome strike me as being so. The whole subplot concerning the self-immolation of the protagonist's friend Domenico (Erland Josephson), who sets himself alight in the Campidoglio after mounting the back of the equestrian statue of Marcus Aurelius, is intractable to Christian interpretation; it belongs, as imagery, to some other worldview – the Viking pyre, perhaps, or the grim godless lessons of the auto-da-fé.

If light is 'obviously' religious, fire, as a symbol, can be, depending on context, both Christian and *not* Christian. At any event, it is difficult not to see that Tarkovsky is in love with its properties. He makes it the climax to the last film he ever made, *Sacrifice* (1986), set in Sweden, in which, in response to a private vow made to God (who has allowed him to survive the night and to save the world from nuclear destruction), the protagonist Alexander makes a bonfire of his house and possessions before surrendering his person to a hastily summoned ambulance crew. He leaves behind a six-year-old son, and this child tends a little tree he has planted beside the ocean.

FIGURE 4 An unintended flavour of paganism? Domenico (Erland Josephson) in Tarkovsky's *Nostalghia* (1983).

So we are left with a feeling of redemption, though the imagery is not transparently that of the Christian story. Still, it is not *not Christian* either! That is how difficult Tarkovsky is. He 'speaks out', but he also hides things. He hates symbolism, but he is a symbolist. If we are looking for the simplicity of an 'edifying parable', we will most likely have to search elsewhere.

*

Let's return at this point to Russia, and to history. With its victory in 1917, and then again in 1921, Bolshevism launched an all-out attack on the past. The intention was to replace traditional religious faith with the newly forged religion of humanity. The godless New Man and New Woman are the subject matter, at bottom, of all art in the Soviet period, though of course how the phenomenon manifested itself differed widely from artist to artist and from decade to decade. The tone at the outset was brashly militant; a certain atheistic dogmatism and truculence seems to be, in retrospect, an inescapable ingredient of the work of the great silent masters, Eisenstein, Dovzhenko, Pudovkin and Dziga Vertov (to take only the four most famous of them). Modern commentary on these filmmakers tends to distance itself from the necessity of taking a position, one way or another, regarding the truth or lack of truth of their ideological *parti pris*, concentrating instead on expounding the formal and aesthetic quality of the art in question. After all (the argument goes), the directors themselves were 'formalists' and when, at the end of the twenties, formalism came under Stalinist interdict they paid a heavy penalty for their predilections. What, anyway, does ideological truth, or for that matter ideological error, mean today, judged by the verdict of history? In our postmodern world, the very word truth is unable to be deployed without the visible or implied support of scare quotes. Nevertheless, the modern reader/viewer can still feel frustrated by a certain lack of candour and even of common sense in discussing the issue. Can there be (one asks oneself) any value in extensive exegesis of a given director's films if the very impulse that guided his or her vision at the outset is never to be openly spoken about? And a further untimely thought insinuates itself: is it actually so necessary that we *like* all these directors?

Among the filmmakers just mentioned I won't attempt to disguise the fact that I have never very much admired Dziga Vertov. His most famous film, *Man with a Movie Camera* (1929), will, of course, continue to find an honourable place in all histories of documentary cinema. Undeniably the syncretic picture of the Russian city at the end of the 1920s given in the film has extraordinary historical and sociological interest. Placing his camera on every imaginable crag and vantage point (the photographer was Vertov's brother Mikhail Kaufman), and editing together the resultant footage dynamically, that is, with a sure sense of rhythm and tempo, Vertov constructs an avant-garde artefact – a formalist tone poem – that may still be viewed today with enjoyment. Yet it seems to me that such enjoyment as we gain occurs in the parts where what we are being offered is, relatively speaking, an ideological holiday. In *Man with a Movie Camera* there are scenes of play and pleasure – there is even a nice extended party sequence with a horse-drawn carriage – which alleviate the otherwise relentless insistence the film maintains on the coming of the new Soviet epoch.

What 'Soviet construction' really amounts to in the heart of a man like Vertov can be more clearly seen in a contiguous film directed by him, *The Eleventh Year* (1928), a would-be heroic account of the transformation of the countryside of the Donbass region in the Ukraine in order to set up a huge hydroelectricity project. The envisaged power will come from two sources: water – for which reason a dam is to be constructed, immersing many surrounding acres – and coal, necessitating a massive mining operation which, no less than the projected dam, will leave savage scars on the face of the landscape. The glee with which Vertov records the disruption of nature has to be experienced to be believed; it takes the ideal of anti-sentimentality in Soviet art to new levels. Colossal explosions, artfully photographed, shatter traditional orchards and meadows, and somehow one knows there is no regret here. Early on in the film, excavating engineers uncover the bones of a 2,000-year-old 'Scythian' skeleton. Most professional people would feel a certain compunction about disturbing the ancient dead. At least one could imagine they would pause for a moment and think back over history, even entertain a few thoughts on the passing of time and the transience of human endeavour. This is not Vertov's way; any unearthed skeletons are taken to be ancestors of communism. Rather than say go away, they will hearken to the sound of the pickaxe! One searches round for comparisons to 'place' such impiety. At much the same time as Vertov was filming *The Eleventh Year*, Platonov in far-away Voronezh was completing his extraordinary novel *The Foundation Pit*, in which the construction of a vast, bottomless hole in the ground is dramatised as the way forward for Soviet civilisation.

In Platonov, of course, the intention is satirical; his characters mouth the clichés of socialism, but they, and the place, and the language they use, are all, in truth, literally godforsaken. This forlorn 'lack of God', more than any other factor, is the measure of contemporary deformation; it is what makes Platonov's writing (for all its human kindness) so genuinely creepy and sinister. By contrast, *The Eleventh Year* produces a similar effect of melancholy, but absolutely unintentionally. In place of

Platonov's literary tenderness, we find in Vertov a strident and humourless positivism. No image in Vertov's film is more resonant, perhaps, than the sight the director grants us of the Triumph of Mining; a bare-footed woman, pickaxe raised, has leapt onto the mine's conveyor belt, from which vantage point she is smashing shards of coal into smaller and smaller fragments. On either side of the moving mechanism, a bevy of female co-workers sift the results of their comrade's fantastical and terrifying labours. A bristling feeling in the back of one's neck accompanies the reflection; this is what Vertov thinks civilisation is.

*

One might expect there to be like moments in the movies of Eisenstein, who, like Vertov (at least in his early professional life), had similarly bought into Bolshevism's all-encompassing vision of the future. There is no sentimentality in the way that Eisenstein treats the old monarchical system, and the religious ideology that supported it, in a movie like *October* (1927). In a famous sequence from that film, following the storming of the Winter Palace and the invasion of the tsar and tsarina's living quarters by an angry mob of sailors, private devotional statuettes of the Redeemer and the Virgin Mary owned by the pair are juxtaposed, by deft editing procedures, with images of grotesque Eastern idols and indolent recumbent Buddhas; undifferentiated tokens, all of them, of superstitious benightedness. The satirical intention is unambiguous. Eisenstein, at that stage, was no friend of the *ancien régime* – and no friend of religion. So indeed it might have continued; subsequent years brought the director into conflict with the demands (aesthetic, ideological) of the new political dispensation, yet at no point is it easy to identify some final irrevocable turning towards dissent. Nevertheless, the case of Eisenstein is fundamentally different from that of Vertov, for reasons which, in my opinion, have seldom been sufficiently dwelled upon. His spiritual and political odyssey seems to me to be one of the strangest of any twentieth-century artist, yet also perhaps one of the most heroic.

Let us begin with the journey to Mexico. In 1929, as is well known, following the failure of his film *The General Line*, Eisenstein was given permission to travel abroad. His high-profile itinerary took him first to Germany, the United Kingdom and France, subsequently to the United States, finally to Mexico where, under the aegis of the writer Upton Sinclair (whom he had met in California), he proposed to make a film about the conditions of native culture, and its relationship to the historical Spanish conquest. The movie was shot but never edited or released. Falling out with his patron and financial backer, Eisenstein found himself called back to Russia, in semi-disgrace, by Stalin. The footage that survived was edited first in the mid-thirties and then again in the 1970s, emerging in the compilation known as *Que Viva Mexico!* But the raw material has more recently (1998) been re-examined and re-edited far more coherently by Oleg Kovalov, whose new version has been released under the title *Mexican Fantasy*. Because the task has been very well done, the viewer finally gets a sense of the grandeur and somberness of the film's original intention. The script, such as it is, has a narrative – enough to avoid the trap of abstraction; we needn't bother outlining the plot here, except to note that the story shows, in some detail, both sides of the Mexican equation: the indigenous culture of the *peón*, and the engrafted (or incoming, or conquering) culture of Spanish Catholicism. It goes without saying that the two sides are in conflict; and that the film's sympathies, in good Marxist fashion, lie with the fate of the *peón*. Wonderfully vivid, monumental and graphic is the imaginative eye Eisenstein brings to bear on those scenes in the movie which conjure up the world of pre-European, non-colonial Mexico; an extraordinary documentary flair (which is at the same time creative and poetic) energises the film at these points and etches it onto the collective mind's eye. Yet at the same time there is a counter-current in the film which allows us to see (what is no more than the truth) that the two cultures have an affinity towards each other. The original Aztec residuum is allowed to meet Spanish Catholicism halfway, so to speak, in their shared love of procession and ritual, along with a certain merry, sardonic and carnavalesque attitude towards death which famously fastens on symbols of mortality – on skulls and skeletons and crucifixes and robed torchlit marches with music. In his attitude towards these public practices of the people it is possible to read Eisenstein departing from a purely satirical viewpoint, towards one that is more geared towards the beauty and grandeur of the object depicted. Leaving behind mere anthropological fascination with the topic, Eisenstein here, for the first time, in some strange way, 'gets' the point of religion.

In *Mexican Fantasy*, you could say Christianity's magnificent churches are as much part of the landscape as the indigenous cactus plants. If anything may be allowed to transform the original peasant fatalism it is, of course, the addition to the equation of the implied presence of Christ himself; the processions now have a focus. How is it that we come to feel, in long-drawn-out scenes depicting a peasant Jesus bearing the Cross on his back and flanked by the two thieves, that in some profound way Eisenstein is *identifying with* the figure portrayed, and with His sufferings? It is uncanny. Eisenstein had, of course, an extraordinarily eclectic personality; his cultural antennae were open to legions of conflicting world influences (including, as is well known, a lifelong interest in the arts of the East); yet, from the beginning of the 1930s, a decade of tribulations for Eisenstein as for all of his compatriots, it is evident that the figure of Christ came to possess for him a secret and particular meaning in the midst of his frequent travails. So it was that when, in the early months of 1941, Eisenstein received a commission from Zhdanov to make a film lauding the nationalist exploits of the sixteenth-century Russian emperor Ivan the Terrible, he seized the occasion to mount an audacious gamble – perhaps the most audacious wager made by any artist we know of in the modern period: he would use the life of Ivan as a mirror in which Stalin would be forced to confront his own criminality. Not merely (as in Hamlet's *Mouse Trap*) would the play (in this case film) 'catch the conscience of the king', but, if things fell out according to plan, the tyrant might even be converted to Christianity, as a prelude to repenting his sins.

The recklessness of such an endeavour in the years of paranoia doesn't need underlining. In all probability, the full majesty of the plan only gradually unfolded itself to Eisenstein himself. Even today, there is much that is obscure about the genesis and reception of the film, but the main strands of the story are simply enough recounted. The first thing that needs to be brought out is Stalin's own collusion in the choice of the topic. As I have said, the film was a commissioned work, as all major public works of art were in that epoch. Boris Pasternak in a February 1941 letter to Olga Friedenberg provides the relevant political context, when he notes to his companion with irony: 'Our great benefactor thinks we have been too sentimental. Peter the Great is no longer the appropriate touchstone. The new model, openly confessed, is for Ivan the Terrible, the *oprichnina*, and cruelty!' Shostakovich – we will come back to him – had been asked at the same time to write an opera on the subject, but declined (no doubt prudently, in view of the mauling meted out to his previous effort *Lady Macbeth of Mtsensk*); while in the field of theatre, the party hack Alexei Tolstoy (a distant relation to the great novelist) agreed to undertake a play about Ivan which only failed to see the light of day because of the premature death of the author (happily, of natural causes).

Thus, *terribilità* was a given from the outset; cruelty and ruthlessness were written into the model being solicited. The only question was what might be done with them; and here it seems that Eisenstein took heart at the outset from a previous celebrated episode of Russian culture. During 1940, in the dark days of the Hitler–Stalin pact, he had planned to make a film about Pushkin. Like many of his projects, it had never got beyond the planning stage, but the example of *Boris Godunov* (both Pushkin's original poem and Musorgsky's later opera) shone a light for him. In a text entitled *Eisenstein in the Reminiscences of his Contemporaries* published in 1974 long after Eisenstein's death (and quoted by Orlando Figes in his indispensable study of Russian culture, *Natasha's Dance*), the writer Iosif Yusovsky gives us a glimpse of the director's contemporary thought processes.

'Lord, can you really see it?' (*Eisenstein is reported to have exclaimed*) 'I'm so happy, so happy! Of course it is *Boris Godunov*! "Five years I have governed in peace, but my soul is troubled ..." I could not make a film like this without the support of the Russian tradition – without the great tradition of conscience. Violence can be explained and legalized, but it can never be justified. If you are a human being, *it has to be atoned for*' [my italics].

Such remarks seem in retrospect astonishingly explicit, and one could wonder how (for all his attested personal bravery) Eisenstein believed he could escape censure – or worse. That indeed is the mystery of this great film; for in order to be able to 'speak truth to power', Eisenstein, at some stage, would have to become open about his aims. The question was when; and indeed, how.

In fact, the adventure of *Ivan* was an affair that lasted most of the forties. And it might be interesting to follow the steps of its progress in a little more detail. As we have seen, the film had its genesis at the beginning of 1941. In the summer of that year came Hitler's invasion. Mosfilm Studios, where Eisenstein worked, were evacuated a thousand miles to the east, to Alma Ata (modern Almaty) in Soviet central Asia. Leonid Kozlov in his essay 'The Artist in the Shadow of Ivan', the best modern account of this episode, makes the point that the period from the autumn of 1941 to the spring of 1942 (during which the bulk of the script was composed) was a time of great spiritual freedom for many Russians; challenged, indeed outwitted, by Hitler, Stalin was no longer God. Citizens were free to have their own private thoughts about him, thoughts that could thrive the further away one was from the centre. In May 1942, following industry practice, the script was published – in two parts: the first showing Ivan's youthful exploits in combating the rule of the Tartars; the second – fated to be more controversial – outlining how Ivan consolidated his Russian domains by taking on the power of the boyars (we can read if we like: 'old Bolsheviks'). Already at this stage, even before shooting had started, there were murmurs of caution among his collaborators. 'Too many executions! Shouldn't you reduce the number?', one asked. 'No, if I do that, the "bare teeth" of the epoch [he means *both* epochs, then and now] would be lost to the audience' (March 1942). Preparations began. The size of the undertaking in the midst of uncertainties about the fate of the nation inevitably gave rise to difficulties and delays. Marshalling of resources and building of sets (adhering closely to Eisenstein's own artwork) took a whole year, so that filming finally only began in April 1943. In the autumn of that year, Eisenstein decided that the boyars plot strand and its ramifications should be extended into another episode, so that now the film would have three parts: part one, as before; part two, the insurrection of the boyars; and part three, the remainder of Ivan's conquests up to the moment at which his enemies vanquished, he stands alone, a victor in an empty world, on the Livonian shore. (This third part was never released – and probably never made, for reasons we will come back to in a moment; but the storyboards Eisenstein sketched for it, along with one or two fragmentary scenes, survive, and show his intentions.)

Continuing with our miniature chronology, it seems that the best part of 1944 was spent in filming, though how much this included the material that was eventually to become Part II, or even Part III, is obscure to me from the sources I have consulted (some of the remainder of the film might have been shot the following year). Part I, at any event, the 'optimistic' and nationalistic section of the epic, was edited and released to popular and official acclaim in January 1945. There was a pause while Part II was made ready. As time went by, rumours began to gather. The director Mikhail Romm was witness to the first private screening of Part II in January 1946, the very month in which Eisenstein received the Stalin Prize – the highest honour in the land – for the already-released section of the epic. 'When the film was completed', Romm writes (he refers to Part II only, not Parts II and III),

> we were summoned to the Ministry of Cinematography. We were told: 'Just look at Eisenstein's film! There will be trouble. Help us to decide what to do with it.' We saw it, and felt

the same alarm and the same disturbed feelings as those in the Ministry. But Eisenstein [present at the meeting] conducted himself with daring gaiety. He asked us: 'What's the matter? What's wrong? What have you got in mind?' But no one dared to tell him that in the figure of Ivan the Terrible was sensed a profound allusion to the dictator, in Malyuta Skuratov an allusion to Beria [chief of the NKVD], and in the *oprichnina* an allusion to his myrmidons. And there was a lot more that we sensed but dared not say.

To which Romm adds: 'In the boldness of Eisenstein's eyes, in his challenging sceptical smile, we felt that he had acted consciously, that he had indeed decided to go the whole hog. It was terrifying.' The die, therefore, was cast. Two months later Stalin saw the film in the Kremlin and got the point of it. 'This isn't a film, it's some kind of nightmare!', he expostulated. The production was held back from release until suitable cuts and alterations should be made to it. What such alterations amounted to was to be the subject of a personal face-to-face meeting between the director and his nemesis which, after numerous postponements, was finally held in the Kremlin in February 1947. A stenographed account of the encounter exists and is in the public domain. One can imagine with what apprehension Eisenstein approached the ordeal. Everything was at stake, including (it is not too melodramatic to say) his mortal survival. The interview was indeed extraordinary, if inconclusive. The cuts that were demanded in the event were fairly trivial, but the wider question of whether Stalin ever *really* intended that Part II should be released, let alone whether the director should be allowed to continue with the third part (not even mentioned in the interview), was left hanging in the air. Shortly after the meeting, Eisenstein suffered a heart attack that effectively finished his working life. A year later, most of it spent in hospital, he was dead.

If one is prepared to talk about miracles in the context of the whole astounding episode (and I don't see why we shouldn't) the miracle surely is that Part II survived at all, and has come down to us. Even with its ghostly third part missing, the film as it stands, supported by Prokofiev's wonderful musical score, is an extraordinary monument to art, and to Eisenstein's bravery. Stalin, of course, died in his bed and unrepentant. The film however survives him, and delivers a definitive judgement. And it delivers it in the context of a recognisably Christian eschatology. How strange to consider that Eisenstein – the Jew, the modern man, the ex-Bolshevik – should come round to thinking in these terms. The very first draft of the film, back in 1941, was written in rhymed Old Church Slavonic, and it is clear that Eisenstein's aesthetic imagination over the years had become captivated by the grandeur and mystery of Orthodox ritual; the cathedral ambience throughout the whole of Part II turns the film into a 'huge day-time opera'. I myself cannot prove, and in a way I wouldn't want to, that by the time he died, Eisenstein was someone who could meaningfully be described as a believer. In truth he was probably, like all of us, several things at once. Yuri Tsivian's monograph on the film (BFI Film Classics, 2002) makes a plausible case for arguing that, as well as 'being' Stalin, Ivan in the film is autobiographically focused; he is Eisenstein himself (just as Charles Foster Kane, while standing for Hearst, is more profoundly a self-portrait of Welles). In great works of art, perhaps, *all* characters are in some sense their author. We have Eisenstein's word for it that in *Ivan the Terrible*, the director identified strongly with the fool, Staritsky, pretender to the throne, tricked by the tsar into making an attempt on his life, and suffering death as a result of it. (From Eisenstein's autobiographical notes, written shortly before his own death: '*The victim of the film, Vladimir Staritsky: an image of Sergei Eisenstein, the victim in real life.*') Among such miscellaneous identifications, the least one can insist on is that the image of Christ, and the impact of His sacrifice, have their own vital part to play in the drama. We may leave the last word to Eisenstein's faithful biographer Marie Seton.

> One day, a little later, after telling me that in all his life he had only put his trust in two people – Tissé (cameraman) and Pera (his wife) – whom he believed would remain loyal to him to the end of his life, he suddenly said: 'I have something to tell you I

have never spoken about. I believe in Christ! I love him as a Saviour whose Passion must be borne by those who believe in him. I have tried to overcome this ... But now I have surrendered.'

*

The present author, who endured a Catholic upbringing during the 1950s in the north of Scotland, has dim and distant memories of a prayer repeated at the end of Mass each Sunday enjoining the 'conversion of Russia'. Why Russia needed converting and what exactly it was that it was to be converted to (presumably Christianity; but then, Catholicism or Orthodoxy?), were mysteries and distinctions beyond my then powers of reasoning to unravel. Thirty years later, at the beginning of the nineties, and following the collapse of the Soviet Union, freedom of worship was indeed given back to the people – one might even claim, miraculously. The bells that had been silenced rang out again; and whatever reservations one may have about post-Soviet Russia (surely for any intelligent person such reservations are numerous) that at least is something to gladden the heart.

The spiritual desolation issuing out of years of official atheism at grassroots level is the subject, or perhaps one should more accurately say *one* of the subjects, of a film by the St Petersburg director Alexei Balabanov. *Cargo 200* (2007), set in the fictional industrial town of Leninsk in 1984, takes a backward look at the last years of the Soviet empire. The moral landscape it invokes is as bleak as can be. The story itself, perhaps taken from one of those *faits divers* one finds in newspaper columns (it has that authentic feeling about it), has a fascinating particularity and complexity. Not all aspects of the plot need be outlined here; suffice to say that among the film's dramatis personae we find in the foreground a cowardly and pompous academic whose professional title is Professor of Scientific Atheism at the University of Leningrad. (One would hope such a post really existed.) Seeking help when his car breaks down on the highway, our not-so-heroic anti-hero finds himself knocking on the door of a dim-looking

FIGURE 5 'A film that [...] delivers a definitive judgement'. Nikolai Cherkassov as the tormented tsar in Eisenstein's *Ivan the Terrible*.

shack at the end of a dirt road that turns out to be a secret hooch-making factory. He had better be careful because, unbeknown to him, he has stumbled into a den of thieves, whose leader (a dead ringer for one of Jean Renoir's favourite actors, Gaston Modot) listens to his tale of woe and invites him to sit down and share a glass of vodka with him.

Soon they are engaged in a full-scale theological dispute. 'So you don't believe human beings have immortal souls, do you?', murmurs our host, with feline irony. It is perhaps one thing to deal with such a challenge in the lecture hall – a simple matter of your professional bread and butter, so to speak – another matter entirely when everything about the atmosphere of the place, and the sinister, invisible air of menace emanating from the room, tells you that at any moment such a proposition is liable to be tested for real.

The scenario that unfolds in due course from this interview – a saga of abduction, rape, execution and multiple mindless slayings – might be envisaged, on one level, as taking place almost anywhere – in the secular West as plausibly as in barbarian provincial Russia. Psychopaths, alas, exist in every society. What is specifically interesting here, however, is that the hypothesis of the absence of God (and therefore of pity, and mercy) should be deemed worthy of having a place, even residually, in this particular movie's overall argument. It is not that Balabanov is in any way 'preaching a cause'; far from it. I have little notion what the writer-director's private beliefs were – it is too late to ask him (he died in 2013) – but I should be rather surprised to find that they lay anywhere in the region of Orthodoxy. Yet, in his grim and slightly decadent way, Balabanov is profoundly alert to the language of religion, and to the consequences of its withdrawal from common discourse. At the close of the film the professor, a shaken survivor of the horror of the events depicted, is seen entering a church and enquiring of an old *babushka* about the availability of the 'ritual' of baptism. 'It's not a ritual, it's a sacrament', the woman corrects him fiercely. 'Go over there and pray while you wait for the priest to come.' Meanwhile the mood of this profoundly unnerving movie may be summed up in an epigram minted by one of its rare positive characters: 'We should all pray to die young', this woman opines; 'there would be fewer opportunities for sinning.'

*

The survival of religion in Russia during the 70 years of its official proscription is, on the face of it, one of the most fascinating anomalies in modern culture, and I intend to talk about it more in the final chapter of this book. Faced with the organisational might of the totalitarian state, religion proved too complicated, too deeply embedded and too multifarious in its manifestations to be eradicated entirely. So it was that, when the pressure towards official atheistical compliance was relaxed in the late eighties and early nineties, the phenomenon reasserted itself more or less from where it had left off; communism turned out to be merely an interlude. Despite the regime's destruction of thousands of churches, the Church as an institution survived, along with its teachings and rituals. This seamless continuity enjoyed by religion in the context of Russian culture may be observed in the final film I would like to look at in this chapter, *The Island*, directed in 2006 by Pavel Lungin.

FIGURE 6   'So you don't believe human beings have immortal souls, do you?' Denizens of a sinister hooch-making cabal in Alexei Balabanov's *Cargo 200* (2007).

Lungin happens to be one of the better-known modern Russian film directors. Whether or not he would wish to be classed as a believer is unknown to me; as with Balabanov, I would rather expect not. What he undoubtedly is, is a story-teller, and an exceptionally fluent one. *The Island* has a 'popular' aspect to it that places it in a different category of aesthetic discourse from some of the films we have been considering so far, *Andrei Roublev* for instance. No matter – it is genuine where it needs to be; in its own way it is as much the real thing as Tarkovsky's film. The tale is set in the 1970s, though in fact it could unfold at almost any time. The island in question, located in some remote corner of northern Russia, houses a monastery, home to no more than a handful of monks, one of whom, Anatoly (played by Russian rock idol Pyotr Mamonov), lives apart from the others in a tumbledown coal shed at the end of the island's jetty. A flashback to World War II establishes how he came to acquire his vocation in the most exacting moral circumstances: captured by a German naval patrol, he had been offered the choice of shooting his commanding officer or perishing himself. Tragically, and on the spur of the moment, he had taken the cowardly option. So there is a large guilt component in his vocation, mingled with a sort of madness that descended upon him in the wake of the horror of the event. We grasp the point that 'becoming a monk' is Anatoly's offering to God in expiation for the fact of his sin and his survival.

The film may be characterised for our purposes by saying that its attitude towards religion, despite the tragic underlying premises of the story, is essentially an easy and natural one. The several encounters between Anatoly and the outside world that structure the narrative are notable for demonstrating a kind of practical Christianity: Christianity 'in action', as it were, with the humour and humanity one would expect to attend such a stance, along with a fair share of darkness. Each of Anatoly's meetings shows a different facet of the man, while the film itself keeps its counsel on the ultimate mystery of the relation between Christianity and madness.

Thus, to take these meetings in the order they occur in the movie: (1) a very young girl from the mainland comes to seek Anatoly's advice; she is expecting a child and wants to know whether she should keep it or not. In fact it is Anatoly's reputation as a teacher and holy man that has brought her to this spot; she has never met him in person and is therefore defenceless against his initial off-handedness and deception. He pretends first of all that he is not Anatoly at all, merely a 'janitor'; and when he owns up to his identity it is only to tell her, rather sharply, to stay away from him and follow her own path. In due course, however, he relents, counselling her to keep the child; somehow we feel that this change of heart towards the girl is not capricious. However it has come about, he understands her, and she him. (2) A contrasting encounter shortly afterwards sets him in contact with a woman who has come to him bringing along her son on crutches. Can, or will, the priest cure the boy? The dialogue in this section is brilliant, complex and refractory. Once again (but differently) a seeming harshness characterises the encounter; in his Aesopian way, he tells her she must choose: her boy or her work? – and that until she has decided which, nothing more can be done for her. (3) An enchantingly humorous section of the film now chronicles the attempts of the prior of the monastery to persuade Anatoly to give up his shed and to come back and live with his colleagues. Father Filaret, the prior, unlike Anatoly, has nothing fanatical about him; indeed he seems, at first, to be woefully lacking in that asceticism we would expect from men of the cloth, especially those living in monasteries. Yet he has sweetness and persistence and humility, as the episode demonstrates. For Anatoly has come to believe that his coal shed is inhabited by demons who must first be 'smoked out' before promises can be made about rehousing himself with the other monks. Poor Father Filaret! The two men barely avoid asphyxiating themselves in their joint endeavours to fumigate the shack, while the prior's prized quilt and his best footwear are immolated in the course of the experiment. (Anatoly is impenitent about this latter loss by his superior: 'Sins gather in the top of bishops' boots,' he mutters heartlessly.) (4) The final and key encounter in the film brings a pair of strangers to the island, a father and a daughter. We will find out shortly (in a plot twist that seems merely right and natural in the context) that the man is none other than Anatoly's ex-commanding officer, Tikhon, who miraculously survived the pistol shot on the waterfront that was aimed to kill him. Meanwhile, his daughter, in her early twenties and rather beautiful, is in serious need of help; the madness that afflicts her has probably a scientific name, but it covers the case sufficiently to say that her wits are astray. Anatoly, for his part, seems sensitised to the implicit challenge of her arrival; there is a feeling in the air that this is what he has been waiting for, and that if the challenge is met he will be able to die in peace (he has already prepared a makeshift coffin on the premises). In any case, a curious affinity appears to exist between him and the girl – they greet each other with strange and heathenish bird-calls. Yet the battle for her soul is real enough when it happens. In the film's intensely dramatic and psychologically riveting climax, Anatoly rows her off to a deserted beachhead and grapples with her physically until the invisible demons part from her body. What is the outcome of this *agon*? A last glimpse of the maiden – inertly stretched out, but calm and even radiant in her stillness – suggests that her madness has been vanquished.

The situation characterised here, in which a holy fool or holy sinner summons faith to his aid beyond the power of ordinary mortals – such faith indeed as may accomplish miracles – is a recognisable trope from a number of classic movies, whether their director be Dreyer, or Tarkovsky, or Bergman, or Rossellini (or even modernist mavericks such as Lars von Trier and Pedro Almodóvar). Miracles are in question once again, and we sense that miracles are somehow at the centre of faith. They are, one could say, that aspect of faith that is most inimical to the scepticism of the rational mind. So it was that when Christianity first came under critical survey by writers such as Hume and Spinoza, it was the credulousness of the faithful towards events that were 'scientifically impossible' that, in the opinion of these philosophers,

FIGURE 7 'Faith that can accomplish miracles'. Monks set sail with Father Anatoly's coffin in Pavel Lungin's *The Island* (2006).

most undermined the power of religion to make a claim upon modern allegiance. And yet somehow, even today, 'the miraculous' is a necessary part of life, is it not? Speaking personally, I have always been unable to feel anything other than tender towards the idea – so much sweetness and piety and hope are involved in it. That miracles may, and in most cases do, have an alternative natural explanation, and that in most circumstances we should want to insist on the cogency of that alternative in discussing the phenomenon, does not detract from the moral, poetic and indeed psychological force of the original credulous wonder that is mythically tied up in such events. Most of us, I think, can deal with both points of view simultaneously. Lungin's film takes a calmly historical view of the oddity, indeed exorbitance, of Russian experience, while leaving open to our conjecture the wider and more interesting question of whether, and in what way, the sights we have been witnessing are momentous.

FIGURE 8   'Premonitions of fate [...] and mortality'. Zbigniew Zapasiewicz and Piotr Garlicki in Zanussi's mordant portrait of pre-Solidarity Poland, *Camouflage* (1977).

2

Poland: A Trio of Catholics

Just as Russia retained a bedrock of Orthodoxy throughout the communist period, so Poland, through its much shorter (1945–89) epoch of communist rule, retained a grounding in Catholicism. Churches, monasteries and convents remained open when, under a stricter secularism, they might have been closed down; while priests and bishops on the whole escaped the more vicious forms of political persecution. In the postwar period that we are talking of it would be wrong to say that the Church was exactly *underground*; career advancement came, of course, through adherence to the Party, but Catholicism existed as a kind of visible counter-culture, with very wide acceptance across the populace and in the universities. When, finally, in the late 1980s, the communist system began to unravel in Europe for the many complicated reasons that it did so, the inspiration of the Polish Pope, Wojtyła, turned out to play a significant part in its downfall. Naturally there were bumps on the way; after the initial triumphs of Solidarity in the late 1970s, eight years of martial law under Jaruzelski had to be endured, years which did indeed include some notorious persecutions of the clergy. But rather more than in neighbouring Czechoslovakia (where, under Havel's leadership, protest was civic and secular), day-to-day resistance to communism in Poland had a recognisably religious tinge to it.

The issue of Catholicism's underground resilience in Poland, and the judgements that can be made about it, are impossible to consider without taking into account the corresponding issue of Jewishness and of anti-Semitism. There are rather few Jews in Poland today, but before the war they amounted to 10 per cent of the population (and up to 30 per cent in the capital city, Warsaw). The presence on conquered Polish territory of the most notorious of the death camps – Treblinka, Chelmno, Sobibor, Auschwitz – has kept alive well into the twenty-first century, as a matter of ongoing controversy, the whole question of what the Poles did to aid the Jews, in a situation where they themselves were often helpless. Central to the shaping of this debate was the appearance, in 1985, of the late Claude Lanzmann's monumental documentary *Shoah* (Lanzmann of course was a Frenchman); the indictment contained in that movie has been echoed by indigenous filmmakers, most notably Paweł Łoziński, whose powerful documentary *Birthplace* (1992) follows the writer Henryk Grynberg as he trudges from farm to farm, in the midst of a freezing Polish winter, trying to identify the man or the men (he knows them to be neighbours of his) who 50 years previously sheltered and then murdered his father.

A similar crime of betrayal is evoked, this time within a fictional setting, as part of the historical background to Pawel Pawlikowski's prize-winning film *Ida* (2014), about a young woman contemplating a novitiate in a Catholic convent who finds out, somewhat late in the day, that she is Jewish.[1] Other filmmakers besides Pawlikowski have explored the complicated cohabitation of the two traditions of faith, and the profound (one should say tragic) ambivalences it gave rise to, in the excruciating circumstances of Poland's occupation by foreign powers. Greatest of these filmmakers I would judge to be Agnieszka Holland, whose personal background – Jewish father, Catholic or at least nominally Catholic mother – has lent seriousness and depth to

---

[1] It is a measure of how sensitive the situation remains in present-day Poland, a quarter-of-a-century after liberation from communist rule, that when *Ida* was broadcast recently on the second public channel, TVP 2, it was preceded by a health warning claiming that the scenes referring to the murder of the heroine's Jewish family by the Polish farmer they were lodging with were not to be taken as 'typical' of general wartime experience.

her exploration of the whole Catholic-Jewish 'rescue effort' in such coruscating movies as *Angry Harvest* (1985), *Europa Europa* (1990) and *In Darkness* (2011). Krzysztof Kieślowski, too, has broached the theme (more than once) – we return to him shortly.

The difficult question of whether one can call Polish cinema *as a whole* a 'religious' cultural artefact escapes the bounds of sensible generalisation; it is simply too complicated to specify. Certainly, Poland possessed (and perhaps still possesses) a sophisticated anti-clerical tradition, visible in filmmakers like Borowczyk, Has and Lenica. The explicitly libertine bent of these artists (Borowczyk and Lenica started their careers as animators) shades into a general predilection for satire and derision observable in the work of a number of the more interesting senior current practitioners: Juliusz Machulski and Wojciech Maciejewski spring to mind. Meanwhile, of the Polish directors who made their names abroad and until recently have continued to practise internationally – Polanski, Skolimowski, the late Andrzej Żuławski, for example – none are recognisably religious artists, unless I have missed something.

That leaves, however, three important directors about whom it would not be inopportune to raise questions of commentary and interpretation that cross over into religious and/or metaphysical territory. Each of them is a major figure in his own right; indeed an argument could be made for saying they are Poland's most important postwar directors. Of course I am referring to Andrzej Wajda (1926– 2016) in the first place. Following him, there are two famous Krzysztofs: Zanussi (born 1939) and Kieślowski (1941–96). Let us look briefly at each of these artists in turn.

Wajda's Catholicism, perhaps we can start by saying, was a by-product of his career-long engagement with Polish history, and specifically of his fascination with nineteenth-century Romanticism as a political response to the nation's devastating partition at the end of the previous century. In short it is part of his liberalism, a pendant to his immersion in the classics. As far as I can see, Catholicism exists in

Wajda's films not at all as a habit of personal piety, nor as an allegiance, explicit or clandestine, to the institutional Church. Significantly older than Kieślowski and Zanussi, Wajda passed much of his career under the constraint of a regime where it would not be considered prudent to profess religious sympathies outright, even if one felt them – which doesn't mean that one can't still be amazed at how outspoken Wajda *was* at certain periods of his career. For over half-a-century he was a central – perhaps indeed *the* central – voice of conscience of his country, and, allowing these things to be said in the right spirit, it is clear that Poland's culture owes a huge moral debt to him.

The complex ways in which Polish Romanticism and residual allegiance to Catholicism fold into each other (making them, in effect, two sides of the same coin) may be illustrated for our purposes by reference to Wajda's most famous film, *Ashes and Diamonds* (1958). Adapted from a 1948 novel by Jerzy Andrzejewski and set in a provincial township in in the turbulent period just after the war when the Communist Party was set on installing itself as a one-party system of government, the film tells the story of an assassination attempt made by an irregular of the Home Army ('Maciek': Zbigniew Cybulski) on a visiting Communist dignitary. The action of the movie is compressed into less than 24 hours, between a first, failed, attempt in daylight and a second, this time successful, night-time strike which has its own consequences; the film ends with the assassin himself brought down on a garbage dump in a hail of army bullets as he attempts to flee through the township's labyrinthine back courtyards.

Maciek stands as an example of the modern existentialist action hero; despite belonging to the wrong side (from the point of view of the regime in place when Wajda was making the film), he is presented as possessing the typical Pole's brave romantic recklessness. *Being* a Pole, he is also a poet and a lover. The 'love interest' in *Ashes and Diamonds* centres on an attractive, thoughtful barmaid ('Krystyna': Ewa Krzyżewska) whom Maciek befriends in the hotel he is staying in as he waits for his prey to present himself. Following a (beautifully shot) rendezvous in the hotel bedroom, they walk out into the street and, sheltering from the rain, end up in a ruined church crypt. The church's crucifix hangs upside down over the altar in the foreground of the scene, subtended from a broken crossbeam.

On one of the walls there is a plaque containing lines of verse which the girl reads out hesitantly in the light of a match she has struck:

Coraz to z ciebie, jako z drzazgi smolnej,
Wokało lecą szmaty zapalone;
Gorejąc nie wiesz, czy stawasz się wolny,
Czy to, co twoje, ma być zatracone?
Czy popiół tylko zostanie I zamęt,
Co idzie w przepaść z burzą – czy zostanie
Na dnie popiołu gwiaździsty dyjament,
Wiekuistego zwycięstwa zaranie...

From you, as from burning chips of resin,
Fiery fragments circle far and near.

FIGURE 9   Polish Romanticism's debt to Christianity; Zbigniew Cybulski and Ewa Krzyżewska in Andrzej Wajda's *Ashes and Diamonds* (1958).

Ablaze, you don't know if you're to be free
Or if all that is yours will disappear.
Will only ashes and confusion remain,
Leading into the abyss — or will the ashes
Hold the glory of a star-like diamond
The morning star of everlasting triumph?

The poem is by Cyprian Norwid (1821–83), one of nineteenth-century Poland's greatest writers, and it seems to be asking what, if anything, can be said to have come out of the famous rebellions against foreign rule that the nation unsuccessfully mounted, first in 1831 and then again in 1848 and 1863. At a certain moment (line seven), the girl breaks off — she can't follow the text any more; and Maciek, who knows the poem by heart, supplies the conclusion of the stanza: 'or will the ashes / Hold the glory of a star-like diamond / The morning star of everlasting triumph?' Here we have the perennial Polish optimism wrought out of suffering and sacrifice, and transferred, momentarily, into the personal sphere of romantic attachment. (When, after a pause, the girl asks him, 'What are we exactly?', the 'terrorist' Maciek is able to respond to her: '*You* [. . .] you are definitely a diamond!') In the scene's superabundance of symbolism there lie, of course, different possibilities of interpretation. Yet it seems clear enough, on the other hand, that religion, love and patriotism are being fused together in a complicated symbiosis, and that the country's Christian past (which the ruined crypt could be said to symbolise) in some mysterious way guarantees this compact.

Nonetheless, Wajda is not a particularly religious-minded director. Even in this film it is possible to query the depth of feeling towards Christianity that the scenario plays with. Maciek knows his Norwid, but the exigencies of his life as a 'guerrilla fighter' have long since precluded any habit of day-to-day reverence. The original ambush of the communist official on which the film opens (and which goes terrifyingly askew when Maciek and his two companions fire on the wrong target) has been set up beside a little wayside chapel. Needless to say, no thought is wasted by the attackers on the fact that this might, in some way, be holy territory they are desecrating. War is war, after all. And in the sequence we have just been analysing, there is a telling and ever-so-slightly deflating aftermath. If the reader remembers, Krystyna's heel becomes detached from her shoe, as the pair of lovers negotiate the rubble. Stepping into the sacristy, Maciek mends it, or attempts to do so, by placing it on the side-altar and bashing it with the near-at-hand consecration bell. No sacrilege, perhaps, in the greater scheme of things – the gesture is well meant and even gallant. Yet the sexton, roused from slumber, is angry with the lovers for another reason: they have failed to notice (and to pay respect towards) a pair of laid-out corpses lying in front of the altar steps – the victims of the previous day's botched assassination bid. The film has, one way or another, an intriguing political ambivalence towards the historical events depicted. On the one hand, there is no mistaking the director's admiration for the wild young man whom Cybulski so engagingly personifies; nor for the lost cause he stands for – Wajda doesn't 'buy' (nor are we expected to buy) the idea that the anti-communist Home Army was made up of scoundrels. On the other hand, the communist victim Szczuca (Wacław Zastrzeżyński), in the few scenes we see him, is drawn with lively human sympathy; at least, he is no arid ideologue. The conflict of interests, in short, is sketched with a certain dramatic evenness. Meanwhile, the bourgeoisie – representatives of traditional, Catholic Poland – appear to be still operative in this society, though this may turn out to be their swansong. Is it predominantly satire or predominantly pity and fellow feeling that we are meant to experience, as Wajda conjures up for us the tipsy polonaise that ends the evening revels – the dancing actors communally oblivious, somehow, to the dark forces that are gathering to shape the future of their country?

Wajda leads logically, and with acknowledged continuity, into the next generation of filmmakers of whom Zanussi and Kieślowski are clearly the leading lights, and whose collective work in the seventies and eighties helped to make Polish film (as Czech cinema was in the sixties) the one national industry from that part of the world that it was impossible for outsiders to ignore. More than anywhere else behind the Iron Curtain, one sensed in Polish film a kind of freedom, independence and tough-mindedness (qualities, one had better say now, that extend themselves to important directors I will not be discussing such as Morgenstern, Kawalerowicz and Zaorski). Zanussi, marginally the older of the pair, if only by a couple of years, is interesting from our point of view in that he is one of the few current directors one can think of who *are* prepared, hand on his heart, to admit to being a Christian. A man of culture and discretion (as all who have met him will testify), he would doubtless own up to the fact modestly and tentatively. Perhaps he would use the word 'Catholic' rather than Christian, though the two things are obviously intertwined with each other – intertwined, though not quite interchangeable. 'Catholic', for one thing, envisages a social and civic-national dimension that is relevant about a man who at different times in his career has been put forward as a possible representative of his country in the diplomatic sphere. Zanussi, in the event, has never become an official ambassador; but there is an 'ambassadorial' side to his work that cannot but be noted. Famously, he made a film about Pope John Paul II (*From a Far Country*, 1981), and another about the Polish priest Maximilian Kolbe (subsequently canonised) who at Auschwitz stepped forward to substitute himself for a group of prisoners condemned to death, by starvation, after a colleague of theirs succeeded in escaping. For all I know, these films have their admirers, but if so I doubt it would be for their respective aesthetic qualities; there are passages in both films that come perilously close to hagiography. Zanussi is an uneven director, and even his strongest supporters (I would certainly count myself among them) would be hard put to deny that he has made some frankly 'bad' films. Even in his finest works, there is an element of the purely edifying. Though he seldom, if ever, descends to simple moralising, it is accurate to call him a moralist. His forte is psychological realism, however. On form, no director is subtler or more discriminating.

The son of an architect, Zanussi followed a university education in science and philosophy, and these preoccupations can be strongly felt in such early films as *The Structure of Crystal* (1969) and *Illumination* (1972) that have a palpably autobiographical feeling about them. Autobiographical and at the same time documentary, the films take us into 'real' laboratories where questions about the nature of material reality – the structure of the universe, the make-up of the human mind – are debated by the film's characters with seriousness and sophistication. Science is seen in these films both as a source of wonder and as reason for possible dismay; what if it were true that there *is* nothing 'beyond' the basic physical substrate of matter? Where then (if anywhere) does Spirit fit into the equation? A young mathematician friend of the protagonist in *Illumination* dies of a brain tumour, and after the post-mortem the brain is examined by a group of curious young doctors. In a way this might be no more than Hamlet apostrophising the skull of Yorick. In a modern film, at any rate, we expect such scenes to lead to atheistical conclusions. It is not, in Zanussi's film, that the opposite case is quite obviously true; but neither are contrary conclusions – metaphysical and even religious – ruled out. The strength of the scene lies in its fearlessness, and in the concrete way the protagonist's reflections are brought home to us. We have seen the brain lifeless, laid out on the mortuary slab. But we have also seen, in a previous sequence, the same brain alive and sentient, in the course of what turns out to be an unsuccessful operation to remove the tumour. I have no idea how Zanussi arranged the filming of this grisly and realistic hospital procedure, nor indeed what the outcome was of the real operation that was evidently used to facilitate this section of the narrative. In any case, the sequence is part of a wider reflection on mortality which the film contains, and which not so much refuses easy answers as dazzles us with its dialectical complexity. A fascinating disquisition is set up in the course of the film's exposition about the meaning of the film's title, *Illumination*. Someone (one of the film's many articulate interlocutors) claims that it is cognate with the idea of ecstasy; yet our protagonist prefers to give it a more sober Augustinian nuance. Illumination, for Frantiszek (Stanislaw Latałło), means understanding, or lucidity. It is linked to the mystery of time. The present and the past, one could say, are 'illuminated' – we know, or we think we know, what happens in them, whereas the future is characterised by darkness. All stories are told in the past tense, as if they *have* happened; yet for the characters involved, the events are still waiting to unfold. Our protagonist is fascinated by prognostication – by that which can be read in the palm of the hand; from time to time he avails himself of fortune tellers. And the director obliges him, so to speak (at any event obliges *us*), by interposing a number of momentary 'flash-forwards' where we are able to glimpse incidents in his life that are yet to take place: premonitions, therefore, of fate – perhaps indeed of unhappy fate. The young man at the centre of the story appears to be living on borrowed time – his physician tells him to slow down or risk heart failure (he is only aged 30). The sense of the fragility of existence that governs the narrative (and that includes, among its episodes, the death of a friend in a mountaineering accident) is powerfully registered, and lends this film a sombre reflective quality. (Let us add an interesting postscript: Stanislaw Latałło, who plays the young man, was himself to die the year after the film's conclusion on a climbing expedition in the Himalayas. A documentary film, *A Trace*, made by his son, and, available on the British DVD, tells the whole story. Naturally, the fact of this happening so soon after the film's release is only coincidence; yet knowing about it somehow adds to the movie's haunting resonance.)

Religion, as human activity, or else as anthropological fact, can be understood in many different ways; there is no single identifiable 'item of belief' that separates the phenomenon from rival non-religious metaphysical systems (thus marking it as different in kind from philosophy, not merely in degree) – unless it is the question of what happens to us after our passing. The 'hoverer on the shoreline of faith' needs to make up his mind whether eternity is only to be understood poetically; or whether there really might be some reality to the idea that spirit, or even life itself, persists beyond the confines of the grave. That momentous question – whatever it really means (alas it may not be so cut and dried as it seems to be) – fascinates Zanussi. In three of his most powerful and interesting films, separated over a long period of years, the lens of enquiry is brought to bear on what is involved psychologically and morally when an individual human destiny faces extinction. In *Spiralia* (1978), a fit and vigorous middle-aged mountaineer (played by Jan Nowicki) finds himself stricken by an unnamed fatal disease – probably cancer. After a failed bid to kill himself by exposure on the mountainside, he is hospitalised and – faced with the prospect of a lingering exit – finds the earliest opportunity to throw himself out of the window of the clinic. The dominant psychological key of the film, in Nowicki's authoritative performance, is rage and derision; confronted by the mockery of an uncalled-for death sentence, he turns his own savage mockery back on the world, refusing consolation with taunts and sarcasm, and deriding would-be well-wishers (the latter category includes a nice young woman (played by Maria Komorowska) who seems determined to concern herself with his welfare).

Dramaturgically, and in terms of the power of its exposition, *Spiralia* represents a peak of Zanussi's achievement. Along with *Camouflage* (1976) it is one of his finest films. In fact, the 1970s were a gloriously fertile decade for this director. Twenty years later he returned to the fray with another award-winning film, *Life as a Fatal Sexually-transmitted Disease* (2000). (The title itself, on the surface, is sardonic and non-Christian, of course.) As with *Spiralia*, the protagonist of this film – a doctor played by Zanussi veteran Zbigniew Zapasiewicz – is faced by the discovery of an incurable malady, though his response is calmer and more stoical than that of the hero of the previous movie. Yet in another way he is equally steely. In the past, he has helped selected patients who have asked him to gain a speedy deliverance – speedier than if nature had been allowed to take her course.

The indications are that, if the pain is too great, he will not be averse, when the time is right, to taking his own life, by injection. Yet he is saved from this drastic step by dying in due time in his hospital bed. Prior to his death there have been odd moments of epiphany – a visit to a church, for example, when he could still 'get around', during which he found himself lighting a candle. During that episode his eye had been caught by the sight of a sparrow perched on a ledge beside a particularly ravishing altarpiece; and now on his hospital bed that same sparrow – or another one? – is back again, a benevolent tutelary presence. There is also the figure of a cowled monk who may have insinuated himself into the hospital ward, and who seems likewise a benevolent presence – a 'real monk', a hallucination or a figment of memory – who can tell? It is not clarified.

Finally, in the third of my examples, it is Zapasiewicz again who plays an elderly diplomat (no less a person than the Polish ambassador to Uruguay) in a movie dating from 2008, *Persona Non Grata*, which I like very much. Here, the focus is not so much human pathology as chronic tiredness, or *mal de siècle*. The man's wife has died; his colleagues, at home and abroad, are ineptly conspiring to have him sacked; he has supped his fill of ideals and delusions. We are allowed to infer that what he essentially wants is *peace*. Blessed by a happy marriage in the past, he desires nothing so much as to die and meet his wife again in paradise – an outcome with which the film's final scenes elegantly conspire to furnish us. (Psychologically speaking, this film is the least 'painful' of the trio.)

All three films under discussion may be said to interrogate death powerfully, and the unbiased viewer is hard put, at first, to say what it is, if anything, that would inflect such enquiries towards religious, or Catholic, conclusions. How are these films different, for example, from a movie like Michael Haneke's *Amour* (2012), where the underlying philosophical presupposition (no matter how tenderly handled is the portrait of the film's ageing couple) seems to be pessimistic, stoical and atheist? In *Life as a Fatal Sexually-transmitted Disease*, as we have seen, there is the question of the 'status' of those hospital visions of the hero: the ghostly monk, the sparrow and so on. What does a sign mean? What does it 'intimate' or point towards? In *Spiralia*, the protagonist, though plainly dead, 'wakes up' after throwing himself out of the window to find himself in a desert landscape with mountains in the distance, towards which he sets off with a stride of mystical rapture and energy. In *Persona Non Grata* the post-life 'snapshot' is static but no less mystical; the protagonist is pictured seated on the rocks, reunited with his beautiful wife, the waves breaking calmly in the background. A kind of paradise, then, in all three cases. But at what level are we meant to take these visions? Beyond the necessity of avoiding kitsch, which all filmmakers must be sensitive to (and none of these sequences, in my judgement, falls into that category), it is surely legitimate for the artist to parry us with different possibilities of interpretation. It is a teasing that is proper to his profession. Wouldn't one be glad, as a Christian, to learn that the aftermath to one's existence *had* been imagined in many different ways, in many different epochs?

Even so central a theological notion as purgatory is a relatively late addition to dogma (indeed it is *not* believed in by Protestants).

FIGURE 10 A domestic affirmation of paradise? Ambassador Wiktor reunited with his departed wife in Zanussi's *Persona Non Grata* (2005).

What religion does teach the penitent soul, or ought to, is how to live well and to prepare for death, in rather the same way as it provides, in its prayers and its ancient incantations, an incomparable spiritual language – an incomparable *story* – with which to confront Death's unspeakable mystery. Zanussi does not 'insist on' Christian trappings in these films – far from it, although as I have said he himself is a self-confessedly practising Christian. In none of the three films I have been talking about is dogma a major dramatic turning point. What religion there is in his films exists as a kind of background in certain characters' lives, or else as a 'way of life' that the seeker might, at a certain juncture or in a spiritual crisis, be drawn towards – an ethic, then, rather than an ideology. He is friendly (at least, not hostile) towards priests, and towards the ideal of monasticism. (One gets the impression that, under other circumstances, that latter path might even have been a vocation for him.) While possessed of a steely, sceptical intellect, a certain predisposition towards charity, honesty and 'openness to wonder' places Zanussi's work, in the last resort, within the circuit of Christian reflection.

*

Zanussi and Kieślowski are (or rather 'were', since Kieślowski is dead) close to each other in temperament. Their plain directing styles share many similarities. Especially during their heyday in the 1970s and '80s, their critique of certain aspects of the Polish political system – its dreariness, corruption and endemic sycophancy in the face of a powerful bureaucracy – had a great deal in common, both morally and stylistically. We are not surprised that whenever Zanussi has occasion to remember his deceased colleague in interviews, it is always with affection and appreciation. In short, they were firm friends as well as mere colleagues. And yet: of course they are different.

Challenged to state where the essence of that difference lies, one might do worse than return to the question of religion. Kieślowski was not really a Catholic, I think. Indeed, was he religious at all? The question

FIGURE 11 A formidable presence on the Polish cultural scene during the 1970s and 1980s: Krzysztof Kieślowski directing Philippe Volter in *The Double Life of Véronique* (1991).

may seem paradoxical, perverse even, in the light of the director's popular 'mystical' image. After all, this man authored a *Decalogue* – ten films in a row, covering each of the Ten Commandments. And in his later films, starting with *The Double Life of Véronique* (1991), and taking in the famous final trilogy *Blue* (1993), *White* (1993) and *Red* (1994), there are intimations, ghosts, coincidences, *clins d'œil* towards the supernatural. Wouldn't any study of religion in cinema delight in having Kieślowski as one of its chief witnesses?

I respond to the appeal of this argument without, as I have hinted, wholly going along with it; though I want to start by making clear my feeling that Kieślowski is *sympathetic to* religion. Yet there are confusions that need to be disentangled. Take the business of the just-mentioned *Decalogue*. This was the cycle of ten hour-long films that Kieślowski and his script-writing friend Krzysztof Piesiewicz made for Polish television in the two-year period 1987 – 8, and on which much of his international fame may be said to rest. The films are given a certain aesthetic unity by being set in the same large housing estate on the edge of Warsaw; but the stories themselves are independent, though from time to time a character from one episode will fleetingly turn up in another. Each story, the viewer would initially imagine, corresponds to a separate Mosaic commandment, so the natural thing to do (since individual commandments are not provided as written epigraphs on the films' opening credits) is to go back to the Bible and check what those commandments are, in the order they are traditionally issued. When we do this we are met with a puzzle. Even when allowance is made (as it certainly should be) for latitude of interpretation, the discovery is soon made that the individual films seem to show little or no correspondence to the numbered Commandments in the Bible. How can this be? Has the viewer missed something? Film two, for example: a slightly obscure tale that seems to hinge on whether it is possible for a woman to love two men at the same time (the woman in question, an orchestra player, is carrying the child of her lover, while her husband lies gravely ill in hospital):

impossible to find the connection between what is going on here and the corresponding second commandment, 'Thou shalt not take the name of the Lord thy God in vain.' Other commandments, such as the third, 'Remember the Sabbath day, to keep it holy,' are equally puzzling in the context of the films they illustrate; in the case of the third film, a story about a woman who descends on her ex-lover on Christmas Eve in order, it seems, to enlist his help in tracking down a previous male friend of hers who may or may not have been injured in a motor accident. (It turns out the woman is a fantasist: the pair drive around the night-time city in vain, looking for him.)

Should one go on? The fifth and sixth films in the series seem to offer a possible crutch to cling onto. These are two films that were taken out of the cycle and separately released in the cinemas in longer versions under the titles *A Short Film about Killing* and *A Short Film about Love*. Very powerful they are too (especially the first of them). There, the commandments seem to jump out at the viewer. 'Thou shalt not kill,' we all know that one. As for the second, 'Thou shalt not commit adultery.' Plain enough one might think (and perhaps it is merely pedantic of me to notice that the female protagonist who seduces the rather young post office assistant in the latter tale is not actually married – so that *technically* it is not adultery that is being spoken about).[2]

All ten films offer their audience complex, sophisticated stories. Some of them have a religious complexion, others seem not to. The first episode, corresponding (or not) to the first commandment 'Thou shalt have no other gods before ME,' shows a father and an eight- or nine-year-old boy living together. Mother is absent, but there is an aunt

---

[2] We should clear up at the outset a possible source of confusion, which is that the Catholic and the Protestant churches traditionally cite the Commandments in a slightly different running order, and with the one crucial addition (in the Protestant case) of a prohibition against worshipping graven images. This latter, coming in as the second commandment, puts all the other commandments out of kilter with the Catholic version (thus the third commandment in the Catholic version is the fourth commandment in the Protestant version, and so on). I have assumed – in the absence of any reason not to – that Kieślowski's *Dekalog* follows the Catholic order.

(Maja Komorowska) who wishes the child to have a Catholic education. The boy is of an age to become interested in metaphysical matters; he has asked about the existence of God and the Soul and received, from his father, sceptical or at any rate agnostic answers on both accounts. Both of them, meanwhile, are fascinated by the new home computer that stands in a prominent place in the living room, and in the workings of which both prove to be quietly expert. By a complicated series of eventualities this will be the boy's undoing, however; he and his father rely on it, one winter's day, to tell them the ratio between the thickness of ice on the lake outside their block of flats and the weight it will bear at any given moment – with fatal consequences, for the ice cracks and the child is drowned. Was the computer therefore a 'false god'? Is that what the episode is telling us?

The Commandments, in their sometimes fierce simplicity, belong, we don't need to be reminded, to the Old Testament rather than the New. In one of the rare places in his excellent autobiography (*Kieślowski on Kieślowski*, edited by Danusia Stok from a series of interviews) in which the director confronts religion head-on, he purports to express a marked preference for the more ancient of the two sacred bodies of text. It is interesting to listen to his reasons. 'The God of the Old Testament is a demanding, cruel God', Kieślowski avers,

> a God who doesn't forgive, who ruthlessly demands obedience to the principles which He has laid down. The God of the New Testament [by contrast] is a merciful, kind-hearted old man with a white beard, who just forgives everything. The God of the Old Testament leaves us a lot of freedom and responsibility, observes how we use it and then rewards or punishes, and there's no appeal or forgiveness. His judgement is something which is lasting, absolute, evident and [...] not relative. And I feel that's what a point of reference must be, especially for people like me who are weak, who are looking for something, and who don't know the answers.

Yet these early films in the cycle don't strike the viewer – this viewer at any rate – as particularly unforgiving or Old Testament. Numbers two and three share, in a way, a similar subject matter; each of them portrays the dilemmas of a woman caught up in a relationship with a man she loves before she has sorted out properly a previous relationship. Both films offer the viewer psychological snapshots of considerable acuity, yet without any obvious didactic moral attached to them – they are simply well-written, self-enclosed short stories. The same can be said of the fourth film in the cycle, about a father and his young adult daughter, and the complicated feelings they adduce for one another. Here the ambience is quasi-incestuous, and ripe for taboo. Yet one could say that this film is rather bold – rather unorthodox – precisely in *not* passing judgement.

As I have already said in so many words, it is not until one gets to the fifth film in the cycle that the director seems to alight on true prophetic fire. Perhaps the outstanding film in the series, *A Short Film about Killing*, recounts, in exemplary Dostoevskian manner, the tale of the murder of a taxi driver by a feckless young drifter whose state of semi-permanent rage against the world seems to have been kindled, years before, by the death of his beloved younger sister in a farm accident. The passionate exhortation against killing which the film maintains is directed, however, not so much against the murder of the taxi driver (shown as it is in shocking close-up detail) as against the subsequent trial and execution of the perpetrator. By showing the process of Polish judicial execution in more harrowing detail than it had ever been seen before on the screen, Kieślowski is said to have contributed, the following year, to its legal suspension. The film is shocking, yet also redemptive (which might seem to push it out of the Old and into New Testament territory). Our young man has lived his life almost bereft of human contact, and it is the kindness of his defence lawyer that opens up, just before the boy's death, a brief glimpse of what it might mean to be human.

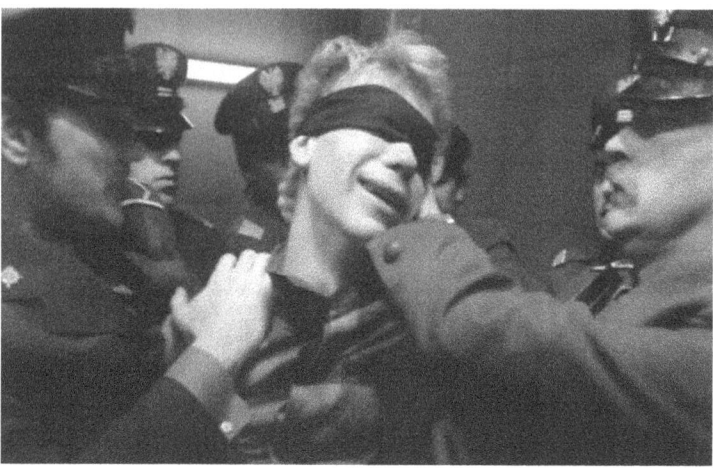

FIGURE 12 'A commandment we all know about.' The execution of the young murderer in *A Short Film about Killing* (1988).

None of the remaining five films in the cycle are pitched anywhere near the key of militant Old Testament austerity that Kieślowski purports to admire so much. Film number six, *A Short Film about Loving*, repeats (but not nearly as powerfully) *A Short Film About Killing*'s theme of redemption. The sexual obsession of a boy with a woman who is a stranger to him succeeds in breaking down her guard. His innocent clumsiness chastens the corrosive hedonism that has been secretly ruining her life, and she ends up taking pity on him, and thereby overcoming her loneliness. Film number seven ('Thou shalt not steal') explores the resentment of a young unmarried mother towards her own mother who, on the pretext of helping her bring up her child, has deprived her of a properly adult role in life. As ever in this series, there is no very discernible moral attached, or illustrated; if the film succeeds in moving us it is, as always, by the quality of its acting, writing and imagination. Film number eight (eighth commandment: 'Thou shalt not bear false witness against thy neighbour') does brush religion, and in an interesting way that might give us reason to pause over it. Zofia (Maria Kościałkowska) is a professor of philosophy approaching retirement age who runs a popular seminar at Warsaw University on ethical dilemmas. Present at this series of lectures is her American translator Elżbieta (Teresa Marczewska) as a guest in the class (it would appear to be the first time she has met the professor in person). At a certain moment this stranger intervenes to ask the students whether she might set them a hypothetical moral test. She requests that they imagine that they are back in the year 1943. In the scenario outlined, a stranger accompanied by his six-year-old Jewish ward approaches a Catholic family involved in resistance work and asks them to extend their protection. The favour is granted, at least potentially, but there is a catch involved, the condition being that the Jewish child shall be brought up in the household to be a Catholic. This turns out to be too much for the couple, who decline the offer and move off to seek what help they can find elsewhere. How would you have behaved (Elżbieta asks the students) in a similar situation, if you were the Catholic hosts? By now we are beginning to guess that it is the speaker herself who was that six-year-old orphan – while the professor must have been part of that Catholic resistance family. Yet, if this was indeed the case, the expected showdown between professor and translator does not materialise. On the contrary, the two women bond with each other! The audience is left to contemplate merely another episode in the perennially fraught history of Jewish–Catholic relations in Poland. No discernible moral is being preached here. No commandment is invoked, or is seen to be broken, or upheld.

A similar conclusion, finally, beckons to the audience in the last two films of the series. These stories (pleasurable enough – the last is a dark comedy about postage stamps) need not, I think, be gone into here. In neither of them, it is fair to say, does religion play even a minor role.

What conclusions are to be drawn from this summary of these powerful movies?[3] If we were to stand back from the *Decalogue* and attempt to characterise it honestly, we would have to confront its anomalous nature; it *purports to* give us an updated version of the Ten Commandments yet in reality it simply ignores them, at least in the majority of cases. (I have attempted to point out the few obvious exceptions.) One might conclude from this that there was something opportunistic and intellectually shallow about Kieślowski's project – the title being no more than a marketing ploy, a conveniently 'sellable' package into which to shoehorn ten otherwise disparate tales. I feel there is some truth in this analysis, though – I don't know if this is paradoxical – the work itself, considered as a whole, is plainly among his finest shots at cinema. I say 'cinema' rather than television, though we need to bear in mind that these one-hour episodes first impinged on the national consciousness via the smaller medium. And that indeed may be their posthumous greatest value – the way that the series entered the Polish home and spoke for a brief moment to the whole nation. The evolution of post-communist Poland in the quarter-century-plus since the momentous events of 1989 has followed many twists and turns – as is the case of course with all the other countries of the ex-Soviet bloc. Materially speaking, entry into the European Union has probably served the country's citizens well; at any event, the standard of living for the majority has improved immeasurably. Yet on the cultural level, the retreat from communism has been followed by a reversion to traditional 'Catholic' values that has seemed at times, from our distant vantage point, to be

---

[3] I hope I have not been unfair to film number eight. Its supposed moral, let us remind ourselves, is 'Thou shalt not bear false witness against thy neighbour.' The conditions of life in wartime Poland opened up many opportunities for spying and tale-telling. Members of the Resistance in particular (like the Catholic family) had to be especially wary of informers, and perhaps they were right to be suspicious about two strangers arriving on their doorstep. In any case, a pervasive aura of civic and neighbourly distrust survived into the postwar settlement, fuelled by the pervasive lies of communism. It is one of Kieślowski's recurring themes in interviews that Poles, in general, are not very 'neighbourly' towards each other.

indistinguishable from mere vulgar authoritarianism. The pressure for conformism in the legislative arena (on such matters as abortion and women's rights) has come close to overturning the very notion of Christian liberalism. In short, a sort of fundamentalism has reasserted itself – as banal and unintelligent, perhaps, as the 'communist' fundamentalism it is a belated reaction against. Here, it could be argued, Kieślowski's *Decalogue* provides a truly precious antidote – precious reminder, if you like, of the complexity and variety of life, and how it is that not every moral dilemma needs be reduced to the simplicities of the catechism. This, then, may be the answer to the puzzle, or paradox, that the *Decalogue* seems to confront the viewer with: it *appears to be* a call for the reassertion of ancient values, yet in fact it is a plea for tolerance and pluralism.

*

Need one return now to the question of whether Kieślowski was, or was not, a Christian artist? For some people, the evidence of his films makes it obvious. Of course, they say, the man is an atheist! Certainly the Catholic Church, or more accurately, the clerical-intellectual (and patently right-wing) part of it, was fond of targeting Kieślowski with accusations of infidelity. One occasion was the release, in 1984 (during the full depths of martial law), of the movie *No End* ('Bez Końca'), a film that concludes with a strange and unmotivated suicide. It is certainly a black piece of drama; I myself remember thinking so at the time, and wondering where such despair would lead Kieślowski to intellectually. For the critic Krzysztof Kłoptowski, reviewing the film in the Jesuit journal *Przeglad Powszechny*, there was at the time only one conclusion to be drawn. 'Kieślowski's films', he said, 'do not belong to the Christian tradition.' Yet in response, Krzysztof Zanussi, in the filmed interview (available on YouTube) mentioned at the beginning of this chapter, can be seen to argue indignantly on behalf of his friend and fellow countryman. 'Kieślowski could be anti-clerical, as many Christians are', he expostulates. 'But his deep metaphysical apprehensions were not in conflict with evangelical teachings.' (One notes the way Zanussi puts it, insisting that his friend actually *is* a Christian.) The mention of 'evangelical teachings' focuses attention, at any event, on the New Testament rather than the Old, allowing us to entertain the reflection that, despite everything we have said about Kieślowski's stated preference for the original Jewish Pentateuch, *part of* his spirit was open to the famous Glad Tidings.

Is it true and does it matter? I have said that Kieślowski was sympathetic to Christianity, and I cannot think of any better way of demonstrating this contention than by having a look in detail at one final movie. *Blind Chance* ('Przypadek', 1981), not mentioned so far, is a portmanteau work that was conceived of in three parts at the height of the Solidarity campaign. It belongs, I think, among Kieślowski's finest efforts. Three films in one – we might note in passing Kieślowski's formal genius for compression. (This is one of the artistic qualities that also shines out of the *Decalogue*.) None of the three stories in *Blind Chance* seems at all cramped; all of them are as long as they need to be. The connected tales emerge out of a single premise, which is: your life can be changed by the simple fact of missing a train – or of catching it. Thus as the film opens we observe Vitek (Bogusław Linda), a young medical student from Łódź, speeding along the platform to catch the Warsaw Express. In the first telling of the tale he succeeds, and, on board, falls in with a group of Party activists. In the second episode he fails, and, in his frustration, becomes involved in a commotion on the platform. Striking a railway guard is a serious matter in any country; after trial and conviction, Vitek is made to undertake a short spell of community service. In the third 'alternative scenario' he also fails to catch the train, only this time there is no fight with the authorities. A blonde girl on the platform calmly observes his frustrated dash towards the disappearing railway carriage. Now she accompanies him back to his apartment, and the pair make love. Shortly, this woman will become his wife.

Three identical openings, three vastly different outcomes. We need to assume – the conceit is successful, I think – that the young man is the

FIGURE 13 Following the path of whim or of providence? Exemplary student Witek (Bogusław Linda) in Kieślowski's *Blind Chance* (1981).

same young man in all three cases, with the same background history (whatever that is – it is left deliberately vague). So these are three different paths that one particular young man's life might have taken.

Who is this person? He is young, as we have said, idealistic, imbued with energy, perhaps a future leader of his country. Whatever happens to him, it is going to be interesting, and he in turn will be articulate and thoughtful about his fate.

We need to start by observing (what may indeed appear obvious) that blind chance is not really a Christian concept. In Christianity, on the contrary, we have the idea of providence. The implication of Kieślowski's title, before we have got any further, is that man is at the mercy of the universe, and that fate can treat us according to its whims. That was how the Romans thought of the matter; and one can see the attraction of this standpoint, too, in an age that recognises the truths of quantum physics. With this preliminary caveat 'out of the way' (a little schematically perhaps), let us see how *Blind Chance* plays itself out in practice.

In the first episode, as already intimated, Vitek meets an urbane acquaintance who tempts him into joining the ranks of the Party. His first task will be to spy on some junior doctors who are leading a protest against working conditions at the local hospital. Accepting the task cautiously, Vitek soon reveals himself morally out of his depth. The Party is discovered to be irremediably corrupt, even if there are nuances among its personnel, as everywhere in life. Would it be possible to rise up through the ranks and preserve one's integrity? Soon enough, Vitek has his answer; and this episode ends in comprehensive disillusionment.

The second episode introduces us into a specifically Christian milieu. While serving his punishment on community service (after striking the railway official on the Łódź platform), Vitek makes a connection with the religious underground – it will be recalled that we are in the time of martial law – and soon becomes involved in their clandestine activities. Inspired by the bravery of a woman who is being harassed by the State for no other reason than her religious convictions, the young man seeks baptism, and teaches himself to pray. When things go wrong (alas they do go wrong) it is because he allows himself to be distracted by a love affair. Time taken out in pursuing this liaison interferes with Vitek's new Christian-civic duties. The samizdat press he is in charge of is raided by the authorities, and Vitek falls under suspicion, among his militant companions, of being a police informer. So this episode too ends in abject failure.

In the final of the three alternative scenarios Vitek completes his medical studies successfully and marries his blonde partner (the woman who was standing looking at him on the platform). A baby follows. The dean of his faculty likes and admires him. When this same dean falls under the suspicion of the authorities for dissenting views, he singles out Vitek (already seen as an ally) and arranges for him to deliver a lecture at a conference in Libya that he himself will now be unable to attend. Our hero postpones his flight by a day so that he can be at home on his wife's birthday. This alteration of schedule turns out to be fatal however, since, shortly after take-off, the plane he is travelling in explodes in mid-air, in front of our eyes. A shocking ending to Vitek's life in this third incarnation, for at last it seemed to be going somewhere positive.

Blind chance, then. Or not? It is true that things 'happen' to us, including accidents. We make our way in life as we can, but we cannot *not* be vulnerable to exterior contingencies. Chance is capricious and cruel, yet still (this profoundly pessimistic film seems to say), within its constraints, human beings may order their fates and attempt to make meaningful decisions. Kieślowski is not a determinist, even if 'fiddling the dice' is the perennial privilege of story-tellers. The aesthetic power of *Blind Chance* lies in its controlled sense of doom and unease, combined with an extraordinary formal openness. The audience is allowed to feel that it doesn't know, in any of the three cases, where exactly the narrative is going, or what will be the final upshot of its incidents.

Meanwhile the Christian elements in the second tale are handled with consummate precision and what I would call an altogether impressive display of knowledge. Faces, dialogues, gestures are continuously convincing. The conversations between Vitek and the priest Stepan (the latter, for unexplained reasons, confined to a wheelchair) go straight to the heart of faith; they do not falter. So we follow Vitek's path to prayer, and witness his first tentative efforts to communicate with God. There is nothing melodramatic or exaggerated in these scenes of simple Christian piety – no irony, no 'attitude'. The Christian religion is evoked by Kieślowski in terms that properly belong to it, and not as a mere anthropological curiosity.

FIGURE 14 'One of the bleakest films in existence': Robert Bresson's *Lancelot du Lac* (1974).

3

France: The Apostasy of Robert Bresson

It is perhaps not saying anything very new to maintain that the predominant mode of writing about culture in general, and cinema in particular, is secular. Of course it is. We live in a secular age. Still, I hope we would feel that, if and when it is appropriate to address the topic of religion in the context of cultural debate, not everyone will have forgotten how to do so. There was a time when a certain expertise in such matters could be taken for granted. Modern French film criticism is as secular as it is anywhere else, yet hidden within it, among practitioners, there has always been a tradition of Christian reflection. The ideological rivalry between France's historically two most important journals of film criticism, *Positif* (founded in 1952) and *Les Cahiers du Cinéma* (1951), was defined, at least partially, on theological grounds – *Positif* being proudly and staunchly atheist (it went with its allegiance to surrealism), *Cahiers* in its heyday much more sympathetic to what might be called Christian social thought (the magazine even had a priest, Amédée Ayfre, as one of its regular contributors). The tone of *Cahiers* was set by its famous first editor André Bazin (1918–58), and in Bazin's personal writings on the artform there is a detectable Christian subtext, albeit socially liberal and non-evangelical. One can discern this influence in the essays of the contributors he drew round him, a number of whom of course went on to become themselves high-profile filmmakers. It would not be right to call Godard Christian, I think, under any circumstances; but the film journalism of Truffaut, Chabrol and Rohmer, to take three of the magazine's then most prominent writing stars, is at times explicitly theological. (Recall the efforts of Chabrol and Rohmer over the years to prove that Hitchcock was a Catholic film artist.) Even when the discussion was ostensibly far from religion, as it is for example in Truffaut's famous essay 'A Certain Tendency in French Cinema' (1954) (his attack on the hegemony of establishment scriptwriters, and a crucial text in the battle to assert the notion of the director as auteur), the writing is powered by a moral discrimination that seems to me to be religious, or at least partly so. Thus, the reason Truffaut hates Aurenche and Bost so much (the two scriptwriters he concentrates on) is not because they are bad writers – on the contrary, he concedes they are consummately professional – but because, according to his reckoning, the view of life put forward in their film scenarios is so drearily and mechanically atheist. (Truffaut was only 22 when he wrote this essay.)

Naturally I am not claiming that the rise to eminence of the New Wave directors unleashed a sudden spate of Christianity into the corridors of French filmmaking, an unlikely outcome on the face of it. As a matter of fact, Christianity had always been 'there' in some sense, on a popular and melodramatic level; witness numerous films about Joan of Arc and assorted female seraphim – what used to be called the 'Sulpicien' school of French filmmaking.[1] On the other hand, it can be said about French cinema in general that, where religion does emerge as a topic of drama, it is dealt with, often, in a sophisticated and intelligent fashion. I find it hard to recall, for example, an English or American movie that captures the simple and impressive piety of monastic life as convincingly as is done by Xavier Beauvois in the film *Of Gods and Men* (2010). We will come back to monastic matters shortly, but in the

---

[1] The adjective makes reference to the pious and sentimental statuettes of saints and the Holy Family on sale in the many little gift-shops surrounding the church of Saint-Sulpice in Paris.

meantime it is interesting to explore further the distinction (where it exists) between films that are 'about religion' in some merely sociological or anecdotal fashion, and other films that it would be proper to call religious in their essence. Perhaps it is harder than one might think to tell these categories apart. Rohmer has been briefly mentioned, and we could take a film like *Ma Nuit chez Maud/My Night at Maud's* (1969) as a critical example of the difficulty. Although a meditation about Catholicism seems to be at the centre of it, this is not true, by and large, of Rohmer's other films, which dwell characteristically, and with consummate scruple, on the deceptions of secular love. So does this film, of course! A respectable argument could be made about it that religion is essentially a subtext, a sort of 'local colouring' or even an added erotic spice, put there to cover the main thrust of the movie's investigation, which lies where it always lies with this director, in deciphering and illuminating the complexities of the human heart.

Yet this doesn't, either, quite get the measure of the movie. For a start, the protagonist's Catholicism is far from being mere camouflage; on the contrary, it seems to constitute the deepest core of his being; it is central to the way that he operates in the world. Admittedly, his stance is idiosyncratic, as perhaps personal belief always is, and different tenets of it, at times, come to seem contradictory (or at any rate, as he himself allows, 'in conflict'). Despite this, he seems to be not *ipso facto* unorthodox. Readers who have seen the movie will recall that the protagonist in question (called Jean-Louis, and played by Jean-Louis Trintignant) is unable to disguise in discussion with his friend Vidal (Antoine Vitez), and later with Maud herself (Françoise Fabian), his antipathy towards the writings of Pascal. In these matters he is on the side of the Jesuits. His disdain is directed first of all against the arbitrariness of the celebrated wager on God's existence, which he sees as prudential and pusillanimous. At the same time he is impatient about the fact that the seventeenth-century mathematician and philosopher never seems properly to make up his mind about anything.

More precisely, Jean-Louis maintains, Pascal 'lacks distinctive passions'. (He would never be caught saying, for example, about the delicious wine of the region, 'J'aime ce bon vin de Chanturgue!') Like many of Rohmer's films, *Ma Nuit chez Maud* revolves around the question of how it is that we decide what sort of life-partner suits us best, and beyond this therefore, in the deepest sense, what our passions *are*. On the one hand the world presents itself as teeming with wondrous variety; on the other hand, for a person of discretion, there will always be, inevitably, distinct types and preferences. Knowing what you want is a sign of character and maturity; but on the other hand, how can we stop ourselves from looking? Jean-Louis is a typically riven member of the species. On the one hand he has met, by accident, the magnificent Maud (how could any man *not* be taken by her?); on the other, there is the awkward fact that he seems to have already made his choice beforehand (despite up to this moment never having spoken to the woman!) when in church one fine day he fastened his gaze on a 'blonde catholique' named Françoise (Marie-Christine Barrault) in the midst of her weekly devotions.

So Jean-Louis is 'riven' by a dilemma, for all that he prides himself on his decisiveness. As evening gives way to night, the question arises of whether and when he should leave. Maud asks him to stay, and he hesitates. Having accepted her invitation to lie down on the bed beside her, he precipitously withdraws from her embraces. (Running naked to the bathroom, Maud lashes out at him with scorn: 'I hate a man who doesn't know his mind.') His fastidiousness, in this episode, might seem merely to expose his humbug. And so it does in a way. Yet in another way it doesn't. *Both* interpretations of his character (his 'ditheringness' on the one hand, his Catholic lucidity on the other) are correct or, shall we say, plausible; this is why the film is so psychologically subtle, and also so hard to pin down. The protagonist is 34 years old. He has had several girlfriends in his life; he may even have been, at one time – it is hinted by his friend Vidal – a bit of a Don Juan (when he lived abroad, in Vancouver and Valparaiso). 'My affairs with women and my Christianity are two different things,' he says to Maud, defensively, and of course priggishly, early on in the course of their night together. Later on, he can be heard qualifying this reticence. The side of Christianity he *doesn't* like, he says, is the part of it that entails minutely accounting for deeds and for misdeeds; whereas where religion comes into its own, he thinks, is by teaching us the virtue of simplicity. He claims, for example, that he doesn't really understand infidelity: 'When you are really in love with one girl, you don't want to sleep with another,' he opines. 'What is important', he declares bravely at another stage in the night's heroic conversation, 'is purity of heart.' Later on: 'Love adds to religion, as religion adds to love.' The viewer may think of him as an ass in certain ways, or else as a hypocrite, but these are magnificent sentiments. So the movie is serious, without sacrificing its undertone of comedy. The Catholicism that it sketches through Jean-Louis precisely benefits (so it seems to me) from an absence of angst and portentousness.

FIGURE 15   'A typically riven member of the species'. Jean-Louis (Jean-Louis Trintignant) stumped for excuses in Rohmer's *My Night at Maud's* (1969).

Ma Nuit chez Maud is an achieved work of art and not a theological treatise. My brief remarks on it have, of course, omitted many if not most of the things that make the film live in the memory, among which we should have to include its marvellously deft sense of place (Clermont-Ferrand in wintertime: the countryside as well as the city, both of them highlighted in luminous black and white photography); also the consummate structural balance of the film which ensures, among other things, that while Maud stays firmly in its centre, the other girl, Françoise (i.e., the 'blonde catholique'), is equally wonderfully drawn, in her own way. Finally there is the exquisitely discreet way in which the twist of the tale – what one might call its incipient 'back story' involving the former life of the innocent Françoise – is made known at the end to the audience. The movie was released in 1969, and one of the most extraordinary things about it is that there is no reference at all – not the slightest allusion – to the fierce moral and political upheavals that had shaken France the previous year. Exotic, perhaps, to us, for that very reason, the film seems nevertheless to take positive pride in its ordinary middle-class normalcy. Whatever might be said about Paris and its revolutions, life in the provinces proceeds in this film as it has always done. Here reign established rituals such as the bourgeois dinner party, the weekend walk in the mountains and (for some at least of the city's intelligent inhabitants) regular devoted attendance at Sunday Mass.

*

Ma Nuit chez Maud is one film out of the 51 that comprise Rohmer's complete filmography. While it shows that he is sympathetic to Christianity, and certainly understands what it means, it doesn't necessarily (in the absence of other evidence, though it is well known that the director was in fact a churchgoer) turn him into a 'Christian filmmaker'. Among Rohmer's compatriots, that label could at least as plausibly be attached to the figure of Robert Bresson (1901–99). Indeed, if one were asking oneself whether there *were* major artists in the twentieth century who could contrive to be called Christian, Bresson surely would be one of the major candidates. Nevertheless, there is a kind of paradox lying at the heart of his work. An enemy, from the start, of sentimentality and emotionalism (the most lucid and austere of filmmakers), he seems at a certain stage to have abandoned the idea of pity and, with it, the visible vestiges of Christian compassion and charity; so that by the time we come to certain late films he seems to be not merely not religious, but even, by certain lights, atheist – as bleakly or blackly atheist, perhaps, as a contemporary of his, Samuel Beckett. This 'peculiarity' in Bresson's artistic trajectory has of course not gone unnoticed by film scholars, but the questions arising out of it are, it seems to me, underexplored. If I have got the trajectory right (I am hoping it is not more complicated than I claim it to be), the crucial artistic question that follows is: which part of his career – his 'believing' or his 'unbelieving' phase – produced the better movies? And how would a critic go about supporting such a judgement?

Bresson's first film, *Les Anges du Péché* (English title: *Angels of Sin*), plunges us by necessity deep into the drama of religion, set as it is within the confines of a nunnery. The order, we are told in the opening credits, has been founded by a certain Father Lataste with the specific purpose of rescuing those who used to be called fallen women. The film is one such case history, a particularly dramatic one, in that the would-be rescuer, Anne-Marie (Renée Faure), a proud and aristocratic young nun scarcely out of her novitiate, comes to flout the convent's unwritten rules in her eagerness to grapple with the soul of a young murderess, and is expelled from the order as a result. Melodrama – a certain wayward emotionalism – is perhaps written into stories that find themselves set in convents. Certainly the film has melodramatic aspects to it (aspects which Bresson himself later came to repudiate). But it would be wrong, nevertheless, to conclude that this is the last word on the subject. On the contrary, the unbiased viewer cannot fail to register how much the film from the start possesses a beautiful documentary seriousness. The rhythm of convent life – the balance between worship and relaxation, between solitude and gregariousness, between public charity and private devotion – is superbly integrated into the film's dramatics. Right from the start the viewer gets a sense of eavesdropping on a world of Christian piety impressive on the one hand for its practical common sense, and on the other for its idealism and innocence. That world does not exist now, I think, for many reasons. But it existed then, in 1943, in the depth of war, when the film was made, and the modern viewer benefits from this.

The main defence against the charge of mere melodrama lies where one would expect it to lie, in the subtlety and intelligence of the film's psychology, manifested especially in the handling of the two main characters. Anne-Marie, as incarnated by Renée Faure, is a beautiful and spirited aristocrat who in the normal trajectory of her class would have been expected to make a 'good marriage' and raise a family, yet who instead feels an inexplicable call to serve Christ. If there is a back story to her decision (an aborted love affair, a broken engagement) we are not vouchsafed its details, beyond discovering, in a magnificent short scene with her mother, that her family is implacably opposed to her calling. We meet her first on the day of her induction and we can guess perhaps that things are not going to be easy for her. Attachment to the world is still there in the way that she glances at herself in the mirror to check that her habit fits neatly, and again, in the visible regret with which she looks longingly at a collection of family photographs before casting them into the fire. Bypassing the details of her novitiate, the film moves on swiftly to the moment when, installed as a young nun, she comes across the woman who will turn out to be (we need to put it like this) her destiny. The prostitute Thérèse (Jany Holt) possesses as forceful a character as Anne-Marie's, but it is set in an opposite mould. Brought to the nunnery from prison against her wishes, she refuses the ministrations offered by the nuns that will smooth her future path; she will hold onto her anger and bitterness. Ages ago, back in the outside world, there was a man who wronged her, and it is not in her heart to forgive him. 'The guilty forgive;

the innocent want revenge!' is one of her icy epigrams. (Another: 'Flayed is right. You can't caress the flayed.') How to conquer this woman's pride and assuage her despair – how, in short, to conduct the soul of Thérèse into the merciful presence of the Lord – becomes Anne-Marie's overriding obsession.

The power struggle that ensues once Anne-Marie has decided on her path constitutes, then, the core of the film. We may skip many of the plot details, pausing only to observe that the stakes are upped, rather evidently, when Thérèse temporarily escapes from the convent to carry out the threat of revenge on her ex-lover. Purchasing a pistol, she murders the man (a dramatically imagined sequence – we only see his shadow in the doorway), before returning to the shelter of the cloister where, for the moment, the secret is hers alone.

Meanwhile, however, Anne-Marie has been having her own troubles. Characteristically outspoken, she contrives to fall out with the deputy reverend mother over the presence of a cat that has been killing the convent's songbirds; and refusing the – rather mild – punishment

FIGURE 16   An underground subplot of melodrama? Night-time Paris imagined by Bresson in *Les Anges du Péché* (1943).

assigned to her, finds herself expelled from the community. A tremendous blow to her spirit! Up until now Anne-Marie has seemed to be not only ardent, but blessed (as the happy are) by good fortune. How will she take her expulsion – an expulsion that will mean, among other things, the failure of her self-appointed task of 'turning' the soul of Thérèse? As the film moves into its majestic final phase, months have passed; we come across the exiled Anne-Marie in civilian clothes, apparently in high fever, haunting the periphery of the convent. A gap in the fence allows her to slip into the cemetery, where she prays at, then collapses on, the grave of the order's founder. Discovered by a party of nuns, she is transported to the convent infirmary. The still-unrepentant Thérèse has been present among the onlookers, and though she alone of the congregating women fails to kiss or comfort her former protector, when the body is gathered up from Father Lataste's grave something for the first time seems to move her.

The last stages of the film show the seeds of this change of heart evolve into a fully acknowledged submission of humility. Bresson uses in these sequences (as he has throughout) all the traditional resources of cinema to make us feel the weight and significance of what is happening. So there is music, but it is discreet and appropriate. And while the *mise en scène* is made up for the most part of looks and silences, the words when they come have a magnificent plangency and simplicity. The staging of the figures around Anne-Marie's deathbed uses classical pictorial techniques of contrast and highlighting – setting the body of the nuns at the head of the bed, where they minister to Anne-Marie's dying needs (kissing her hands and folding them in prayer), at the same time isolating Thérèse at the foot of the bed in preparation for the moment when, at last, she leans forward and kisses her passionate mentor's feet. The rhetoric that Bresson uses here finds a culmination in the wonderful extended travelling shot that closes the movie, showing the chastened Thérèse arise from her knees, process past the massed assembly of nuns down the corridor – out towards the doors of the convent where she will place her hands in the manacles of the waiting policemen. 'Submission' in all senses, therefore – but freely bestowed, and, in that sense, her first truly existential act of liberty.

Roland Barthes penned a celebrated essay on this film. Since it is by Barthes, it is no surprise that it should be well written. Yet the odd thing perhaps is that he should like the movie so much. Against what he acknowledges to be the 'perils' of its setting (a nunnery) and its argument (Christian redemption), he absolves Bresson of resorting to sentimental cliché. 'The convent is delicate, tender, clean', he writes.

> Not too much chapel; from time to time a linear cloister; more often, a sunny little garden, a workroom, a kitchen, a corridor, no organ, and a bell only once or twice; a little evensong; the dialogue simple, decisive, quite virile. Bresson's nuns are reliable; they know how to wear their habits; they know how to walk, pray, speak; they don't keep raising their eyes to heaven, nor casting them down to the ground; they are fresh without being freshly painted, and charming without being provocative.

The 'quite virile' language of the film that he admires is glossed in the following way:

> The dialogue [written by the playwright Jean Giraudoux] required only his talent, not his famous manner; and such talent is enormous. To listen to this film is a great pleasure for both mind and heart. Not one sentimental or pedantic sentence; no effusions, no catechism; a human mode of speech, full of grandeur and kindness, which grips the soul and embraces it without any of the tricks of religious eloquence.

Still, it is with that mention of 'religious eloquence' (and its implied deceptiveness) that one seems to encounter the limits of Barthes's sympathies. Redemption as a central aspect of human experience he can't in the end take seriously, and throughout the rest of the piece a light tone of incredulity reasserts itself ('one doesn't die of a thunderstorm', he remarks at one point). I think his irony is misplaced. For me (it should perhaps be obvious by now) the experience of the film doesn't warrant any such barbed condescension. Certainly, the conventions of our age make it foreign, if not downright incomprehensible, that anyone should ever kneel to anyone else, or bow the head in reverence; but the Christian notion of the soul's salvation (so magnificently and theatrically dramatised, as it seems to me, in this film) is merely the poetic rendering of a psychological habit of being that in the end is accessible to all of us. To appreciate what is at stake, it is irrelevant whether we 'belong to' the church in a confessional sense. For what is redemption after all except freedom from suffering, anguish, self-laceration? It is peace with oneself: a universal desideratum. That such a state of grace may be achieved, against the perverse and refractory urgings of the will, ought to be nothing but moving and wonderful.

*

Bresson's next film, *Les Dames du Bois de Boulogne* (1945), a dark and sophisticated drama of revenge, with dialogues by Cocteau, is certainly a classic, but it is not really relevant to our argument here, so we will quietly pass it by in order to look at the film he made after this, *Le Journal d'un Curé de Campagne/ The Diary of a Country Priest* (1951) – by any criterion one of the great films of the twentieth century, and central to any serious argument about cinema and Christianity. Part of such greatness is ascribable to the force of the original source material, Georges Bernanos's novel of the same name that was published in 1931. Yet a film and a book are two different entities. Just as there are things that literature can do but films can't, so film, too, has its own vocabulary, its own syntax and rhythm, which are ultimately autonomous and independent. If the spoken dialogues of the characters are part of the 'given data' that is available to be shared between book and movie, everything else depends upon the artistry, taste and interpretive skill of the adapter. To take just a few examples at random: the timbre of the voices, the relation of spoken dialogue to interior voiceover (crucial in a diary-film like the one we are talking about), the play of glances in a given scene, the distribution of music, the choice of location, the physical appearance of the actors, the alternation of light and darkness over the human countenance (what one might call the movie's chiaroscuro) – these are all things that are in the film but not there in the book, whatever compensatory advantages belong, traditionally and rightly, to the privilege of the printed word.

Since I have mentioned the face, we might move on from there; it seems a good entrance into a movie about which Truffaut said memorably: 'Every shot is as true as a handful of earth.' The actor Claude Laydu, who died only a short while ago, appeared in several films in the course of his career, but here we have one of those roles – like that of Falconetti in Dreyer's *La Passion de Jeanne d'Arc* – where the actor simply *is* the character; what he gives to this film is not really acting at all but, as Bazin might have put it, metaphysical presence. In an important but hard-to-define way, his face is the meaning of the movie. I say 'face' here, but it is also the body – the parched, ascetic body of a man whose diet, it is easy to believe, has reduced itself through circumstances to a staple of bread sopped in wine. The curé of Ambricourt is new to a parish in rural northern France where God seems to be only just hanging on by His fingernails. The priest's duties are the standard ones: offering daily Mass, organising catechism classes, burials and weddings, plus getting to know the community socially (where it chooses to reveal itself) so that he may deliver himself of what humble solace lies within his powers. His powers, he recognises, are weak: they would be nothing at all without the authority of priestly office. Our man is young and inexperienced. And yet he seems to bear within him some secret aptitude. Without knowing where it comes from (this is crucial), he belongs, as his neighbour Doctor Delbende comes to realise, to the race of men who 'hold to it', needing no instruction, no encouragement even, in the sacred pursuit of their calling. Never in the history of film, I think it is safe to say, has the meaning of vocation been more subtly and movingly dramatised than it is in these scenes showing the priest going about his daily business. What gives the portrayal its extraordinary authenticity is the combination of humility with inner strength which Laydu brings to the part, and which allows the parallels with Christ's earthly journey to emerge with a natural, unforced and finally momentous authority. Bazin, as usual, puts the matter with classical precision: 'Bresson, like Bernanos', he says in a famous essay on the film, 'avoids any sort of symbolic allusion, and so none of the situations, despite their obvious parallel to the Gospel, is created precisely *because of* that parallel. Each bears his cross and each cross is different. But all are the Cross of the Passion.'

The film is rather well known, and different readers will have different memories of its high points. When a film really works, all details, even the minor ones, are important, making up as they do the integral stitches of the tapestry. So we have here the 'minor' character of the doctor (Antoine Balpêtré), already mentioned, and his friend the

FIGURE 17   'Every shot is as true as a handful of earth.' Claude Laydu as the curé d'Ambricourt in *The Diary of a Country Priest* (1951).

curé de Torcy (André Guibert – in real life Bresson's psychoanalyst), around whom the director weaves a parallel meditation on the hesitations of faith and despair. Torcy is the opposite of our hero: bluff, pragmatic, unoccupied by interior strivings. In the early stages of the narrative he is free in his criticism of the new country priest's social gaucheness; such naive theological earnestness, he implies, can only lead to trouble. And yet even as he delivers this advice something seems to strike him about its inadequacy. It is relevant and interesting that his own best friend should be the doctor, whose pitiless and disillusioned view of the world in due course issues in suicide. Evidently there is an affinity between the two older men – affinity of experience, and even of worldview. Beneath his bluff and professional exterior, Torcy is alive to the logic (or perhaps one should say the attraction) of atheism, so that when it comes to his dealings with the priest it is a beautiful feature of the film that Torcy, the ostensibly 'stronger' man, as he is certainly the senior, should be shown slowly coming to recognise, and finally to find strength in, the power of the priest's moral steadfastness. Still, Torcy's amazingly hopeful speech on the interceding powers of the Virgin Mary when he comes to say goodbye to the curé remains, I am sure, for many people besides myself, one of the absolute vivid high points of the movie.

But not the *very* highest point, surely! That distinction must be reserved for those twin battles of the will that take place between the priest and the countess on the one hand, and on the other, between the priest and the countess's daughter, Chantal. *Le Journal d'un Curé de Campagne* strikes me as being remarkable, among other reasons, for the subtlety of the portrayal of its women characters. Let us pause briefly to remind ourselves of who is involved here. Outside the perennial and necessary figure of the housekeeper (all priests have housekeepers), there are in fact five main female figures in the movie: in order of appearance, the child Seraphita (the star of the curé's catechism class); the governess Louise (the count's secret mistress); the countess herself; her daughter Chantal; and finally, towards the end of the film, the girlfriend of the seminarian-turned-chemist Dufrety. It would be fair to say that three at least of these characters – Seraphita, Louise and Chantal – are strongly aware of the priest as a sexual being: temptation, in this austere film, is 'in the air'. But it is not in itself the *subject* of the movie. The sexual ambience serves, rather, as a sort of physical medium through which matters of the soul, as well as questions of ordinary tenderness, are identified and come to the fore. Two scenes in particular, of stark confrontation, lift Bresson's exposition into the realm of the sublime and stamp the film with the authority of a masterpiece.

Let us examine first of all how Bresson deals with Chantal, played with extraordinary finesse and delicacy by the young actress Nicole Ladmiral. The girl has been profoundly shocked by two things: the discovery of her father the count's adultery, and at the same time her mother's contemptuous acquiescence in this state of affairs. So her soul is in the kind of turmoil that may be identified as defiance of adult authority: indifference towards her father, contempt towards her mother – plus murderous hatred for the governess-mistress as the instigator of her uninvited torment. Into this cauldron steps the priest, the newcomer; she will seek him out in church and ask his counsel.

Yet is it really counsel she is seeking, or something else? For her vehemence, alas, goes with slyness and knowledge of her own incipient beauty; and it would be satisfaction of a sort – a strangely sexual satisfaction – to shock *him* as profoundly as she herself has been shocked. I will hold back from analysing the extraordinary scene in the confessional box (extraordinary in both its purity and its eroticism) in which the curé turns the tables, so to speak, by persuading the girl to hand over a letter of revenge addressed to her father (which he promptly burns); and move the reader forward instead to the related yet equally haunting scene towards the end of the movie in which, as the priest packs up to leave for medical help in Lille (he thinks he is consumptive, though in fact he has cancer), Chantal makes one final bid to penetrate his defences.

Her purpose in one sense is an innocent one; she wants to know from someone she respects (and possibly even fears a little) what that person thinks of her; in a way, as before, she is only asking for guidance. But the request is disingenuous, firstly because it is inflected by flirtation, and secondly because it is accompanied by the subterranean desire – futile as it turns out – to place her interlocutor at a moral disadvantage. The subtlety of the scene depends, as always in Bresson, on an interplay between the trenchancy of the dialogue and the precision of the *mise en scène*: the pauses, the hesitations, the choice of the moment at which the camera moves into close-up, the sobriety of the surrounding atmosphere and so on. Mere description can only hint at the nuances conveyed. Yet perhaps it is worthwhile to listen to the dialogue that transpires between the pair, if only to remind ourselves how confidently, at this stage in his career, Bresson handled the exigencies of drama and psychology:

[*The girl has snuck into the room while the priest is packing his boxes*]
Chantal [*smiling foxily*]: 'Are you ever going to come back?'
Curé: 'That depends...'
'On you?'
'On the doctor in Lille.' [*Pause, then, indicating his suitcases*] 'Help me, since you're here – against your father's will, I might add.'
'You certainly keep your cards hidden. May I ask what you think of me?'
'A priest has no opinions.'
'You have eyes and ears, and make use of them, like everyone, I suppose.'
'They would tell me nothing about you.'
'Why not?'
[*Hazarding a diagnosis*]'You're always restless, happy to conceal the truth of your soul. Or perhaps to forget it.'
'I'm not afraid of the truth. And if you're daring me –'
[*Vehemently*] 'I'm not daring you. I'd only agree to hear your confession if you were in danger of death. As for absolution, it will come in due time, I hope, and from another hand than mine.'
[*Pause: Chantal proceeds*] 'That wasn't hard to predict. [*Slyly*]

Anyway, father will have you transferred. Everybody here takes you for a drunkard –'
[*He gives her no reply. They walk together into another room. He puts his notebooks in a suitcase*]
Chantal [*suddenly earnest*]: 'If you only knew what I think of life [...] I want everything. I'll try everything. I know plenty of others have died without managing to do that. If life disappoints me, so be it. I will sin just for sin's sake.'
Curé [*after a pause*]: 'That's the moment you will find God.'
Now it is her turn to pause. 'I feel like – I don't know – insulting you. You think you can decide my fate against my will? I'll damn myself if I please.'
Curé [*with great sincerity and simplicity*]: 'I answer you, soul for soul.'
Chantal: 'Are you just saying what strikes your fancy? I was at the window when you spoke with Mother. All of a sudden her expression became so gentle. I don't believe in miracles any more than I believe in ghosts, but I think I know my mother. She cares for fine phrases like a fish cares for apples. Do you have some secret?' [*eagerly, as if she really wants to know*]
Curé: 'A lost secret. You will find it and lose it in turn. And others will pass it on after you.'

This quiet, grave and momentous scene ends with a close-up of Chantal's face, as she takes in the impact of his words.

I shall not reproduce (though if there were space I would like to, since it's so surpassingly marvellous) the dialogue of the other great, complementary scene that stands out in this film, which dramatises what I have been calling the 'struggle for the countess's soul'. For, in a way, the dialectic here between the spoken word and the movement of the camera is even *more* subtle than in the scene just described, if that were possible. Just to remind ourselves: the priest has come up to the chateau to warn the countess of her daughter's defiance; the girl's desperation has struck him as being so serious that he thinks it may issue in suicide. But the news fails to impinge on the woman it is delivered to. Her mental space is wholly taken up by the memory of the beloved son whose accidental death years before our story started has locked her into a permanent soul-sulk. And this despair too is 'defiant', like Chantal's, taking the form of an implacable rage against the Almighty, along with a refusal of the consolations of the Church. As for the priest: her scorn towards the Church's representative is the habituated scorn of her class: 'God has ceased to matter to me. What will you get by making me admit that I hate Him, fool?', she throws out at one stage in their confrontation. At the climax of an interview that takes up several minutes of screen time (and that is clandestinely witnessed, as we have just seen, by Chantal, hidden outside the window) the countess rips off her necklace and throws the attached medallion into the burning grate, from whence it is retrieved by the priest who goes down on his knees to rescue the object. But the gesture turns out to be the countess's breaking point – the priest's words have already penetrated her soul, even as she finds herself repudiating them. Already (it is quite miraculous how we sense this) the momentous step has been taken. Different critics have found different ways of summarising the scene, but Bazin, as usual, cuts to the heart of the matter. 'It is unlikely', he says, 'that there exists in the whole of French cinema, perhaps even all of French literature, many moments of a more intense beauty than the medallion scene between the curé and the countess. The overpowering severity of the dialogue, its rising tension and its final calm, leave us with the conviction that we have been the privileged witness of a supernatural storm.' In front of our eyes we witness a conversion. Has this ever happened before in cinema, I wonder? Here without further comment I quote from the film's dialogue one last time, citing the scene's epilogue, the beautiful letter which the countess writes to the curé after the event, and which he reads to himself out loud by candlelight that evening in his lonely bedroom:

> 'The hopeless memory of one young child had me isolated from everything in a terrifying solitude. And it seems as if another child has drawn me out of it. I hope I don't hurt your pride by calling you a child. You are one, and may God keep you one

always. I ask myself how you did it. Or rather, I have ceased to ask. All is well. I didn't believe resignation was possible, and in fact it's not resignation that has come over me. I'm not resigned. I'm happy. I desire nothing. I had to tell you these things this very evening. We shall never speak of them again, shall we? Never. It is good, that word "never". I feel it expresses, beyond words, the peace you have given me.'

Le Journal d'un Curé de Campagne, I am claiming here (not the first person to do so, of course), is a masterpiece. Whereas, in some adaptations, the very 'thickness' of a novel can stand in the way of what may be successfully put over to an audience in the time the filmmaker has at his/her disposal, here one feels the 'fit' between original and adaptation is one of those miraculous pieces of serendipity that can never happen twice. Certainly the movie is austere – what Bresson film isn't? – but it is important to grasp that it is not minimalist in the derogatory sense. On the contrary, the film has surpassing richness and variety of tone. In an *extended epilogue* that takes us out at last from the constricting environs of Ambricourt, it even goes so far as to introduce several new characters: Chantal's brother, the ex-seminarian Dufrety, and the touching girl this man refuses to marry. It closes, too, with an entirely appropriate and exquisite cadence: the letter by Dufrety describing the priest's death read out in Torcy's gentle voice on the soundtrack, while on screen appears the outline of a cross accompanying the movie's famous final words: 'All is grace'.

*

In *Diary of a Country Priest* (as in Bresson's previous films) the acting is naturalistic – at least, not notably un-naturalistic – and there is an undisguised interest in, as well as mastery of, psychology. Yet as we know (it is one of the best-known things about Bresson), the acting of the day, either on stage or on screen, was not really his 'thing'; he seems to have felt it gave too much away to be congruent with genuine artistry. The films that he made from the middle of the 1950s onwards can be seen as so many attempts to pare back the expressivity of conventional mime in the interests of a deeper inner mystery. Partly this was a formal preference, but by the same token it cannot have been *purely* formal – he genuinely thought his unique new methods, using amateur actors, brought in their wake greater and greater artistic-spiritual authenticity. His drive towards ever more sober minimalism, he would say, was in the interests of Truth. Nor was there ever, it seems to me, an absolute cut-off point; the acting in the later films is still expressive, in its way. Yet overall there is no denying that it becomes harder to read Bresson, and harder to say therefore where his films have alighted on the total religious spectrum.

There are ten further films in question. The reader will be pleased to hear that I have no intention of considering all of them in detail. Still, it is interesting to reflect on the subsequent course of Bresson's career at least briefly. So let us divide these movies, for convenience, into two groups of five and try to work out where the problem lies. The first group is the easier one to deal with. With *Un Condamné à mort s'est échappé/A Man Escaped* (1956), *Pickpocket* (1959), *Le Procès de Jeanne d'Arc/The Trial of Joan of Arc* (1961), *Au Hasard, Balthazar* (1966) and *Mouchette* (1967) there is a recognisably Christian ambience, although towards the end of this list (with *Mouchette* in particular) there is room for argument. Then Bresson made a further five films in the last decade of his career, all of them in colour, and these are the ones that are vexing. Whatever one's ultimate artistic verdict, they are surely his darkest works. The films in question are *Une Femme Douce/A Gentle Creature* (1969), *Quatre Nuits d'un Rêveur/Four Nights of a Dreamer* (1971) (adapted from Dostoevsky), *Lancelot du Lac* (1974), *Le Diable, Probablement* (1977) and his swansong, *L'Argent/Money* (1982).

Later works of Robert Bresson

We should start with *Un Condamné à mort s'est échappé* (1956), released three years after the success of *Diary of a Country Priest*. The Polish filmmaker Agnieska Holland remembers the overpowering effect this movie had on her as a girl. 'I saw *A Man Escaped* for the first time in a ciné-club in the sixties in Warsaw', she writes. 'I was about fifteen years old and I felt this film as I had felt no other. It is difficult to express, but the experience was an absolute awakening for me.' (We have all had such experiences, I suppose. These early encounters with art are vital mileposts in any adolescent's moral development.) A similar epiphany had struck the Spanish filmmaker Victor Erice a few years earlier, in Valladolid. 'What I most remember', he says 'is the unforgettable title: *Un Condamné à mort s'est échappé*. Unforgettable because the image it conjured constituted for me a kind of revelation, that is to say, a type of mental experience that changes one's whole idea of cinema.' We can agree how beautiful the title sounds in the original French – hinting as it does that we might already be in allegorical territory, and that the escape spoken of refers not just to the contingent fate of one man, the hero of the film (still to be encountered in the darkened cinema), but, biblically and spiritually, to all of us. All of us, then, are condemned to death; and yet mysteriously (for those who believe in such things) there remains the reality of Christian hope. I don't want to over-interpret the film before we start, but the epigraph that follows from the film's title needs to be cited too at this point – the strange and haunting words of Christ to Nicodemus: *The wind bloweth where it listeth* (John 3:8). The meaning of the relevant chapter from the Gospel is as open to dispute, perhaps, as any comparable passage from the Bible, but *part* of what makes this episode mysterious is the way that Christ seems to be saying to Nicodemus, at one and the same time, that grace and salvation are open to all, and yet that their dispensation is arbitrary. What is grace? And what is miracle? What is this 'wind' that bloweth where it 'listeth'? The film's plotline, evidently autobiographical (Bresson himself had been a prisoner of the Gestapo), concerns the successful breakout from jail of the resistance fighter Fontaine (François Leterrier), so *he* certainly escapes, and perhaps miraculously; but on the way, there are many who fail to escape, as there are others who die without reason. Clearly, there are few just deserts in these matters; and the film's crucial questions, both psychological and spiritual, revolve largely around the assorted prisoners' mental attitudes.

Here Bresson seems to me to be admirably even-handed. If the film's overall emblem is indeed Christian hope (as I believe to be the case), there is plenty of space given to portraying, for example, the atheistical despair of the 'man in the hat', Blanchet, to whom Fontaine attempts to give succour; time to meditate, too, on the brutal unfairness attached to the capture and death of Fontaine's lively comrade-in-arms Orsini. Other bitterly arbitrary deaths follow: the execution of a 19-year-old French fellow-inmate imprisoned for killing a German, in a banal dispute over a girl. Caught up in these events as they happen, the protagonist tries to make sense of them. Central to the tone and wisdom of the film is the lengthy and inspiring friendship sketched (this part also evidently autobiographical) between our dogged and reticent hero and the Protestant pastor De Leiris (Roland Monod). The encouragement given to Fontaine by the modest fortitude of this exemplary priest is surely one of the most beautiful aspects of the movie – a lesson to us too, if we choose to hear it, in the beautiful *habit* of prayer.[2]

---

[2] It is necessary to insist on the mystery of providence, and to be cautious about any notion that prayer *leads to* (or even 'may' lead to) miracles in such unimaginably awful circumstances as those connected with Nazi captivity. In memorable passages in his book *The Drowned and the Saved*, Primo Levi records his disgust at the idea that prayer could be said to have played a part in individual prisoner's salvation – the whole notion of being kept alive in order to 'witness' is repugnant to him. 'The experience of the Lager with its frightful iniquity has confirmed me in my laity', he writes. 'It has prevented me, and still prevents me, from conceiving of any form of providence or transcendent justice.' It is surely understandable that the existence of the death camps signals, for survivors like Levi, the very proof of religion's futility; and yet the opposite case surely also needs to be listened to. Contemplating Auschwitz, the Polish philosopher Stanisław Krajewski has this to say about the necessity of religion: 'The place intrigues because it places before us the most profound dimension of human existence. It is not an easy task to capture it and it is even more difficult to describe it, but one thing is certain: all religions refer to this dimension.'

Is it absurd to suggest that there is Christianity in the way that Bresson shoots the sequences of Fontaine's efforts to forge the tools that will make good his escape bid? The subtle religious atmosphere that encloses the entire movie ensures that the memorable scenes of shaving and planing of woodwork that Fontaine is involved in – of measuring, sawing and 'fitting' – resonate in the viewer's unconscious with childhood memories of Christ the Carpenter. (As usual, there are no *explicit* parallels.) Yet it seems to me one need not, anyway, be overly defensive in discussing these matters, since transcendence is so plainly there in Bresson's impeccable choice of music. Extracts from Mozart's Mass in C Major are threaded throughout the film, resonating above all at its magnificent climax when the screen shifts into black and 'holds' the audience in the presence of the sacred liturgy for the duration of a full minute, before allowing us a glimpse of the end-titles.

Music, in general, is crucial in cinema. Yet Bresson's attitude towards it was strangely ambivalent. Sometimes (as here) he sees the

FIGURE 18   'Measuring, sawing and fitting [...] the whole film is caught up in a subtly religious atmosphere.' François Leterrier in *Un Condamné à mort s'est échappé* (1956).

point of it – you could say he sees the *necessity* of it. At other times – increasingly in his later films – he seems to have felt that the use of musical extracts would only have introduced the sentimentality he was perennially rebelling against (in rather the same way he was rebelling against 'acting'). At this stage he was still using music confidently: here (supported by Mozart), and in the next film, *Pickpocket*, and in the two films after that, *The Trial of Joan of Arc* and *Au Hasard, Balthazar*. Yet when, finally, he comes to take his strictures literally, and abandons music altogether (as he does in his last film, *L'Argent*), it will be one of the clearest possible indications that the Christian framework of understanding the world no longer holds any heft for him.

We haven't yet arrived at this point, however. In *Pickpocket* (another masterpiece – *the* favourite for a number of viewers) the music is by J.C.F. Fischer and Lully, and its redeeming aspect is the more marked in that, far from the heroism of the Resistance, we have moved into an outright ambience of crime. *Pickpocket* shows the redemption of a thief through the pure love of a girl, so it is unsurprising to find the concepts of sacrifice, choice and election lying at the very heart of this drama. Michel, the protagonist (Martin Lassalle), is one of those Dostoevskian figures whose recourse to criminality springs out of a mixture of timidity and arrogance. And as in *Crime and Punishment*, the desire to cheat and outwit goes with a strong counter-element of *wanting* to be caught. The psychology may be summed up along the lines of 'Dare to arrest me. Judge me – so that I can exist!' (Most of us, somewhere in our own lives, have encountered such desperate wagers.) The idea that rescue from such a state of lonely and benighted defiance shall come in the form of a chance encounter with a woman who is open to love and to pity is not in itself, of course, an especially original contribution to screen-writing: the plot – *as* plot – is as old as the oldest written dramas. But, as in *The Diary of a Country Priest*, Bresson handles the unfolding of the moment of grace with exceptional beauty and sensitivity. I have not the space here to go into the outcome of the film more than very briefly, but some aspects at least of the *mise en scène* may be pointed to. The fact that we *hear* the boy's voiceover is crucial, I think ('My heart pounded as I read her letter' – suddenly, with these words, Michel becomes human and vulnerable). Then there is the perfect rhythm of the final scene's unfolding – the fact that from within his prison cell he has sent Jeanne away, and that despite her discouragement she has not lost faith in him. All this is immensely simple and moving. When, next day, she does come back, there is the exquisite calibration of the final encounter as, stepping out of the shadows, he kisses her forehead through the bars, and kisses her *again* after she has bent forward to kiss his knuckles. Finally, his last words to her: 'Oh Jeanne, to reach you at last, what a strange path I had to take!' – such a plangent and eloquent cry from the heart. Coming from a screenwriter of Bresson's emotional reticence, it sears the viewer with its spiritual forthrightness.

Should we go on? Yes, we have to. Bresson's next film, *Le Procès de Jeanne d'Arc/The Trial of Joan of Arc* (1961) (his third in a row to contain a prison setting) is Christian almost by definition, so there is something to be said, along the lines of a self-denying ordinance, for not lingering on the obvious – though I do want to add my conviction, and not merely dutifully, that this too is an extraordinarily profound movie. Like Dreyer's great silent version of the story made more than 35 years previously (we will come to Dreyer in another chapter), Bresson's film limits itself to the authentic words used by Joan herself, as recorded in the contemporary deposition of the trial, that 'greatest document of our history' as Dreyer so wonderfully calls it. (Elsewhere I have seen it referred to as 'the fifth gospel', so perpetually wise and imbued with true religion are Joan's responses to her inquisitors.) Between the merits of Dreyer's and Bresson's respective versions, there will always be room for debate. If the prestige of the Dane's film seems at times to carry the whole majestic weight of silent cinema on its shoulders, it could equally be argued that the very addition of sound which Bresson brings to the story has an incalculable poetic value in its own right, not only in our being able to *hear* for the first time Joan's miraculous responses, but in the manner in which the whole universe of ambient sound is opened up for us: the portentous drumbeats of the soldiery mingling with the far-off ringing of the Easter bells, while the friction of Joan's shackles as they drag against the stone floor gives way to to the final sharp crackle of the kindling as the martyr steps onto the pyre. Of this film more than almost any other one can think of, it could be claimed that it is the *photography* that supports the *soundtrack*, rather than (as more usually) the other way round.

Two further films communicate to us with an 'obviously' Christian resonance: *Au Hasard, Balthazar*, made in 1966, and *Mouchette*, released a year later, represent a further step taken by Bresson in the exploration of human depravity – small-scale depravity, on the whole, in that the set-ups are unmelodramatic, the crimes portrayed, in other words, tending to be derelictions of the spirit rather than legally visible felonies – except in the crucial case of rape (there is rape in both films). *Mouchette*, like *Le Journal d'un Curé de Campagne*, was adapted from a novel by Bernanos; only in this film the ambience of rural provincial France (we are in the Vaucluse region, south of Avignon) is perhaps even more godforsaken than it was in the earlier masterpiece. The church exists as it does in every corner of France, but there is no priest in sight – and no charity in the surroundings. The rich old lady who donates her cast-off dresses to the 14-year-old Mouchette (Nadine Nortier) does so not from kindness of heart but out of perverse *méchanceté* – she gaily tells the child how much she prefers the dead to the living! In this village, too, the bottle is everywhere in evidence; Mouchette herself comes from a long line of drinkers. As so often in *la France profonde* (though these days perhaps less than used to be the case?) despair comes pickled in alcohol. Meanwhile, village life in *Au Hasard, Balthazar*, situated close to the Pyrenees, is equally benighted and melancholy, though perhaps no great point is being made of this – it is not rubbed in by the screenplay. On the surface, a kind of normalcy reigns – we are recognisably in the modern world, with its cars and bakeries and petit bourgeois-housing plots. In this movie, what one

FIGURE 19 'In rural France of that epoch [...] the bottle is everywhere in evidence'. Typical bar scene in Robert Bresson's *Au Hasard, Balthazar* (1966).

might call Bresson's long-range fascination with sin finds its focus in three brilliantly sketched studies in perversity.

The film's anti-hero first of all: he is Gérard (François Lafarge), the leader of the band of rural *voyous*, who in their worst depredation violate the film's heroine Marie (Anne Wiazemsky) before casually skipping off. Gérard's actions encompass a sort of motiveless malignancy. His type is that of the fallen archangel, beautiful and intelligent (he sings in the village choir). His flaw is affectless *ressentiment*, dramatised in two further non-relationships, firstly with the baker's wife, who loves him and takes him in (but whom he betrays and steals from); and equally viciously, with a harmless wandering drunkard named Arnold (Jean-Claude Guilbert), whom Gérard goes out of his way to persecute.

In the Bible, the archangel's sin was Pride. Pride too is the downfall of a second striking figure in this movie, Marie's schoolteacher-turned-farmer father (Philippe Asselin). Initially presented to the audience as an upright and honourable member of rural society, he becomes mired in litigation over an inheritance and, refusing all counsel (including that of the parish priest), falls into pitiful despair. Everyone remembers the bleak scene in which, visited by the priest while lying ill in bed, he turns his back on the curé to face the wall in implacable silence. Father he may be, and respected owner of property; but he offers his family neither succour nor solace.

No prayer or supplication in heaven or on earth, I suppose, could reach the third of Bresson's exemplary sinners, a character known as the 'miser'. His profession is that of a grain merchant. Played with icy authority by Pierre Klossowski (in real life, brother of the painter Balthus), he is a man who has cast off all obligations to his fellow creatures except those governed by what can be bought and sold in the marketplace – a peasant hoarder, in other words, straight out of the pages of Balzac. When first met with, the man is cracking a whip at the patient donkey named Balthazar, recently come into his ownership. During a nocturnal storm, rain-soaked Marie knocks at the door of his barn, seeking refuge both from her family (who have rejected her) and from the attentions of Gérard and his associates. The miser tells her to take off her clothes. Glimpsing her nakedness, he throws her a duvet to cover herself with. There follows one of those riveting dialogues at which Bresson excels, where a pitiless vision of the world is laid out and forensically dissected. As we have said, the origin of all action, for this miser, lies in the cash nexus, so the question arises, as the night goes on, at what stage he will tempt her to sleep with him – that negotiation being made possible at all by the fact that, after a terrifying series of humiliations by Gérard, Marie no longer feels herself to be 'innocent'. She sizes up the situation from her own point of view as pitilessly and bleakly as he does. There seem to be no illusions left in the world, only a terrifying and lucid moral blankness. Is this, we ask ourselves, what the world is *really* like? Where are hope and charity? Whatever happened to the parable of the Good Samaritan?

I am trying to sketch here the kind of bleakness that is characteristic of Bresson's late cinema. The argument could be made – and often is – that the vision we are confronted with is *so* pitiless that it would be absurd to go on talking about such movies as being Christian. But maybe such judgement is premature. People interpret, of course, how they want to interpret. In art, as in criticism, it is seldom a matter of 'proof'. Yet it is impossible here not to take in the fact that if Marie is the heroine (the fallen heroine) of *Au Hasard, Balthazar*, the strange and beautiful protagonist of the film is – a donkey! At different times this animal changes hands (we have already seen that at one stage he comes under the ownership of the miser); and the film is structured, more or less, round the incidents which the said donkey could be said to 'witness' during its different and patient peregrinations. Of course Balthazar is only a brute beast, and we don't know what he feels, or even if he feels; at any event, he has no way of telling us. But viewers understand, I think, without needing to be told, that behind his ceaseless journeyings and changings of hands, there subsists an obscure religious parable.

FIGURE 20   'Whatever happened to the parable of the Good Samaritan?' Marie (Anne Wiazemsky) beaten and humiliated by a gang of rural voyous in *Au hasard, Balthazar* (1966).

Or maybe not so obscure after all. The donkey, surely, is part of the imaginary universe of all people brought up in Christian countries. The beast's emblematic meaning is instilled in us through childhood exposure to countless scenes of the crib at Christmastime, and sustained in adulthood every time we visit an art gallery in which Old Master paintings are hanging. The donkey is not only present in the manger (along with the ox and the lamb) as one of the wonderful mute witnesses to the Nativity; he is also the animal which bore Mary and the Holy Child on its back during the flight into Egypt; he is the very beast that Christ rode on in his entry into Jerusalem on Palm Sunday. In his patience, fortitude and meekness under blows – in his serene indifference to the buffets of the world – the donkey is, of course, finally, Christ himself. Obviously, this can't be *said* by the filmmaker in so many words, else the mystery is lost, and the tale becomes mere edifying homily. But *some* parallel is nevertheless felt by every viewer at what I would like to think of as an appropriate level of poetic suggestiveness.

To put it like this is to put it too explicitly. It is to come down with a reading of the film that is several times more fixed than I want it to be. There is no escape from the fact that the late films of Bresson *are* haunted by atheism! The heroine of *Mouchette* – a 14-year-old girl violated by a local poacher, and worn down by the burden of caring for a dying mother (the father is nowhere to be seen) – commits suicide by rolling down a bank into a shallow stream (several attempts are made to perform this act before succeeding). On the surface, it is hard to reconcile the terrible finality of such a deed with any notion of Christian salvation – suicide being, by definition, the ultimate act of rejection of God's mercy, at least, in traditional Christian theology. But viewers of the film are not limited by Christian orthodoxy in these matters – as, in practice, the Church isn't either. (One small but vital consideration: the draconian prohibition against the burial of suicides in consecrated ground is nowadays not consistently enforced.) Bresson is dealing, of course, with a human soul, the soul of an innocent child. Everything in the scenario is designed to show the way that, throughout her travails, Mouchette remains, somehow, impervious to the world's surrounding corruption, and unblemished in her mysterious solitude. All the director's energy goes into putting this conviction across concretely, from the initial choices surrounding the casting of the girl (what she looks like, what she shall be able to communicate to the audience in terms of gravity, candour and intelligence) down to the smallest details of *mise en scène* including editing, lighting and musical punctuation (the sacred music used here, with its tragic and sombre indications, is by Monteverdi). Mouchette herself, in a word, is presented as a 'real child', rather than a pious saint from a nineteenth-century oleograph. Her clogs are caked with real peasant mud (which she grinds into the rich widow's carpet). Bresson's grasp of psychology seems to me as convincingly rich in this film as it is in any of the previous works we have been looking at – particularly memorable being the sequences that follow on from the rape scene, before the gravity of the violation has sunk into her consciousness. One remembers the individual touches: Mouchette at home, going about her household duties, opening her shift to warm the bottle of her baby sister's milk against her body, then pausing to comfort her dying mother before retiring to bed in the deserted roadside shack that serves as their shared home, where the noise of the passing cars and the beam from the headlights eventually lull her to slumber. Deep in *this* night of her soul, Mouchette awakes; a sharp editing cut reveals her stationary against the wall of her bedroom in the light of the street lamp, tears streaming down her cheeks. There is not much in cinema, perhaps, that is quite as desolate as this image – or quite as tender and compassionate.

'I try to use a filmmaker's tools to represent a human being, by which I mean someone *with a soul* (not merely a juggling puppet). I don't think that speaking of God or saying the word "God" necessarily indicates His presence. Yet if the human is present, so is the divine', said Bresson in an interview recorded in the mid-1960s.

France: The Apostasy of Robert Bresson   99

FIGURE 21 'A real child, rather than a saint from a nineteenth-century oleograph.' Nadine Nortier in Bresson's *Mouchette* (1967).

And in another interview, recorded just before *Mouchette* went into production:

> I believe I'll manage to show how, despite appearances, this transformation of the soul still occurs – but in secret! It will be expressed through images, and by the relationship between images and sound. Redemption isn't achieved in death – we don't know what happens after death. Redemption must occur *now*, while we're alive. Christ redeemed us with his death, *but we must redeem ourselves with our lives*. For it's up to us to choose to be saved.

Saved or not saved, then? The five final films

Theoretically, those words of Bresson could be used to cover the remaining five films of his career: those movies from the late sixties onwards that throughout this chapter I have been calling vexing or problematic. The divine is *always* in the human, Bresson says. Surely that is a simple and satisfactory way to look at the matter. Even in the direst circumstance, grace is incipient and beckoning. We are human and therefore 'salvageable'.

And yet, is this how we actually experience what Bresson is saying in these final five works? I wonder.

Let us briefly remind ourselves what films we are talking about. Their plots can be given concisely. (1) *Une Femme Douce* (1969) is adapted from a short story by Dostoevsky. A young woman commits suicide by leaping out of a window. With her body laid out in the parlour, her husband (a pawnbroker and jeweller by profession) revisits in flashback the history of their marriage, and attempts to work out what went wrong with it. (2) *Quatre Nuits d'un Rêveur* (1971), also from Dostoevsky (the novella *White Nights*): a young woman, contemplating killing herself by jumping from the Pont des Arts, is rescued by a youthful poet who subsequently falls in love with her. His kindness awakens in her feelings of love and of gratitude. But when, eventually, her boyfriend reappears (his desertion was the cause of her original despair) she quits her new companion on an impulse in order to pursue the profitless original relationship. (3) *Lancelot du Lac* (1974): a retelling of the Arthurian legend that emphasises the confusion of allegiances, and the futile vendettas, that follow from Guinevere's adultery. In Bresson's version, no attention is paid to the Grail quest, and the film concludes with the knights slaughtering each other. Few bleaker films in existence! (4) *Le Diable, Probablement* (1977): in Paris a group of young people drift in and out of relationships while debating how the world might be run better. Charles, the most intelligent of the comrades, is also the most pessimistic. Suicide is constantly on his mind. Indeed, in the concluding sequence of the movie he persuades a friend to shoot him at night-time in the Père Lachaise cemetery. (5) *L'Argent* (1982) is loosely adapted from a late Tolstoy novella, *The Forged Coupon* (1911). This story recounts the descent into crime of a young man of respectable background (vide *Pickpocket*). As one misfortune leads to another (desertion of wife, loss of child, imprisonment), his grip on morality weakens. Offered succour by a kind woman, he responds by senselessly murdering her, along with her crippled granddaughter (his weapon of despatch is an axe). The film ends abruptly; part two of Tolstoy's tale, showing the character's eventual redemption, is rudely and deliberately omitted.

Stylistically, these films are not different from the films that preceded them. There is the addition of colour, but, apart from that, the same kind of editing procedures operate. There is a similar sparsity of dialogue and a general austerity which together serve to identify the films, clearly enough, as bearing Bresson's signature. For those who enjoy Bresson's rhythms (surely one of the most enjoyable things about his movies), the pleasures remain; there is no falling off in technical mastery. It could be argued that the world was always dark in the Bressonian version of events and there is no change now. Yet in the midst of that gloom – as I have tried to indicate – there were, at one time, these piercing epiphanies of hope; in a way, this is what *made* a Bresson film. And if there was a clarity about these passages it came, often, from their being positioned at the work's climax: that was what one took away from the viewing, its overall 'sense', if one can put it like that. I am thinking of something like the scene at the end of *Au Hasard, Balthazar*, with the wounded donkey lying in the field, the sheep grazing about him, their bells tinkling, Schubert beautifully playing on the soundtrack. Such profound peacefulness, such pathos! Or take the extraordinary end of *Pickpocket* when the young man at last cries out his acknowledgement of the succour given him by his faithful companion Jeanne. Or the decision to end *Mouchette* with a whole section of Monteverdi's *Magnificat* while the audience is still sitting quietly in the darkness. These are affirmations that arise logically and organically out of their preceding dramas; they are what make Bresson's cinema *thrilling*. And they have to be there, surely, concretely and physically – they cannot merely be intuited. We are discussing, as so often in this chapter, the outer reaches of minimalism. Bresson *is* minimalist, of course. But that minimum inside the minimalism has got to include – it cannot *forget* – the thing that is being 'said', or else we fall into bathos. I know that *L'Argent* has its admirers, but I simply don't follow their thinking. Why *omit* the second part of Tolstoy's tale, where the anti-hero finds his redemption? It can't be – or can it? – that Bresson expects his audience to supply the missing salvation out of their own reading of the tale. (That would be unfair to the people who *haven't* read the book.) Questioned on just this matter by Michel Ciment in an interview he gave late in his life, Bresson, citing Stendhal, grounds his defence of the omission in the power of the tale's psychology:

> Why did Julien Sorel kill Madame de Rénal? Did he know five minutes before doing the deed that he was going to do it? Of course not. What happens at that precise juncture? The forces of rebellion are suddenly unleashed within one, with all the hidden hatred that builds up inside. I was more interested in Tolstoy's account of that than in his religious ideas, fascinating though these are.

Tolstoy's religious beliefs are of course famously idiosyncratic; and it might well be true – indeed, I think it would be obvious – that cinema is *not* the place to 'discuss' them. But I find myself saying now, in conclusion, that what is wrong, or at the very least aesthetically unsatisfying, about *L'Argent* (and the other four late colour films) is exactly that they lack the 'breath of religion'. It makes of Bresson's oeuvre an extraordinary case, in my view. Consider: films such as *Les Anges du Péché* and *Le Journal d'un Curé de Campagne*, from early on in his career, are among the most beautiful Christian films of the twentieth century; they could be singled out to show us how cinema and Christianity are absolutely congruent. Yet by the end of his career Bresson has cast himself off from such sublimity. The final films I have been discussing are among the darkest and most serious films in the whole canon of cinema (despite their being conceived of in colour). 'Hide the ideas, but so that people can find them. The most important will be the most hidden!' said Bresson in one of his aphorisms. Yet one can hide things *too* deeply, perhaps. Then they will simply not be there when one digs for them.

In Bresson's favour, we can agree that this director was fearless. Reason enough to salute him. There is more than a grain of truth in what Tarkovsky said: 'The only one who is afraid of nothing is Bresson.'

FIGURE 22   The meek shall inherit the earth. François Périer and Giulietta Masina in Federico Fellini's *The Nights of Cabiria* (1956).

4

Italy: Christianity and Neo-Realism

Probably in no country in Europe are the contrasting origins of our civilisation – going back to paganism on the one hand, to Christianity on the other – more visible than they are in Italy. One speaks of these strands of civilisation as 'contrasting' or 'opposite', but the truly miraculous thing about them is surely their harmony. One can never be too amazed, I think, by how it came about that, at the time of the Renaissance, painters of all stripes were able to explore the myths of the classical world and the truths (as they saw it) of Christianity with equal conviction and beauty.

The pagan gods and goddesses, along with their supporting armies of nymphs and putti, have largely declined, in the intervening years, to mere decorative background status. But Christianity is – or was, until recently – still a living thing. Its presence is visible wherever one sets foot on the peninsula; in the vast number of churches and holy buildings as much as in the continuing validity of religious processions on saints' days. A plethora of icons and holy images dangle from the key rings of cab drivers, as they decorate the interiors of workplaces (barber, chemist, beauty salon). It may be true that such images have had to compete, over the years, with more or less glorified portraits of secular political heroes from Garibaldi onwards; still, it remains a fact that likenesses of the Virgin, and the currently reigning pope, confront the tourist pretty much everywhere.

The culture of the country is Catholic, then, even today; so much is obvious. And it means that, without anyone intending it, a typical Italian film will carry these ineradicable residues with it; the movie in question will be inflected with Christianity even when Christianity, as such, is far from being the film's ostensible subject. There will be gestures, recognisable situations, reminders. Shortly in this chapter we will attempt to broach the question of whether, or how much, neo-realism itself can be said to possess an intrinsically religious underpinning. Just for now we limit ourselves to noticing that the surface of life in Italian films, in so far as they speak of traditional village and bourgeois culture, has the body of religion built into it.

I am talking here about the perennial ceremonies that cement civic life. When you get married you need a priest; just as you need a priest, and a sexton, to bury you; all phases of existence from the cradle to the grave are – or were (one has to keep saying 'were') – conducted, in Italy, within the sound of church bells. Religion is so much a part of the daily texture of life that piety doesn't really come into it. And yet surely popular piety *is* there, not far from the surface – or else (to say it yet again) 'was' there, not so very long ago. So for example I doubt very much that a film from 1945 like De Sica and Zavattini's *La Porta del Cielo* (*The Gate of Heaven*), about the cult of Loreto, could be made today – it is altogether too friendly to godliness. But the fact that it *was* made, within living memory, and with evident conviction, is more than merely interesting for our argument. In the filmography of the celebrated pair of neo-realist cineastes (De Sica the *metteur en scène*, Zavattini the scriptwriter) this movie is perhaps not widely known, so there may be reason to dwell on it briefly here. We start by admitting that, unusually for the filmmakers in question, the film bears the hallmarks of officialdom; a note appearing after the credits informs us that it was made – with the backing of the Vatican and the Catholic Cinema Centre – 'to celebrate the importance of the Christian faith in the late conflict'. Good – we know what to expect, then: there is bound to be an element of religious propaganda about it – though possibly, with any luck, not merely that. Loreto, in the Marches, is or was one of the chief Catholic shrines in Italy, its cult centred on the dwelling place of the Virgin known as the Santa Casa, or Holy House, supposedly transported intact from Nazareth, by angels, late in the twelfth century, when the Crusaders were finally thrown out of Palestine. Encased in a handsome classical cladding designed and constructed by the Renaissance polymath Bramante, and situated plumb in the middle of the cathedral where it stands with impenetrable authority, it has served for centuries as a pilgrimage goal for Italian Catholics from all walks of life seeking consolation, succour, and deliverance from their manifold ailments.

Towards this destination comes a trainload of pilgrims from Rome, in different states of neediness. There is a crippled boy, in the care of an interesting girl not much older than he; an elderly housekeeper, escaping the confines of a quarrelling bourgeois family; a good-looking pianist, one of whose hands mysteriously froze one fatal evening in the middle of a concert; a worker who has lost his sight in an industrial accident and so on. The back story of these various individuals, told in extended flashback scenes, forms the bulk of the movie in running time, and these scenes are brilliantly handled, with that sure sense of sardonic idiosyncratic realism that is characteristic of De Sica's cinema, lifting the intrigue far above conventional melodrama. On the train too are various nurses, railway officials and hospital authorities. The rules are strict, and kindliness, when it appears, is doled out only in the shadows. As Bert Cardullo has observed (in his excellent book on De Sica), there is probably no film from the period that better shows the weariness, nervousness and general bad temper of the civilian population in the immediate aftermath of five years of harrowing conflict.

The climax of the movie, necessarily, lands our party of travellers at the basilica in Loreto – or at least what looks like this place. (The real church, Cardullo tells us, was unavailable for shooting purposes, so the sequence in question was set up in one of Rome's vast supernumerary cathedrals – St Paul's Outside the Walls – where elbow room had to be shared, apparently, with 3000 tired and hungry displaced persons who, in the aftermath of war, had taken shelter there.) It is night-time when we arrive, and the entire space is packed with pilgrims. The whole panoply of Catholic ritual is out in force: choirs, candles, incense. By the side of the altar an impressively voiced monk on his knees whips up the congregation into an ecstasy of expectation. Yet when the longed-for miracle occurs – as we feel it *must* occur – the recipient of divine grace is not any of the characters we have just been spending time with; no, it is a total stranger, a woman (unseen until now) from the midst of the congregation who puts aside her crutches and propels herself on risen legs towards the altar. In a beautifully angled crane shot, the rest of the congregation rise to their feet and mysteriously follow her; and the film ends with a surge of emotional affirmation that one can't imagine the steeliest non-believer not, somehow, responding to.

No ambiguities there, then. Or at any event, only the right kind of ambiguity. We do not have to feel that the director or writer are themselves 'implicated in' Christian dogma and worship – merely that they respect and see the point of it, as part of the fabric of the society they are committed to observing and dramatising. Such a friendly stance towards religion is not true of all Italian directors, of course (and not always true of De Sica, as we shall see in due course). Neither, I think, is Christianity the territory of a Visconti, an Antonioni or a Bertolucci, for example. And there are out-and-out atheists like Monicelli. On the other hand, religion *does* figure in the thinking of a rather large number of the others, among whom one would have to mention Rossellini and Fellini in the first place, but also in their train Pasolini, Olmi, Castellani and several more. Fellini's is an interesting case, and we should probably approach him first, for he too was fascinated by popular religion in all its wayward enthusiasm and emotionalism. In one of those magnificently shot sequences that in their totality make *La Dolce Vita* (1960) such a masterpiece, a crowd of people converge upon a field where a child is reported to have had a vision of the Virgin Mary. Illuminated by the light of car headlamps, the sick are hastily brought along on stretchers in the hope of a miracle; journalists mill about looking for 'human interest' stories; a couple of priests are interviewed. Yet amid all the noise and commotion, Fellini's stance (in contrast to De Sica's in the final sequences of *Gate of Heaven*) is plainly satirical and sardonic; we are merely invited to see the parallels with showbiz.

Such a point of view is congruent with the cynical, disillusioned tone of the film overall – observable from the celebrated opening sequence onwards, in which a larger-than-life statue of Christ is seen being helicoptered across the roofs of Rome while, from within the cockpit, a grinning crew of newshounds wave cheerily to a group of beauties they have spotted sunbathing underneath their flight path. This, then, is the emptiness of modern religion: the sign is there, but the substance has vanished. Irrecoverably? Fellini's take on modern mass religion is not – was not – always quite so brittle or damning. In *Le Notti di Cabiria* (*The Nights of Cabiria*) (1956) there is another of those scenes depicting mass popular emotion. A bevy of prostitutes, among them Cabiria herself (Giulietta Masina), have turned up at a country church where an icon of the Madonna presides over an annual massed pilgrimage. Each of the women bears in her heart different things she intends to pray for, whether it be for a villa in the countryside, or else (in Cabiria's case) the profound hope that she may have the strength to change her lifestyle. It is a bright sunny day and the atmosphere, as often on these occasions, is festive and carnival-like. Outside the church, along with the candle-sellers, are hawkers of figs and prickly pears. (A picnic is scheduled to follow the procession.) Yet the ceremony itself, in all its jostling chaos, is presented by Fellini on its own terms and entirely without irony. Once again, a priest whips up the congregation, inviting the women (they are mainly women) to advance towards the icon of the Madonna, where they may 'look into her eyes' and experience her piercing rays of mercy. Cries of

'Viva Maria!', 'Gratia Madonna!' echo to the rafters. Cabiria, of course, is immensely moved by the spectacle – overwhelmed indeed; but very beautiful, it seems to me, is the way that Fellini films the *other*, anonymous pilgrims present. The camera that travels across the rapt, singing faces seems to me to be working here in truly documentary-like fashion; these 'extras' are not actors so much (as it were) as the real article. And this seems to be a 'real' ceremony we are witnessing (though of course it is not – it is only a pageant on celluloid). In contrast to the De Sica film we were discussing earlier, no actual miracle is provided by Fellini. The crippled uncle of one of the pimps – he has invested a lot of energy (along with not a little money doled out to the candle-sellers) in finding a cure for his lameness – collapses on the floor when he attempts, prematurely, to abandon his crutches. Yet strikingly, this anticlimax is presented neither comically nor satirically. For when we next see the man, all is normal again; he is lying comfortably on a rug at the picnic, tucking into a healthy snack of grapes and cheese.

FIGURE 23   Everyday Christianity in *Nights of Cabiria* (1956).

The everyday and the sacred subsist together, then, in living harmony, in Fellini's universe. That's how it has always been in Italy – Fellini does not seem to want to depart from the orthodox consensus. As Geoffrey Nowell-Smith puts it nicely (in his liner notes to the DVD of *Il Bidone*): 'There are no miracles in Fellini's films. But they are suffused with an atmosphere of faith, as if a miracle may happen any moment.' His films chronicle (with superb sociological acumen) those stages of Italy's postwar modernisation when traditional truths and beliefs were everywhere cast into doubt. Yet he himself is not obviously in favour of their overthrow. Beneath the lively social comedy that all Fellini-viewers delight in, his work has a melancholy, reactive undertow. I should not want to make him out to be a graver man than he was historically – ebullience, certainly, was central to this wonderful artist's character – yet his interviews and writings make explicit an essentially conservative allegiance to Christian values. In the collection of essays published under the title *Fellini on Fellini* (1996) one is confronted, across the book, with the evidence of this loose Christian humanism. 'What does it mean, to be a Christian?' he asks himself at one point; to which he answers in the next sentence:

> If by Christian you mean an attitude of love towards one's neighbour, it seems to me that [...] yes, all my films turn upon this idea. There is an effort to show a world without love, characters full of selfishness, people exploiting one another, and, in the midst of it all – especially in the films with Giulietta [Masina] – a creature who wants to *give* love, and who lives for love [...] Even *La Dolce Vita* may be defined in this way.

His train of thought continues: 'I know little about Catholic dogma and I may be a heretic. My Christianity is rough and ready. I'm afraid I don't go for the sacraments. [But] I believe in Jesus: he is not only the greatest person in the history of the human race, he continues to live on in anyone who sacrifices himself for his neighbour.' It is Cabiria who is being focused on here ('especially in the films with Giulietta'). Yet the idea is applicable across all his filmography.

Cabiria, prostitute and sinner, belongs to the recognisable literary-artistic category of the 'holy fool'. There is something a little bit simple about her. Her inexhaustible ability to trust in the men she meets will only ever bring grief; and yet by the same token we are meant to see that this is also the precondition for salvation. This can be dramatized sentimentally, or else it can be done (as here) with sublime authority. Surely there can be few more beautiful sequences in the whole of Italian cinema than the clifftop scene at the end of *Cabiria* when our heroine comes face to face with the realisation that the man she is betrothed to, the gentle charming businessman Donofrio who has rescued her from poverty, and in whose company she may at last say goodbye to her 'profession', is nothing but a thief and a conman – a conman, moreover, who is looking at her with murder in his eyes. 'Here, take it!' she cries, proffering him her pathetic handbag with all her savings in it, before falling to the ground with the plea 'Kill me, kill me! I don't want to live any more!' Extraordinarily however – the film is so daring in this respect! – this isn't the end of the road for her – the film doesn't conclude here as it so easily might have done. There is the coda in the woods where she meets a band of young people and, within minutes (so to speak), refinds her equilibrium. There can't be a worse social hazard, I suppose, than to be credulous and gullible and perpetually open to deception; yet Christianity habitually looks at the matter differently. Few enough are the films which *really* convince the viewer that the meek shall inherit the earth! Yet this is one of the great subjects of Italian cinema in general, and of neo-realism in particular.

In a short film called *Il Miracolo*, directed by Roberto Rossellini in 1948 (the second episode of a diptych released under the title *L'Amore*), Fellini, this time as actor, plays a peripatetic shepherd who seduces a simple robust countrywoman. (The actress is Anna Magnani.) 'Simple' really means simple in this case: she has convinced herself, that sunny afternoon on the hillside, that the handsome apparition she is speaking to is either St Joseph, or else the Holy Spirit. When, nine months later, she gives birth to a child, it is logical for her to claim, and more importantly to believe, that the baby is none other than the Infant Jesus. The plainness of this tale, as recounted by Rossellini, leaves plenty of room for irony. Thus Cardinal Spellman, in America, sensing blasphemy, called for the movie to be banned. Yet although there is nothing overtly 'pious' about the scenario, there is, equally, nothing anti-religious either. The attitude of the director, for those who can see, is surely one of compassion – and enjoyment.

There is nothing problematic about the religion of the people, then. It exists without having to be intellectualised. For the educated person, alas, it is a more difficult matter. The contrast between 'simple faith', on the one hand, and the anguish of the over-sophisticated, on the other, is the subject – or more accurately, one of the subjects – of a later film by Rossellini, *Viaggio in Italia (Journey in Italy)* (1953) starring the director's then wife Ingrid Bergman, along with the British actor George Sanders. Together they play a wealthy upper-class couple who are visiting the south of Italy to settle a property matter. The marriage is shaky, for the man is a bully, and Katherine Joyce (our heroine's name in the movie) finds herself seeking more and more time on her own. She uses her freedom to explore the Italian countryside. Excursions take her to the ruins of Pompeii and the main museum in Naples where she views the naked statuary; also to the catacombs with their fearsome collections of skeletons; and to the sulphur-leaking slopes of Vesuvius. These sequences have a rare unvarnished beauty not witnessed again in cinema, probably, until Antonioni's *L'Avventura*. The sights shock her in complicated ways; they stir up powerful feelings that have hitherto been lying dormant. Reunited, finally, with her husband (in person if not necessarily in spirit), she finds herself witnessing preparations for Naples's famous annual miracle, the decongealing of the blood of St Januarius, and for one terrifying moment gets swept away by the crowd.

At this point the film ends, a bit abruptly. Katherine is restored, if only temporarily, to her husband's arms. Are we to take it that St Januarius's 'miracle' (the word here needs to keep its inverted commas) has somehow saved their marriage? That we have been present in some way at a 'conversion'? Certainly, some viewers (including the great critic Bazin) have veered towards this interpretation. Yet I personally don't get the sense that this is what Rossellini is really telling us. If any particular emotion is being dramatised in these final scenes it seems to me more like fear, isolation, bewilderment and (once Katherine has achieved the safety of her husband's arms) sheer animal relief. In an interview published ten years after the film's release, in the journal *Filmcritica*, Rossellini insists that people, even intelligent people, often miss the point about simple things – just as Katherine does here: '[Katherine] is always quoting a so-called poet who describes Italy as a country of death. Imagine, Italy a country of death! Death doesn't exist here. It's so much a living thing that they put garlands on the heads of the dead! To them [i.e., Katherine and her husband] death has an "archeological" meaning; [whereas] for us it is a *living reality*.'

'For us', he says, placing himself in the camp of those pagan-Christian southerners (the indigenous populace, the 'people', the worshippers at the shrine of St Januarius), as opposed to nervous rational English-speaking foreigners. The puzzle of Rossellini's

FIGURE 24 'A shaky marriage ...' Ingrid Bergman and George Sanders in *Viaggio in Italia* (1953).

personal allegiance to Christianity is an intriguing one, to which there doesn't appear to be any simple answer. He was brought up in a religious household which at the same time was wealthy and worldly. Educated at a Catholic establishment (the Collegio Nazareno in Rome, run by the Scolopi Fathers), he passed his youth in a riot of indulgence. (Tag Gallagher, in his exhaustive biography, provides the details.) This playboy lifestyle lasted well into his maturity, and in some ways he never really outgrew it; up to his death he loved champagne and fast cars. At the same time, a capacity for hard work seems to have come easily to him. Eventually, aided by the luck that everyone needs, he found his way as a filmmaker. The advent of World War II was crucial for him – crucial, I mean, in enabling him to become serious. Thus, at a certain stage of the conflict, Rossellini passed from being a more or less complaisant servant of the regime towards a stance of out-and-out anti-fascism. The ideological positives observable in his breakthrough film *Roma, Città Aperta (Rome Open City)* (1945) – breakthrough not just for him, of course, but for the whole of postwar Italian cinema – are Catholicism on the one hand, incarnated in the heroic priest, played by Aldo Fabrizi, who dies for liberty; but communism on the other: the tortured freedom fighter Manfredi (Marcello Pagliero) is portrayed as belonging to – deriving his strength from – the Party. Between these two rival worldviews one can imagine Rossellini hovering, if not for ever. In his heart I think he was never an extreme leftist, although democracy (openness, dialogue, enquiry) formed, of course, a major part of his personal ethic. A turning point seems to have been his meeting with the monks of the convent of Baronissi, just south of Naples, whom he encountered when scouting locations, in 1946, for his next movie *Paisà*. The monastery in question (transported, so to speak, from southern Campania to northern Romagna for narrative purposes) in due course featured in that movie, in the episode in which a group of Allied military chaplains find themselves billeted in the countryside during a lull in the last stage of the fight against the Germans.

In the movie, these monks are presented as simple men, as they must surely have been in real life. Yet their faith is put to the test when they discover that among the three 'men of the cloth' whom they have welcomed as visitors, one is a Protestant, while another is – consternation! – a Jew. (The leader of the group, meanwhile – the only one who speaks Italian – appears to be reassuringly Catholic.) So they proceed to pray for their souls, pray that the pair of heretics among the trio shall be converted. We ourselves would not nowadays, I think, countenance such solicitude very happily – indeed we might think the monks' attention impertinent: a mere sign of ignorance and bigotry. So it is in a way; but in another way *not*. The scene in which the three visitors, guests in the refectory, discover that their hosts are not eating, and then discover *why* this is so (the monks have decided to go on a voluntary fast to prompt God to make an intervention) is wonderful in its delicacy; while the noble, immediate and unembarrassed speech of thanks delivered at this point by the Catholic padre (the actor is Bill Tubbs) ranks among the finest speeches in the whole of Italian cinema – one of many reasons why *Paisà* must be regarded as a masterpiece.

The friars in question were Franciscans, and the idea took hold with Rossellini that it would be interesting to devote an entire film to the origins of that movement and to its charismatic early thirteenth-century founder, St Francis. Moreover, wouldn't it be interesting, he thought, to do it with *these monks* as the leading actors? Permission was sought from the monastery. And thus it came about: *Francesco, Giullare di Dio* (*Francis, God's Jester*, also known as *The Flowers of St Francis*) premiered at the Venice Film Festival in the summer of 1950, four years after the release of *Paisà* (other films, as we shall see shortly, having been made in the interval). The scenario had been pieced together with his friend and colleague Fellini's help, based on certain episodes of the *Fioretti*, the so-called 'little flowers' of St Francis, pious tales about the founder of the order compiled, in Latin, in the fourteenth century, by a certain Ugolino di Monte Santa Maria.

Francis in his lifetime rose to become a figure on the world stage – friend of popes, and inspirer of Crusades. But these tales, by contrast, concentrate on the earliest and most authentic part of his ministry, when he set out to preach the word of God locally, with a small group of dedicated companions. As such, then, we have 'primitive Christianity' represented on screen in starkly documentary fashion: the simplest and most direct acts of charity, dramatised within an enclosing atmosphere of poverty, chastity and humble good humour. The words 'simple' and 'silly' are etymologically cognate, and Rossellini does not hold back from giving us episodes where silliness is indeed the governing sentiment; a brother, for example, sends himself off to steal a pig's trotter for the communal pot, to predictable protests from the neighbouring farmer (who owns the still-living creature), and there is another episode where the same brother (Ginepro, the youngest and most innocent of the band), in order to free himself up for preaching, disastrously decides to cook all the food the friars require a fortnight in advance. Total chaos ensues. Mingled with such scenes of almost slapstick comedy (slapstick too marks the film's single longest episode, where Ginepro sends himself off to preach peace in neighbouring Viterbo, where a siege is in operation, and runs into problems with the local tyrant) there are graver, quieter scenes, as when Francis, praying at night-time alone in the fields, encounters a leper and forces himself to embrace the man lovingly.

Beautiful as this particular episode is in execution, the tone of the film eschews tragedy and deep feeling, so one isn't surprised to hear that some of the more habitually anti-clerical critics of the epoch reacted to the film's release with savage derision. 'A monument to stupidity [...] never before have Christianity and cretinism been so close to one another', observed one of them, acidly, while another (Pierre Leprohon, author of a still useful survey of Italian cinema) spoke for many of his colleagues, perhaps, in dismissively referring to the monks whom Rossellini admired so much as 'childishly playful imbeciles'. *Francis, God's Jester* belongs, I think, and will probably always belong, to the category of films that one 'gets' or one doesn't get. I myself find it

FIGURE 25   The origins of the Franciscan order reimagined with documentary simplicity: Roberto Rossellini's *The Flowers of St Francis* (1950).

hard to put into words why I find it so charming. False simplicity and genuine simplicity are sometimes separated, in art, by the smallest of margins. Yet to me the film has a great sense of liberty about it – a wonderfully fresh innocence. There is absolutely no padding in the screenplay. Each episode is the right length. Individual sequences have a laconic 'rightness' about them that is inseparable from the proverbial, legendary origin of the incidents they are drawn from. More than anything else, perhaps, the film benefits from being presided over by a beautifully convincing acting performance, that of Nazario Gerardi (a monk himself, of course, in real life), who manages to incarnate the saintly founder of the friars with a lovely open cheerfulness.

Francis, God's Jester, as has been said, premiered at the Venice Film Festival in August 1950, at the same time as another, darker, Rossellini film completed a few months earlier. *Stromboli – Terra di Dio* was the first of the four films Rossellini was destined to make with Ingrid Bergman, who had artlessly presented herself to him as a long-distance fan. In a famous letter to the Swedish actress setting out the aims of his proposed new movie (she was still in America and personally unknown to him when he wrote it) it is clear that the spirit of St Francis – the spirit, as he said, of 'true Christianity' – was again very much on his mind. It was going to be a film about conversion, about the providential finding of God in the midst of a secular life crisis. Inspiration for the tale came from one of those postwar epiphanies that had etched itself onto his memory: the sight of a tall Nordic-looking woman standing alone on the periphery of a refugee camp, lost in thought and unhappiness. Taking the first opportunity to escape from her confinement, this woman (so Rossellini claimed he had subsequently learned) managed to marry a fisherman, with whom she went off to live on the Aeolian island of Stromboli. What would have been her cultural expectations? Would she have found contentment there? he wondered. Imagining how difficult it would be for her to prosper there – up against the problems of language, the differences of cultural expectation, the hostility that might be shown towards foreigners by the native populace, womenfolk in particular (all such problems summed up under a general heading of 'loneliness') – Rossellini and his collaborator Sergio Amidei constructed a story that aimed to show the heroine at a moment of crisis casting aside her egotism and going along with the wisdom of her fate. 'Suddenly the woman learns the value of the eternal truth which rules human lives', Rossellini wrote, a touch grandiosely, in this same expository letter to Bergman I have already quoted from. 'She understands the mighty power of he who possesses nothing, this extraordinary strength which produces complete freedom. *In reality she becomes another St Francis*. An intense feeling of joy springs out from her heart – an immense joy of living!'

Still, the film itself is not very joyful – one could even say that this is what makes it interesting. The cogency of his heroine's conversion depends, of course, on the turmoil that precedes it. In the finished film, there is something odd, and striking, about the way Rossellini seems to go out of his way to make the character so hostile to the environment she finds herself in, so refractory as a personality, so 'sharp' and frankly unsympathetic. It is probably important not to exaggerate this aspect of the film; in real life Bergman was nice as well as beautiful, and we can't forget Rossellini was in love with her. So the camera is in love with her too; her attractiveness 'comes across' – you feel while watching the film that she's a person with a soul. This seems to me the movie's great distinction – the rigour with which Rossellini keeps to his brief that this is a damaged woman we are looking at, who has been scarred in mysterious ways by her forced wartime peregrinations; unable, therefore, in crucial ways, to see what is in front of her eyes: above all, the integrity and simplicity of the people she has fallen among. *Stromboli* is classically neo-realist in alerting its audience, documentary-style, to the harsh, poverty-stricken lives of the islanders – their ceremonies, their prejudices, their ancient rhythms of life. Yet cut off from the world as it is, the community is far from being godforsaken. Church services are kept up, and the villagers go to them. The fishermen in their boats pray and sing; while the parish priest (in the absence of other visible civic or feudal authority) presides over the moral lives of the villagers with what can only be called insight and tolerance.

Which brings us back to the issue of the heroine's epiphany. Perhaps I should fill in the context leading up to it. There has been a series of dramatic incidents one on top of one another, starting with a terrifically staged tuna-catch that Karin – Bergman's name in the film – has witnessed close-up, in all its thrashing violence. (As the enormous beasts are hauled aboard the boats with pikes and grappling hooks, their vast miserable eyes seem mutely to solicit pity from her.) And now, shortly afterwards, no sooner has she announced to her husband that she is pregnant than the volcano above them erupts in fell fury! It peppers the village with bolts of burning lava and forces the inhabitants to take to the boats again, for safety and refuge. The eruption, this time, is short-lived, however, and the village is saved; but it is too much for Karin who, despite the fact that she is bearing her husband's child, determines forthwith to leave him.

Humiliating complications follow that we need not concern ourselves with here; the upshot is that she finds herself alone on the mountain, heading towards a fishing village on the other side of the island, from whence she plans to catch a boat for Messina. And at first all goes well; she makes good progress. Yet panic ensues as the still-smoking volcano wafts its fumes towards her, enveloping her in its sulphurous miasmas. Lost and overcome, she sinks down on her knees in despair. It is then that the vision assails her. 'Oh God, if you exist, give me a little peace!' she cries tearfully. As if in answer, the mist clears and the stars come out. Karin sinks into sleep. The screen dissolves. Next morning, the sun comes up on her sleeping form; and as she opens her eyes she is able to murmur: 'Oh God. What beauty! What mystery!'

That ought to be the end of the matter, but strangely it isn't. Instead the sequence continues with Karin struggling to her feet and continuing her journey. Breasting a rise, she pauses to take in what has

FIGURE 26 The loneliness of a Northerner among Southern peoples. Ingrid Bergman as Karin in Rossellini's *Stromboli – Terra di Dio* (1950).

happened, and now once again her tone seems to catch an echo of the previous night's despair. 'I can't go back', she cries out to the empty valley. 'I don't want to! They're horrible. It's all horrible', while she sinks to her knees, adding to herself in an undertone 'They don't know what they're doing. But I'm even worse!'

The last words of the movie (the *really* last words) find her promising herself to 'save her child', if the Lord will grant her 'strength, understanding and courage'. With this she sinks into silence.

'In reality she becomes another St Francis.' That was what Rossellini said in the initial letter to Bergman. Well, does she? Are we convinced she has managed to shake off her 'egotism'? Will she go forward or go back? The ending of the film is profoundly ambiguous. And yet *something* momentous (and even, perhaps, something 'beautiful') has happened to her; we respond to it, while being pulled in different ways. The musical score (pervasive in this film, composed by Rossellini's brother Renzo) urges transcendence. But the words, and the gestures, leave the content of the experience deeply open to doubt.

*

There is something rather odd, one could almost say tragicomic, in the solemnity of Rossellini's 'meditation on religion' being accompanied in the wider world, at the time the film was made, by an atmosphere of frank scandal. The issue was the adultery of the principal players, Bergman and Rossellini, at first a mere matter of rumour, subsequently – by the time the movie was due for release – publicly acknowledged. To be together, both parties abandoned their respective spouses. (Rossellini abandoned a mistress as well, Anna Magnani, but that is another story, with wondrous dimensions of its own.) If Ingrid Bergman had to put up with being denounced from the floor of the United States Senate, Rossellini faced the harsher interdict of excommunication. Not that that worried him overmuch; his lifestyle had never been conventional, nor had he ever mingled in higher

Church circles. Still, Europe then was different from Europe now, and it is difficult to believe that the issue of respectability didn't impinge *at all* on his thoughts – on 'their' thoughts. Apparently they faced the guns bravely, before deciding to marry. Should the matter of what kind of a person an artist is play any part in our critical estimate of the value of their finished work? We tend to keep the two things in separate compartments, and not just for fear of being judged sanctimonious. Naturally, it *is* the work that matters in the last resort, not the morality of its begetter. Pia Lindström, Bergman's teenaged daughter, was unimpressed (Gallagher tells us) by her new stepfather: she thought him a hypocrite. 'He used to stand in front of the fireplace and tell us how religious he was', she is quoted as saying. One can imagine the scene, and even smile about it. Yet, in certain cases, the gap between the beauty of the work of art, and what is known about the artist who produced it, is *so* startling as to require commentary, and even judgement.[1]

*

I don't know if this is the case with Pier Paolo Pasolini, episodes of whose life (not least, his abject manner of parting from it) were as notorious in their time as the scandals that beset Rossellini. The Friulian cineaste, poet and essayist was a Catholic Marxist in an epoch when those two systems of belief were not seen to be *ipso facto* incompatible. Films of his as different as *Accatone* (1961) and *Teorema* (1968) are susceptible to Christian interpretation (I mean they have

---

[1] Before taking leave of Rossellini, I should mention some later relevant films of his. Not all his movies with Bergman broached or skirted religious topics; *Paura* (Fear) (1954), for example, is a shot at the genre of *film noir* (not wholly successful). But *Europe '51* (1952) is interesting: a profound investigation into misunderstood sainthood, strongly influenced by the writings and personality of Simone Weil. Outside the Bergman corpus, it is also important to mention *Germany Year Zero* (1948), the bleakest of all his movies (yet according to Gallagher 'the most religious'). Later in his career, Rossellini made films for television about Blaise Pascal (1971) and Augustine of Hippo (1972), as well as a Life of Jesus (1975).

parabolic elements that draw on raw Christian imagery, *essentially* perversely so in the latter case, I think). Yet if Pasolini finds a place in this chapter, it is to acknowledge and (why not?) to praise the grand simplicity of a single film of his that stands out in the history books: *The Gospel According to St Matthew* (1964). The movie is addressed (without any irony) in its opening credits to 'the fond, happy, friendly memory of Pope John XXIII'. This stark, neo-realist and, indeed, frankly proletarian version of the Holy Story, shot entirely with amateur actors and vividly embellished with a magnificent musical score, is too well known to warrant extensive description here. The reader may recall that it was originally planned to be shot in the Holy Land. An hour-long publicity film made by the director, *Sopralluoghi in Palestina* (*Scouting in Palestine*) (1965), shows Pasolini location-hunting in the region in the company of a priest, Don Andrea Carraro. Watching this documentary, the viewer can't help being struck, I think, not only by the intellectual distinction of Pasolini's voiceover commentary (a lost art, in so many ways), but by the kindness, courtesy and general deference with which the cineaste treats his clerical companion. Pasolini knew the clergy intimately; he knew how to speak to this class. His take on the Gospel of St Matthew in the finished movie (which in the event was shot in southern Italy) emphasises, as we would expect, the most vehement aspects of Christ's teachings. But the inflammatory oratory belongs to the holy text itself, and is not an invention of the film director. Neither is the film defined by this vehemence. It contains, as the viewer would hope (and to balance its revolutionary fierceness), many lovely, tender images that impress themselves permanently on the memory. As much as Fellini or Eisenstein, Pasolini was a connoisseur of the human figure; he was a master finder of faces – not only the young and androgynous (the Angel of the Lord in *Matthew* is a particularly fine example, I think), but also the old, the vulnerable and the weighed-down-with-sorrow. So the film has depth, and pathos, and staying power. And it possesses too a fascinating *doubleness*: there are a lot of things going on beneath the surface. This 'underground narrative' – underground, almost, in the psychoanalytic sense – comes into its own with the characterisation of Judas, and in those sequences towards the climax of the movie that dramatise the events leading up to Christ's betrayal. Is it something about the look of the actor playing this disciple that alerts the viewer to the fact that Pasolini here identifies in some profound way with the inner life of the treacherous apostle? But then he identifies with Christ too! Such is the narcissism of masterpieces.

Pasolini went on to make a series of colourful and patently 'exotic' movies – *The Decameron* (1970), *The Canterbury Tales* (1972) and *Arabian Nights* (1974) – that brought him renown on the international art-house circuit, before signing off his career (though he couldn't have known it would be his last work) with *Salò* (1975), one of the most brutish films ever made. I think it is fair to say that none of these films is brushed, even residually, with the spirit of Christianity. Their atmosphere is pagan and libertine. There is no need to dwell on

FIGURE 27   'A master finder of [...] beautiful faces.' The Angel of the Lord outside the Empty Tomb in Pasolini's *Gospel According to St Matthew* (1964).

them, I think – or indeed, any longer, on the tortured journey of their *auteur maudit*, to whom we say goodbye with the thought that *if* one can be damned one can be saved. Certainly, *Salò* is a damnable movie, the movie of a lost soul, a soul in torment. It is good to move on to another, somewhat lesser-known director at this point who, as much as any other cineaste I have mentioned, deserves an honoured place in our dossier. Ermanno Olmi's life (1931–2018) was as low-profile and blameless as Pasolini's was public and notorious. Based initially in Milan, where he was employed during the 1950s as an in-house documentary-maker for the industrial concern Edison-Volta, Olmi emerged on the international stage with the success of two small gems of perfect late neo-realism, *Il Posto* (1961) and *I Fidanzati* (1963), both of them marvels of low-key observational naturalism. In their humour and humanity they uncannily prefigure, if by only a few years, the later work of Czech cinema; they are closer in spirit to Menzel and Forman than they are to Antonioni, for example. *Il Posto* is about the awkwardness attending the search for a first job in a large city, and, having found such a 'post', adjusting as best one can to the petty restrictions – the footling demands of hierarchy – that plague the life of a typical office junior. The movie had an enormous *réclame* in America and one can see why; it is full of beautiful anthology pieces, such as the marvellously observed works dance sequence which, starting out in frozen inhibition, moves slowly (and with exquisite comedy) into an atmosphere of frank unbridled licence.

I Fidanzati, the follow-up film, is less conventional in almost all respects, and less overtly placed in the comic register (though the comedy of *Il Posto* is bitter-sweet, and informed by the sadness of life). A Milanese engineer in his early thirties is sent by his employer to Sicily to take up a post in an oil refinery. It will mean leaving behind his fiancée, as well as adjusting in all sorts of other ways to the challenging environment of what is – for a Northerner – another country. The film provides a fascinating snapshot of the South at a crucial moment of industrial modernisation (such a different Sicily than that glimpsed in

L'Avventura, for example). The protagonist, as said, is an engineer, but he is not at all prominent in the hierarchy. The comforts provided by his firm are few, or non-existent: he faces the prospect of having to endure for a few years, in his rented lodgings, a lonely bachelor existence without distraction. How, in the meantime, will his relationship with his fiancée evolve – or survive even? What sort of love do they bear for each other? This is the enigma of the film that is kept salient through the use Olmi makes of startlingly modernist editing techniques, full of daring ellipses and tantalisingly constructed flashbacks taking us to the brink of, but not beyond, revelation. Slowly, what emerges is the seriousness of the man's faithfulness – the sense that the couple's love for each other (which seems so fragile at the beginning) is going to stand the tests of time that have been forced upon them. If one had to have a shot at saying what, if anything, is religious about this movie (right from the beginning, Olmi seems to have been happy to see himself defined – by his enemies – as a 'stuffy old Catholic director'), it is surely the way that it illustrates, or dramatises, the Christian virtue of patience – patience *as* a virtue, that is: a manner, or ethic, of living in the world.

FIGURE 28   The trials of faithfulness. Anna Canzi as the lonely fiancée in Olmi's *I Fidanzati* (1963).

Olmi's two other 1960s films – *E venne un uomo* (1965), a homage to Pope John XXIII, the moving spirit behind the Second Vatican Council, and *Un certo giorno* (1967), an attempt to dramatise a set of fairy tales in modern rural surroundings – have their interest but need not detain us. And the work that Olmi did for Italian television in the 1970s remains buried for the most part in those particular archives until they are uncovered. He was always an artisan filmmaker and in 1974 he set up his own studio in the town of Asiago in the Veneto, nestling in the foothills of the Alps. From here the director re-emerged on the international scene at the end of the decade with what is probably his best-known film, *L'Albero degli Zoccoli/The Tree of Wooden Clogs* (1978), winner of the main prize, the Palme d'Or, at that year's Cannes Film Festival. This lengthy and impressive epic poem (three hours long and photographed, in ravishing colour, by the director himself) attempts to dramatise incidents from the lives of a group of peasants inhabiting the region of Bergamo, northeast of Milan, at the end of the nineteenth century. The evocation has an extraordinary particularity; one really feels that this is what it might have been like to live and be sentient in that epoch in that part of the North Italian landscape. The emphasis is on the perennial round of daily events that follow the unfolding of the seasons. Labour, of course, is at the heart of this life; the peasants in question live in feudal dependence on the local landowner, whose rents are collected by a bailiff. There are children to be schooled and daughters to be married. A young lad is apprenticed to a miller. A pig is fattened up and slaughtered. On special occasions the two or three families that occupy the same set of farm buildings sit around the fire in the evening and tell each other ghost stories. And because this is when it is, at the end of the nineteenth century, before modernity had carried the day, each of these activities is carried out, somehow, within the compass of a sacred dispensation. Prayer is part of daily life, formalised by the rosary and the angelus. The parish priest is a presence in these peasants' lives, respected for his learning and friendliness; in this film, at any event, he is a guide and not an enemy. And so the washerwoman with six children who simply can't go to church on Sunday isn't chided – he goes out of his way to let her know that God cares for her. Elsewhere socialism is on the move, but these peasants are as yet unaffected by it. In a memorable sequence, the newly married son of the main peasant family makes a journey by canal to the city of Milan in the company of his newly married bride; they have come to visit the bride's aunt who years ago had taken vows at a convent there. Sweetly welcomed in the quiet of the cloister (in sharp contrast to the outside streets where the mounted police are quelling a demonstration of workers), the couple are led to a dormitory where two beds have been placed together to form a primitive bridal couch. 'This is the first time we have welcomed newly-weds!' the aunt says, with touching simplicity. The convent is a haven for orphans and abandoned children, and the next day this same nun offers them one of these infants to adopt. 'Take him – open your arms to him!' she urges, holding up the baby she has chosen. It is a gesture that perhaps none of us has ever witnessed, nor ever will witness, modern adoption rules being what they are. Yet were such an offer to occur, through some unimaginable contingency, one might hope that, like the film's ingenuous couple, one would step forward with similar cheerful courage.

As has been said, these peasants depicted by Olmi are ignorant of the winds of change represented by the growing tide of socialism; perhaps it would be better for them if this were not the case. Without solidarity, they are perpetually vulnerable to the whims of their feudal superiors. For *The Tree of Wooden Clogs* is a tragedy as well as an idyll. The 'tree' of the title is a sapling in a row of saplings bordering a drainage ditch, axed down one morning by the peasant paterfamilias to fashion a replacement clog for his school-age son. The remainder of the stump is spotted by the bailiff and, after investigation, the 'theft' of the tree is traced back to the family in question, who are summarily evicted with their chattels. The final scenes of the film depict the cart loaded with their possessions clattering out of the courtyard, at night-time, followed by the family and watched in helpless silence by the neighbours.

A vivid sense of the unfairness of the system was always part of the ideology of neo-realism; meaning that the films that emerged from this movement could be claimed by the secular left as well as by more moderate Christian opinion. Sometimes these two cultural entities – which we could sum up as communism on the one hand, Catholicism on the other – coexist harmoniously; at other times they pull against each other. Is neo-realism *essentially* Christian, or essentially 'socialist' and militant? It is an interesting question. The profound and touching humility of the protagonists of films like Umberto D (De Sica, 1952) and La Strada (Fellini, 1954), as well as films we have already talked about such as The Nights of Cabiria (1956) (and also the film we have just been considering by Olmi), exhibit, I think, an unmistakably Christian inflection; but other films, it could be argued, point in different directions.[2] The critic André Bazin, who theorised neo-realism as well as anyone, was, as a Christian himself, naturally attracted to a religious interpretation of the phenomenon; but he was acute enough (and sympathetic enough, in that epoch, towards socialism) to see that in some of the greatest neo-realist films – Bicycle Thieves for example – there are strong criticisms made of the Church. Thus, referring to the sequence in which Ricci and the little boy Bruno pursue the phantom thief (a man they think has stolen the father's bicycle) into a church where a dole is being organised for the poor of the neighbourhood, Bazin writes in best 'quasi-communist' vein:

---

[2] We should not leave The Tree of Wooden Clogs without mentioning, by way of comparison, a film that came out two years earlier – I mean Bertolucci's Novecento (1976), along with The Last Emperor probably the most ambitious film this director ever made. Here, as with Olmi's film, we have a huge fresco of the Italian peasantry, concentrated this time in the Po valley and viewed via a narrative that takes us from the death of Verdi in 1901 up until the end of World War II. Bertolucci's film unlike Olmi's foregrounds the bourgeoisie, the 'landed' class of the period, who are criticised for their complaisance towards fascism. The peasantry on the other hand march forward under the banner of socialism. Bertolucci's film (as well as being operatic and spectacular) is militant in its sympathies. It need hardly be added that religion is entirely absent from its scenario.

'The cumbersome paternalism of the Catholic "Quakers" is unbearable, because their eyes are closed to [Ricci's] personal tragedy while they in fact actually do nothing to change the world that is the cause of it.' (Bazin adds blandly: 'On this score the most successful scene [in the film] is that in the storm under the porch when a flock of Austrian seminarians crowd around the worker and his son. We have no valid reason to blame them for chattering so much, and still less for speaking German. But it would be difficult to create a more objectively anti-clerical sequence).'

So religious truth, or even religious feeling, is far from being the point of at least one of the major landmarks of neo-realism, according to Bazin. When it comes to the question of where De Sica and Zavattini's truest sympathies *do* lie, he carefully distinguishes the positive secular tenderness of their vision from what might be termed biblical *caritas* – yet without, it seems to me, disparaging this latter virtue. The whole passage shows Bazin's discrimination at its most typical (and most wonderful). 'The tenderness of De Sica is of a special kind, and for this reason does not lend itself to any moral, religious or political generalisation', he writes.

> The ambiguities of *Miracle in Milan* and *Bicycle Thieves* have been used by the Christian Democrats *and* by the Communists. So much the better: a true parable should have something for everyone. I do not think De Sica was trying to argue anybody out of anything. I would not dream of saying that the kindness of De Sica is of greater value than either charity or class consciousness, but I see in the modesty of his position a definite artistic advantage.

Love, modesty, humility – the values that the film quietly endorses – are, in this interpretation, the exclusive property *neither* of the Christians *nor* the communists. 'The Neapolitan charm of De Sica becomes, thanks to the cinema, the most sweeping message of love that our times have heard since Chaplin. To anyone who doubted the importance of this love, it is enough to point out how quick partisan critics were to lay claim to it. What party could afford to leave love to the other?' Yet it remains an odd fact (which needs to be acknowledged) that the Christian Democrats, as a political organisation, were often grudging about the classic films in question.[3]

Bazin's essays on neo-realism, contributed to a variety of forums over the years until his death in 1958, give the fullest possible picture of the phenomenon unfolding in the present tense, so to speak; so let me end this chapter by looking at two more films the great French critic paused over as he asked himself the question what might constitute, in the world of modern production, a genuinely Christian scenography. Both films I think are masterpieces. Though they were famous in their time, they are now, possibly, more than a little obscure – reason enough, I hope, before leaving 'Italy', to throw a glance at them. The films in question are *Cielo sulla Palude* (*Heaven over the Marshes*) directed by Augusto Genina in 1949; and *Il Cristo Proibito* (*Forbidden Christ*) directed (his one and only shot at direction) by the writer Curzio Malaparte, which came out the following year. Bazin appreciated their qualities with his usual insight, although the second film he had many reservations about.

*

Heaven over the Marshes tells the true story of Maria Goretti, a 12-year-old child of poor peasants honoured by the Church for forgiving, on her deathbed, a youthful neighbour who had violently assaulted her. Bazin titled the article he wrote on the film 'A saint only becomes a

---

[3] Bert Cardullo tells us in the introduction to his selection of Bazin's writings on neo-realism that 'in 1952, Giulio Andreotti, State Undersecretary and head of the Direzione Generale dello Spettacolo (a powerful position that had direct influence on government grants as well as on censorship) published an open letter in the Christian-Democrat weekly *Libertas* bitterly deploring the neorealist trend in the Italian cinema and its negative image of the country – a letter that was quickly reprinted in other journals. Andreotti took direct aim at De Sica, who was castigated for exhibiting a "pessimistic vision" and exhorted to be "more constructive".' (*André Bazin and Italian Neorealism* (London, 2011), p. 26.)

saint *after* the event', the point being, of course, that *before* becoming a saint (the Church canonised her) she was an ordinary child; and it is this 'ordinariness' that the film dwells upon as a means – the only artistic means, Bazin would claim – of approaching what is 'extraordinary' (in the sense of sublime, other-worldly and religious). First of all, then, the film is remarkable for its realism. The location of the drama is the Pontine marshes, near Rome, in the epoch before motorised transport – a desolate, rain-sodden region that is captured in G.R. Aldo's black-and-white photography with absolute precision and authority. (Nowhere is there any hint that sets have been constructed.) Authentic also, in a way that is reminiscent of Olmi, is the characterisation of peasant life – without a trace of sentimentality, yet at the same time without any tendency towards melodrama or 'miserabilism'. The cast was made up of non-professionals who speak the dialogue of the region (remarkably for the time, the director insisted on using synchronised sound recording), and from whom Genina succeeded in coaxing performances of overwhelming natural simplicity. Maria (Ines Orsini) is the eldest child in a family that, on account of seasonal unemployment, has been deprived of the use of its homestead. After wanderings in the neighbourhood, the little group is billeted, on the orders of the local aristocrat, with a widowed tenant farmer and his son, who repay this imposition on their space by making life as difficult as possible for them. Soon after, Maria's father dies of malaria, and their co-tenant begins to pester the child's mother. Meanwhile, a more dangerous pestering begins, with Maria as target; Allesandro, the farmer's adolescent son, has had his eye on her, and he is cunning in pursuing her on the little errands (to fetch water from the well and so on) that, after her father's death, have become an inevitable part of her duties as the eldest of the children. During this period she has been going to catechism classes in preparation for her first communion. Indeed, at last the great day arrives. The horses and carts taking the family to church are decked out with simple floral decorations. There is happiness in the air. It is beautifully conveyed (not without an accompanying underlying pathos) that, in this particular milieu, the ceremony in question, for an adolescent girl, will be just as important as her wedding day.

No wedding day will ever be in store for Maria Goretti, of course. When, in the wake of the festivity, the young man finally launches his attack on her – it is a hot afternoon in the threshing yard some months later, and he has succeeded in dragging her up to his bedroom – the assault is conceived with a pitiless realism. There is an absolute lack of *pudeur*. Genina's decisions are all correct here. The event is immensely violent, but it needed to be shown, and experienced (with its sexual element properly acknowledged), in order to impart to viewers the authentic dimension of tragedy.

The upshot of the attack is not fatal – at least not immediately. As the drama enters its final act, however, the scene shifts to the nearby hospital where nuns are tending the stricken child who is just conscious enough to convey (in her dying breath) that she pardons her youthful assailant. Here, of course, we do inevitably move into the realm of the 'edifying' – but not the 'merely' edifying. It is hard to exaggerate how touchingly her simple speech of forgiveness is made to resonate by means of the actress's artless diction; and at the same time how strongly we are made to feel that what we are listening to, once we have taken in its import, is the opposite of mere pious formula.

The final moments of the film – its final cadence, you could say – are arrived at with the same artistic delicacy that governs the whole enterprise. A large crowd has gathered at the hospital, drawn thither by sympathetic curiosity. The onlookers stretch in a line from the threshold of Maria's bedroom, down the corridor and stairs and out into the hospital's courtyard. When it becomes clear at last, by some mysterious group telepathy, that Maria's soul has departed from her body, the supporters kneel down spontaneously in a single wave. Men in the crowd doff their hats. Everyone makes the sign of the cross. These simple gestures of respect bring Genina's film to a close with immense power and pathos, directing the audience's emotions, in a human way, towards the realm of 'final things'. What else can this be called except a 'Christian' movie, and a great one?

That was Bazin's conclusion at any rate, praising *Heaven over the Marshes* as 'that rare thing, a good Catholic film.' For the Frenchman, its quality was absolutely tied up with its plainness, and paradoxically, with its total *lack* of piety.

> There are no unusual mitigating circumstances (*Bazin writes*). Maria Goretti is neither Saint Vincent de Paul, nor Saint Teresa of Avila, nor even Saint Bernadette Soubirous of Lourdes. It is to Genina's credit that he made a hagiography that doesn't prove anything, above all not the sainthood of the saint. What was Genina's starting point? It was not simply to reject all the ornament that comes with the subject matter – the religious symbolism and, it goes without saying, the supernatural element of traditional hagiographies (a film such as Léon Carré's *Monsieur Vincent* also avoids these stumbling blocks) [...] Genina's bias in favour of realism made him go so far as to prohibit in any of his images the supposition of his protagonist's 'sainthood', so afraid was he of betraying the spirit of the endeavour. Maria Goretti's sainthood is served in the only valid manner possible, by a film that expressly sets out *not* to demonstrate it.

*

Forbidden Christ, by Malaparte, has a wholly different theological flavour from *Heaven over the Marshes*, though both films are anchored (part of their strength) in a hyper-realistically depicted locale: a deserted peasant hamlet in Genina's case, and a populated hill village, with church, piazza, and streets of artisan dwellings, in Malaparte's. Bazin's essay on the movie (published in *Cahiers du Cinéma* in the summer of 1951) starts off with the observation that, even as he likes the film, he can't abide its author. It is true that a whiff of D'Annunzian notoriety had always attached to this 'man about town'; a prominent diplomat, journalist and editor in the fascist period, Malaparte had gradually shifted his ideological allegiance (suffering bouts of imprisonment on the way) so that now, in the postwar epoch, he was, if anything, a partisan of the communist cause. Opportunist he may have been, yet I think he is too powerful and too interesting a personality to be summed up by this epithet; his harrowing despatches from the Russian front are among the most vivid pages in the annals of war journalism; just as there is no stronger or more terrifying fictional account of close-up combat to be found than in his brilliant and notorious novel *Kaputt* (1944). Bazin doesn't like him – we have to accept that fact (indeed at one stage in his essay he goes so far as to speak of Malaparte as being 'wholly deprived of nobility'). Nonetheless, he stands by the movie's quality; the truly astonishing fact about the film, according to Bazin, is not that it was the first and, as it turned out, the sole film of a director-writer who was 51 years old when he made it (where on earth did he acquire these cinematic skills?) but that he managed the task so successfully.

It is hard to disagree with this verdict. The technical skill of the film extends to all departments – writing, scenography, camera-work – yet is registered best of all in the quality of performance Malaparte succeeds in eliciting from his actors. Let us take, for example, the scene in the bedroom where Bruno, the film's protagonist (played by Raf Vallone), coaxes from his former girlfriend Maria (Anna Maria Ferrero) the admission that while he was away fighting on the front, she had been temporarily unfaithful to him. The girl is in her nightgown sitting up talking to him, while Bruno in his day-clothes is perched on the mattress close beside her. There is a stunning moment in the course of this dialogue when Bruno stretches back against the bed-rest facing her, in order calmly to take in the import of her confession. No melodrama: instead, an incredibly natural gesture, of astonishing intimacy; yet just one example among many of the extraordinary subtlety, and precision of tone, that characterise this movie throughout its running length.

Il Cristo Proibito is the story of a quest, with vengeance as its psychological engine. Bruno's brother has been murdered in his absence, and, in the face of a wall of silence and solidarity raised by the remaining villagers (including his mother and fiancée), he is determined to find out who the killer is. His own pride and disdain also comes into the matter. Though his mother may be secretly willing to tell him, she is one person he will not deign to ask. Meanwhile, however, a more promising (as well as more acceptable) source of information is sensed to lie in the mysterious figure of the village carpenter Antonio (Alain Cuny), a personal friend of Bruno from pre-war days. After their initial reunion, Antonio invites him to a night-time rendezvous at his workshop, where without provocation he proceeds to tell Bruno a story about his past life, and how it came to be that, long ago, he had been forced to murder an enemy. So there is blood on his hands, this placid man implies, whose stain is all but ineradicable.

To the listening Bruno, there seem to be two possible things going on here: on the one hand, the tale might be a warning *not* to go ahead with the sought-after vengeance – it will only lead to remorse and melancholy (the kind of melancholy which is perhaps the secret of Antonio's strange empathy). On the other hand, perhaps the parable is meant to harbour another meaning? Could it not be a way of hinting that, far from happening 'long ago', this killing Antonio speaks of is a recent event? Might it be that Antonio himself – the man sitting opposite him, and speaking so calmly and lucidly – is telling him now, in a roundabout way, that *he* is the man he is looking for?

The scene in which this conversation takes place is another of those dramatic highlights of the movie I hinted at earlier, extraordinary for its 'present-tense' intensity. Editing cuts are minimal; instead, the camera circles round the carpentry table, while the boldly stylised lighting picks out in sharp relief speaker and listener sitting menacingly opposite each other. At a given moment, Bruno makes a fatal decision: the knife that he carries on his person whistles through the gloomy atmosphere and pierces his friend to the heart. (A sequence that has taken place the previous day at the fairground rifle range has already established for us that Bruno possesses 'unerring' accuracy of aim.)

From now on events move swiftly. Abandoning the corpse, Bruno stumbles home, where his mother, in panic, blurts out the name of the

FIGURE 29 A psycho-metaphysical thriller with God at its centre. Curzio Malaparte's *Il Cristo Proibito* (1950).

real killer: 'Pinin', the brother of a beautiful female neighbour we have met earlier (not the fiancée). Forthwith, Bruno summons the man to accompany him to a high spot outside the village, where (judging from his challenge and bodily posture) it looks very much as if the game will be up. Perhaps not, however! For now, as if in delayed reaction, the horror of human judgement begins to dawn on Bruno. The man facing him may have killed his brother – what will killing *him* achieve in return? And hasn't he himself, anyway, just killed his best friend in error? So, ignoring Pinin's pleas to 'get it over with quickly', Bruno throws down his weapon and retreats with as much dignity as he can muster to the village to face the judgement of his neighbours.

'He has already paid for it.' Those are the words Bruno was muttering to himself in the moments leading up to his decision. The 'he' refers, the viewer must assume, to his best friend Antonio rather than to the real murderer Pinin (though maybe to Pinin as well). The weight of the film's Christian meditation is tied up, evidently, with the repudiation of vengeance and the necessity of mutual forgiveness. But the dramatic kernel of the movie lies in the extraordinary sacrifice of the carpenter Antonio; perhaps this man had tempted Bruno to kill him so that he wouldn't have to wreak vengeance on the real killer? In taking the burden of the real murderer's sins on his shoulders, Antonio, of course, imitates Christ, in some way. This 'forbidden' Christ (why forbidden? Because 'exiled from the twentieth century') is the figure that each of us must take to our hearts if war and discord are ever to be eliminated. While the 'message' of the film is the simple New Testament gospel of brotherhood, its energy and power derive from Old Testament origins. As the theme of 'brothers' runs through the course of the movie (Bruno linked with his brother, the 'beautiful neighbour' with hers), the viewer is made to reflect, inevitably, on Cain and Abel's rivalry, multiplied millions-fold by the turmoil of the late global conflict. At the heart of *Il Cristo Proibito* there is something furious, biblical and prophetic that strikes the contemporary viewer as far more important than its (occasional) excesses of rhetoric. Indeed, the rhetoric and the artistic sincerity must ultimately be judged to go hand in hand. As we have seen, not a few among the director's contemporaries judged Malaparte to be a phoney. Yet the film itself is decidedly *not* phoney. It remains, in its odd way, one of the strangest and most powerful Christian movies on record.

FIGURE 30 'Artistic options continue to be envisaged [...] within the traditional language of religion.' Medieval Dance of Death in Ingmar Bergman's *Seventh Seal* (1956).

5

Scandinavia: Lutheran Interludes

The landscape of Scandinavia, like that of the British Isles, is littered with small parish churches that continue to function much as they have always done; they constitute a living tapestry. Danish, Swedish and Norwegian citizens have the option to pay a small portion of their income in the form of an upkeep tithe, and most of them choose to do so – that is why these buildings usually look so handsome. The school system is modern but the different national songbooks that are in use on an everyday basis make little formal distinction between poetry and hymn. The songs in question, committed to memory from an early age, are brushed with a Christian flavour. In May of each year in the provinces, as the beech trees burst into leaf, the streets are crowded with spruce little boys, and girls in white dresses, attending their class Confirmation.

Under a certain light it is quite easy to believe that Christianity hasn't given up here. Nor has it. But these visible manifestations of tradition are also quite illusory. Scandinavia is as secular and multicultural as anywhere else in Europe – perhaps indeed more so. From the time of Ibsen and Strindberg, Swedes and Danes (and Norwegians too) have taken delight in championing the modern in all its forms. They are, as it were, pioneers of secularism in art, in design, and in social thought, sometimes a trifle complacently, but usually with the easy tolerance born of the fact that, on the whole, democracy reigns, and the social-political system functions efficiently.

Just as Strindberg and Ibsen can be said to stand for a certain kind of theatre that revolutionised stagecraft at the end of the nineteenth century – and not merely stagecraft, but the whole notion of where theatre stands in terms of a spiritual enterprise – so too in the twin figures of Ingmar Bergman (1918–2007) and Carl Theodor Dreyer (1889–1968) Scandinavia gave birth to two cinematic giants who have come to epitomise the potential of film as a medium of spiritual-poetic exploration. In many ways they are quite different from each other (just as Ibsen is different from Strindberg); but in both cases, if from very different angles, God is somehow part of the equation.

One writes 'somehow'; it is a feeble word. A number of the greatest films by either director have strongly marked Christian themes; but in neither case is Christianity the director's exclusive concern. Bergman, like Bresson, could be said to have abandoned religion in the later part of his career – without much regret, if we are to judge by remarks made in interviews. Less clear is Dreyer's case. He never succeeded in making his great planned film about Jesus. It is nonetheless true that there is a measurable gap of temperament and preoccupation separating *Ordet* (1955), where religion is central, from the Danish director's famous swansong *Gertrud* (1964), a spiritual-erotic melodrama from which most traces of Christianity have been eradicated.

*

Bergman tackles God – this much is obvious. But where exactly? The early films are not patently religious, either in theme or inflection, though they are clearly brilliant: right from the beginning this man had a stance and a signature. There cannot be many directors who produced so many masterpieces in such short order – successive masterpieces, exclusively from his own pen, so to speak. Unlike Dreyer, whose skill lay in the adaptation of already existing literary works, Bergman was a thoroughgoing auteur who wrote and developed his own material. One looks at these early films and marvels at their teeming inventiveness: *Three Strange Loves*, *To Joy*, *Summer Interlude*,

Summer with Monika, Sawdust and Tinsel, A Lesson in Love, Journey into Autumn, Smiles of a Summer Night; in the space of only five or six years (from 1949 to the middle of the 1950s) they tumble out one after another, with astonishing poise and assurance. Their genre, however, is that of psychological drama (sometimes mixed with comedy). Religion is not really their subject matter.

The first explicit encounter in Bergman's art with the velleities of Christianity can be said to be felt in *The Seventh Seal* (1956), one of his subsequently most famous works, and it seems to arise naturally enough from the medieval period in which the film is set. (One cannot really deal seriously with the Middle Ages, I suppose, without bringing in Christianity somewhere; though of course what one says about it – what one's stance is towards Christ and the devil and the society of believers – needn't for that reason be 'Christian'.) *The Seventh Seal* was followed by *Wild Strawberries* (1957), another high point in the Bergman filmography; and after that by a return to medieval themes in *The Virgin Spring* (1959), where Christianity is again evoked masterfully. Three further films in succession, often spoken of as a trilogy (though Bergman himself tended to play this down), can be said to complete the Swede's formal preoccupation with religious matters, the movies in question being *Through a Glass Darkly* (1960), *Winter Light* (1961) and *The Silence* (1962). Two later films, both masterpieces, *Cries and Whispers* (1971) and *Fanny and Alexander* (1982), are notable, by contrast, for their distinct anti-clericalism. With *Persona* (1965) Bergman's career had moved into a new phase, certainly a glorious one in most people's estimation, with many triumphs as well as moral and aesthetic setbacks, but not quite so relevant for the purpose of our current study, except in so far as they throw retrospective light on their predecessors.

*

Classical, accomplished and marvellously memorable – one wouldn't usually think of *Wild Strawberries* as a Christian work. Its theme, insofar as it can be summed up in a single phrase, is disappointment. An old professor, Isak Borg, is travelling from Stockholm to Lund with Marianne, his daughter-in-law, to receive an honorary degree from the university there; but this public recognition of his achievements is undercut by a pervasive private anguish. Flashbacks in the course of the car journey show us that his marriage has been a failure, and that the professor's fatal inability to communicate emotion has been passed on hereditarily to his son who, now married himself (to the beautiful and tender woman who is Borg's travelling companion), refuses, out of a mixture of pride and existential despair, to contemplate bringing children into the world.

I first saw the film when I was rather young – 13 or 14, it must have been – and I can remember very clearly the moral impact of the scene in which Evald, the son in question (played by Gunnar Björnstrand), conveys this bleak and adamant decision in the pouring rain, as he sits side by side with his wife in their motionless motor vehicle. 'It's unfair to bring children into the world, the world being what it is!' Did married adults – *could* married adults – really speak to each other in such tones? Evald's bodily posture is haughty and vehement; he refers to children as 'wretches'. The poor wife (the actress is the beautiful Ingrid Thulin, in perhaps her greatest performance) can do nothing, in the meantime, but sit back and grimly accept his verdict.

The film is famously haunted by dreams and premonitions, starting with the professor's nightmare in which the coffin that has fallen from the horse-drawn hearse as it clatters through the silent township slides open to reveal to him his own doppelgänger, a 'living corpse' that grips his wrist and attempts to draw him forward to join him in the darkness of the tomb. Subsequent dreams, as complicated, refractory and lucid as they are in real life, return to the idea of the sterility of adult relationships, and to the shocking notion – shocking at any event to me then, as a sheltered youngster – that in not every case is the birth of a child to be welcomed as a blessing. Certainly there is anguish and neurosis in the film – who can forget the image of the empty cradle, the jagged branch and the cry of the jackdaws! – and yet even at the time of first seeing it I must have noticed too that darkness wasn't the last word. A broad countervailing swathe of sanity was provided by the ingenuous presence of a hitch-hiking trio of young persons, two boys and a girl, whom the professor and his daughter-in-law pick up on their journey southward; as it also made itself felt in the beautiful family flashback scenes, full of laughing cheerful children, that emerge out of the professor's reverie when the party makes a stop near an old lakeside summer house at which it turns out he passed much of his childhood.

I call these family flashback scenes 'beautiful' in shorthand; no more appropriate adjective presents itself. Overall, the film has a tender moral beauty, a sort of elegiac hopefulness, that makes itself especially felt in the concluding sequences which show us the ceremony at which old Borg (the professor, played by the Swedish veteran film director Victor Sjöström) finally receives his honorary degree, along with the background preparations leading up to this moment (preparations, incidentally, during which it becomes apparent that Evald may change his mind about starting a family). Yet the really great Christian scene of the film – so quiet and self-effacing that the viewer could almost pass it by without noticing – occurs a little time before these satisfactory outcomes, in the form of a peaceful interlude in the middle of the car journey.

The little band, consisting of the professor and his daughter-in-law, along with the hitch-hiking trio (pipe-smoking Sara (Bibi Andersson) and her two male companions) stop off, then, for lunch, at the professor's invitation, at a terraced restaurant in the countryside, where it seems they may be the only customers. The meal, we are informed in the professor's gentle voiceover, is a great success and the five of them linger afterward in the open air, over port and coffee. The two young men, rivals for Sara's affection (one of them, in fact, is engaged to her), have been quarrelling good-naturedly about theology; the fiancé is

FIGURE 31 'Where is the Friend I seek where'er I'm going?' The meal on the terrace from *Wild Strawberries* (1957).

planning to enter the church. Asked by Sara to adjudicate the intellectual merits of the disputation, old Isak Borg smilingly declines. After a few moments of silence, he proceeds instead to recite a poem that starts, 'Where is the Friend I seek where'er I'm going?' At different times in the recitation, different listeners round the table take up the thread of the verses; evidently the poem is well known among Swedes. Its author is a nineteenth-century archbishop named Johan Olof Wallin (1779–1839), but we needn't be cognisant of this historical information to grasp the yearning, idealistic tenor of its discourse:

> *Var är den Vän som överallt jag söker?*
> *När dagen gryr, min längtan blott sig öker*
> *När dagen flyr, jag än ej honom finner,*
> *Fast hjärtet brinner.*
>
> *Jeg ser hans spår varhelst en kraft sig röjer,*
> *En blommer doftar och ett ax sig böjer*

Uti den suck jag drar, den luft jag andas
Hans kärlek blandas.

Jag hör hans röst där sommarvinden susar,
Där lunden sjunger, och där floden brusar;
Jag hör den ljuvast i mitt hjärta tala
Och mig hugsvala.

Ack, när så mycket skönt i varje åder
Av skapelsen och livet sig förråder,
Hur skön då måste själva källan vara,
Den evigt klara!

Where is the Friend I seek where'er I'm going?
At break of dawn my need for him is growing.
At night he is not there to still my yearning.
My heart is burning.

I see his footprint here in nature's power
The weighted wheat that bends, the scented flower.
His love is in the very air I'm breathing,
The sigh I'm heaving.

I hear his voice where summer breezes quiver
Through leafy boughs or on the foaming river;
And in my heart it can most sweetly move me:
Its balm can soothe me.

Oh when such beauty everywhere is showing,
In every aspect of creation glowing,
How bright must be the source of this reflection!
What pure perfection!

Here and yet not here, the 'Friend' can be none other than Christ – we take this in subliminally. We feel that it is He (or the absent He; the longed-for He) who presides over the whole wonderful summer afternoon epiphany. The words of the poem are full of yearning, yet the peace they conjure up in the open air is experienced by the little band (and by us too, privileged witnesses of the scene; we can almost smell old Borg's cigar smoke!) as happiness. There are, perhaps, few graver or more delicate scenes in the whole of Swedish cinema.

The sense of ordered calm and reflection communicated in this lovely quiet passage of the film finds its counterpart in the perhaps even more celebrated sequence in *The Seventh Seal* in which the chess-playing Knight (Max von Sydow) comes across the little travelling circus family consisting of Jof, the juggler, his wife Maria (Bibi Andersson again) and their infant child as the trio are resting beside their caravan in the countryside, on their way to Elsinore. It is evening – one of those long summertime dusks where darkness doesn't really settle in until midnight – and their sturdy horse, unharnessed, is chomping grass on a hillock in the background. Mia is comforting her husband who has just returned from a nasty scrape in the tavern, and he sits there now strumming his lute wistfully. The seated couple offer the Knight a share in their simple snack of milk and wild strawberries, whereupon the Knight, accepting this hospitality, answers them with supremely gracious words, indicating that (taking into account everything that has led up to it, and we are surrounded here by plague and violence) this is a moment it will be impossible to forget: 'I shall bear this memory between my hands, as carefully as this bowl of fresh milk. And this will be a sign, and a great content.' He sips the milk from the wide-brimmed bowl and strolls off down the hill, to where the hooded figure of Death is waiting for him, chessboard at the ready.

The mythical-religious (and indeed allegorical) overtones of the scene are unmistakable, but at the same time delicate. We recognise on one level that the little wandering trio with their caravan has parallels with the Holy Family (as the horse has parallels with the ass), but the symbolism, such as it is, isn't importunate; it doesn't force itself upon you, any more than the milk and the strawberries demand to be read as some kind of poetic equivalent to the Eucharist. What is clear – and it suffices – is that the moment is sacred. Or else, to put it another way, that even if nothing else can be agreed upon, the sacred 'exists'.

Scandinavia: Lutheran Interludes 149

FIGURE 32 'I shall bear this memory between my hands, as carefully as this bowl of fresh milk.' Max von Sydow as the Knight in Bergman's *Seventh Seal* (1956).

The sequence exemplifies merely one of several ways in which the divine is encountered in this movie; here, we could say, we have the popular or even artless level of ordinary everyday piety and goodness. Yet of course there are other more sophisticated levels, represented firstly by the soul of the Knight, calm here, but tormented beneath the surface with his apprehension that God has withdrawn from the world. And other levels too – the 'institutional' level of the Church itself which, in the face of the plague threat, has responded with a sort of encouraged mass panic (processions of flagellants whipping themselves). Finally, of course, on the other side of religion altogether, there is the spectre of atheism, represented by the Knight's no-nonsense squire (Gunnar Björnstrand) who regards with a grim and satirical irony the antics of his fellow men and women as they jostle to save themselves – an irony that doesn't preclude (for he is not at all a bad man) the occasional bold act of practical charity. In the midst of these perspectives, the film does not press an agenda, and it is difficult to gauge where Bergman himself stands on the spectrum between faith and disillusionment; the film, it seems to me, isn't open to certainty. All we can say is that the metaphysical options are envisioned, or rather dramatised, *within the language of religion*, still treated as living iconography, as in the famous Dance of Death sequence at the end of the movie, where, against a skyline of storm clouds, hooded Death with his hourglass and scythe is seen guiding the Knight's party towards who knows what final destination.

Bergman returned to the Middle Ages a couple of years later in *The Virgin Spring* (1959), an adaptation of a thirteenth-century Swedish ballad called *Töres datter I Vänge* (Töre's daughter at Vänge) that recounts the tale of a rich farmer's daughter who is raped by a pair of ruffians and their boy assistant as she rides through the forest to church on Candlemas Day. Having stripped her of her jewels and finery, the assailants make the mistake of trying to palm the material off on the wife of the owner of a neighbouring farm where they seek shelter for the night. Alas for them, it happens to be the homestead of the girl's father. A swift and terrible vengeance ensues – the trio slain as they lie dozing on the hearth after supper – after which the farmer (perhaps we should call him local chieftain; he seems to belong to the minor nobility – at any event he is magnificently played by Max von Sydow) sets out to search for his daughter's body. On the spot where she is found, a spring miraculously gushes forth. Both poem and film end with Töre promising to erect a church in her memory.

> Now Töre casts his knife away
> 'O Lord, forgive my deed this day.
> How can I this deed atone?
> To God I'll build a church of stone.
>
> 'Gladly shall we do such work
> Cold is the forest air –

Kärna shall we call this kirk
When green the trees are there.'

Just like *The Seventh Seal*, the film has a beautifully physical texture; it is set in spring and one can really feel the water unfreezing as the girl rides through the pristine forest air accompanied only by her female servant Ingeri, of whom more shortly. I haven't seen it discussed in print, nor read of it in any interview with Bergman, but the conception of the movie – both its 'look' and its spiritual worldview – seems to owe something to classic Japanese cinema. Certainly the rape scene, which is exceptionally graphic and violent (and which ran into censorship difficulties on the film's release), is reminiscent of the famous mother-and-child ambush sequence in Mizoguchi's *Ugetsu Monogatari* (three drunken spearsmen murder an unarmed woman and her baby as they attempt to make their way home through the battle lines); while prior to this, the image of the mounted female noblewoman on the caparisoned steed conjures up similar graceful forest images from the beginning of Kurosawa's *Rashomon* (this latter also a rape drama of course). In general it could be said the Japanese template is an excellent model; in its classical period, no national cinema, perhaps, was better at evoking the Middle Ages. Bergman wrote the script of *The Virgin Spring* in partnership with Ulla Isaksson, and together they introduced one new element into the story that isn't there in the original ballad: we could call this its pagan undertone – though maybe 'undertone' is too mild a word; the dramatic contrast between Christianity and paganism is a constitutive element of the film's meaning and impact. Sweden, of course, by the thirteenth century had been thoroughly Christianised, but there remained, we are led to believe, pockets of resistance where Odin and the old gods continued to be worshipped. Ingeri the servant girl (Gunnel Lindblom) is one of these secret resisters; on the journey to Mass accompanying her mistress, she finds an ally in an old pedlar living by a ford (he is brilliantly played by Alan Edwall) who deals in dark spells and

FIGURE 33 A face-off between Christianity and paganism? Birgitta Pettersson and Gunnel Lindblom in Bergman's *The Virgin Spring* (1959).

incantations. (One thinks of the extraordinary sequence in *Andrei Roublev* where the monk comes across the naked pagans celebrating their summer solstice on the riverbank; at a certain stage in our history, strange as it may seem, these rival 'forms of thought' coexisted.) One reading of *The Virgin Spring*, therefore, would want to stress the fragility of the newer religion in the face of older chthonic certainties, and to question whether we are supposed to entertain the idea that Christianity has ever really 'grafted'.

That is certainly how Martin Scorsese remembers the movie, in his contribution to a lively filmed discussion about Bergman's work (*Trespassing Bergman: A Documentary* by Jane Magnusson (2013)): the pagan is *stronger* than the Christian – it is deeper, darker, more 'authentic'. 'Remember the sagas!', Scorsese says. Evidently, we are not being asked to decide the matter definitively. The important issue is how the ideological rivalry comes across in the movie. And here I am struck by the calmness and freedom of Bergman's handling of the Christian elements of the tale. Revenge, of course – the slaying of the assailants – is *not* Christian; but the repentance that follows most definitely is. The final scenes in the glade when the body is discovered keep faithfully to the ballad's simple piety. As the miraculous stream gushes from under the girl's raised head, there is no hint of twentieth-century irony; no quotation marks. This is what happened, the film seems to say, take it as you will. Töre's vow to raise a chapel on the site of the body of his murdered daughter and have Masses given there in perpetuity is presented with the power and the pathos of all such similar tragic vows that have come down to us in the historical record.

*

The three films discussed so far have evident connections (if only through chronological propinquity) but they are not usually thought of as a trilogy, I think. That designation is customarily reserved for the trio of films that we need to consider next, produced as they all were within the short period 1960–2. The movies in question – available on DVD in a single Criterion box set – are *Through a Glass Darkly* (1960), *Winter Light* (1961) and *The Silence* (1962), and the first question to ask, if only to get it out of the way, is whether they do indeed constitute a 'trilogy'. The idea appears to be that the movies in question partake of a shared spiritual quest and that for all their surface dissimilarities of milieu and psychology they significantly cohere together.

Yet in fact this apprehension may have more to do with accidental correspondences in their release pattern, and in the way they were marketed, than with genuine marks of identity. We are conducting our enquiry here (a partial enquiry, as I have said from the beginning) into Bergman's religious preoccupations, and in at least one of the films at issue – the last of the three, *The Silence* – such preoccupations of the spirit, I am forced to conclude, are non-existent. Which doesn't mean that this film isn't interesting; indeed, it is possible (or at least not self-evidently absurd) to think of it as one of Bergman's most distinctive masterpieces. Dwight Macdonald, among the cleverest of Bergman's contemporary reviewers, thought that *The Silence* is spoiled by a kind of given or unexplained quality in the initial enmity between the principals of the film, two sisters temporarily thrown together during a heatwave in a vast deserted hotel in some mysterious foreign city. Yet granted that these women (Ingrid Thulin and Gunnel Lindblom are the actresses) *do* hate each other – for whatever familial or ancestral reasons – the playing out of their mutual anguish constitutes, surely, one of the most extraordinarily imagined psychodramas that up to that date had ever been put onto celluloid. The sexual exploration in this film is audacious, leading on, portentously, to similar preoccupations (of inter-female jealousy, rage and rivalry) that were to be magisterially dramatised in *Persona*, and later still in *Cries and Whispers*. Of religion, however – religious feelings, other-worldly yearnings, perspectives on the transcendent, and piety – there is not the slightest trace, I would say. That is not the world which the movie inhabits.[1]

By contrast, the title of the first of the three films seems to be clear enough. It is taken from one of the grandest passages in the Bible, the verses in Corinthians (I.13:12) where Paul defines the radiance of divine love (or 'charity', as he calls it) by contrasting it to the limitations of ordinary human knowledge: 'For now we see through a glass, darkly: but then [i.e., when we come to accept Christ in our hearts] *face to face*; now I know in part; but then shall I know even as also I am known.' The beautiful phrase 'through a glass, darkly'

---

[1] Despite its title, which might be said to point us in a direction that has been important for theology and for prayer – the so-called Silence of God. It is evidently a concept that had fascinated Bergman in the past, most notably in *The Seventh Seal*, in relation to the Knight's spiritual travails. *Le Dieu caché* (The Hidden God), Lucien Goldmann's study of seventeenth-century French sacred literature, came out in 1955 and was widely discussed at the time. It is possible that Bergman may have been influenced by this book. Nonetheless (the reader is entitled to disagree with me), I don't believe that that is what *this* film is about.

(*Såsom i en Spegel*) is used in this film's title to refer not so much to the partial human knowledge which is the fate of all of us in the fallen world as, specifically, to the benighted, murky confusion of the film's principal character, a beautiful young woman ('Karin' – Harriet Andersson) who is suffering from chronic schizophrenia. Her illness is a sort of religious madness, taking the form of encounters with, and yearnings towards, Rilkean angelic creatures, one of whom, as described in a memorable nightmare sequence, morphs into a gigantic threatening spider. The substance of these visions, then, is straightforwardly illusory: Bergman's treatment of the woman's mania is entirely – and convincingly I would say – psychological, the origins of her delusion lying somewhere perhaps (we are allowed to speculate) in her strained relationship with her father, a mysterious patriarch played, with customary stern intelligence, by the great Gunnar Björnstrand. 'Material mind', therefore, rather than metaphysics, is at the core of this film. In so far as religion *is* visible, it is encountered only towards the end of the tale, in concluding sequences that have sometimes been criticised as perfunctory.

The critics in question constitute a formidable authority, including as they do Bergman himself (in his autobiography *Images*), along with Dwight Macdonald again, and the English writer Robin Wood (in my opinion the finest of all Bergman's historical interpreters). For all that, I am not sure that I agree with them about the 'perfunctoriness'. The bone of contention lies in the remark that the father passes on to his son in the aftermath of the girl being taken away to hospital (in a helicopter – they are living on an island). 'I don't know if love is proof of God's existence, or *if love is God himself*,' he says. And the son concurs: 'Yes, for you, love and God are the same.' (It takes us back to that passage from Corinthians.) The anxiety felt by all three critics here, I can see, is that there is too much signalling and straining. The epigram comes across as the 'message' of the movie, a sort of ersatz reassurance tacked onto the body of a drama whose real implications (our critics think) point to a far darker pessimism. Would a father in such circumstances speak in such a way? One has to look carefully at the sequence itself to make a judgement. Yet for me the conclusion works. Indeed I find it a very beautiful coda, one that gives no hostage at all to the question of how much prayer and love really *do* combine to help our fellow human beings. Privately, the father has written in his journal that he thinks his daughter's illness is incurable. The contrary hope expressed to his son (an appropriate hope in the circumstances, one might think) represents, for him, a submission: a lightening of his spiritual load, and a necessary reprieve from his lonely existential anguish.

With *Winter Light* (1961), the middle film of the so-called trilogy, questions of religious evasiveness (or religious sentimentality) do not apply. Faith, and its difficulty, are straightforwardly the subject of the movie (as they were in *The Seventh Seal*). A widowed middle-aged priest Thomas Ericsson (Gunnar Björnstrand) is in the throes of getting over an affair with one of his parishioners, who is still in love with him. He finds himself faced by the modern reality of dwindling congregations. At Sunday morning service in wintertime there are as few as five communicants at the altar rail, not counting the sexton and organist. The gestures of the liturgy can be got through, and the sacrament delivered, but when it comes to pastoral fire our priest has forgotten, if he ever knew, how to speak words that give inspiration and solace.

The crisis has come to a head on the very day that we meet him; one of his parishioners, haunted by visions of nuclear catastrophe, has committed suicide. The scenario of the film, which is constructed in real time (or more accurately, as if to cleverly imitate real time) follows the priest in the three-hour interval between noon (the main Mass of the day) and three o'clock (the beginning of the afternoon service) while he attempts to deal with the consequences of this tragic event – at the same time as grappling with another moral crisis, brought on by the demands of his mistress Märta (Ingrid Thulin) that he clarify once and for all the contours of their failing domestic relationship.

Imminent loss of faith, and what to do about it, is the subject of *Winter Light*. The submission to prayer that is at the core of the religious life no longer makes sense to this pastor. Launched into the void, his words meet with no comforting response, no confirmation. Can it be any kind of comfort to remind himself, as the priest tries to, that Christ too journeyed through similar anguish? In that fearfulness – in that sense of incipient desertion ('My God, my God, why hast thou forsaken me?') – lies much of Christianity's sublimity. Alas, to feel this solace 'theoretically' is one thing; to feel it as Truth is another. And the priest is only too aware that the parallel evoked, in conversation with his sexton Algot (Allan Edvall), between his own *via dolorosa* and that of Christ on the Cross may merely be, at bottom, further indication of his vanity and worthlessness.

On the afternoon we are concerned with, the priest summons sufficient energy to go through the necessary forms (talking to the police authorities, visiting the dead man's widow, confronting Märta in her schoolroom and listening to her tearful expostulations), but nothing in these conversations is edifying, all of it in a certain sense is humiliating. When finally his duties are done, and he arrives at afternoon service, there is no one in the congregation except Märta. Under these circumstances, he asks himself, should the service go forward? The film ends at the moment when, robed at the altar, he turns to his spectral congregation reciting, or perhaps better to say merely mouthing, the words from the liturgy: 'Holy, holy, holy is the Lord God of hosts. The whole earth is full of His glory.'

In the pause of darkness before the credits come up, one can only be struck by the devastating emptiness of it all. What is there 'glorious' in anything that we have witnessed here? And yet: the solemn words of the liturgy (even without music to support them) do, somehow, put claims forward that have their own irrefutable resonance. Could it be that there is something to be said, beyond mere stoicism, for going through the motions? Crises, after all, *can* come to an end, and sticking to the path of duty is one way of making them do so. One of the great successes of the film is the way that Bergman and his cameraman Sven Nykvist manage to suggest minute changes of light as the hours go by. At the zenith of the day a pale effusion from the sun floods into the church and vestry, bathing the architecture in extraordinary radiance. That effulgence in turn makes a significant subliminal contribution to the sense we take away from this movie – not, paradoxically, of despair, but of quiet and moving exaltation.[2]

It was the beauty of the Swedish language to my untutored English ear which as much as anything else fired the precocious love of Bergman's films which began in my adolescence and has lasted ever since. When finally, however, I came to know something about Scandinavia at first hand, it was through Danish rather than Swedish mediation; the newly set-up film school in Jutland, where I arrived by a roundabout route to teach film history in 1993, was situated at the romantic address (so it seemed to me) of no. 1 Carl Th. Dreyers vej, Ebeltoft. ('Ebeltoft' = Apple Hill.) Dreyer, one knew, was the Danish Bergman – though of an older and more remote epoch, the majority of his films belonging to the silent era. We are still (as I write) awaiting the definitive biography of the director promised by the film scholar

---

[2] Bergman's much-disliked father was a bishop who had faced similar crises. In his memoir *Images: My Life in Film* (London, 1994), the Swedish director recounts an anecdote that is relevant to the reading I am giving here of *Winter Light*. He was in the company of his father, and they were visiting a church near Uppsala.

'It was an early spring day with mist and bright light reflecting off the surrounding snow. We arrived [writes Bergman] in plenty of time at the little church north of Uppsala to find four churchgoers ahead of us waiting in the narrow pews. The churchwarden and the sexton were waiting on the porch while the female organist was rummaging in the organ loft. Even after the summoning bell had faded over the plain, the pastor still had not appeared. A long silence ensued in heaven and on earth. Father shifted uneasily in his seat and muttered to himself. A few minutes later we heard the sound of a car speeding across the slippery ground outside; a door slammed, and after a minute the pastor came puffing down the aisle.

Casper Tybjerg, and there remains much that is genuinely unknown about the man. In those days, 30-odd years ago, one had to refer for contextual information to Maurice Drouzy's biographical essay in French, *Carl Th. Dreyer né Nilsson* (Éditions du Cerf, 1982) – 'né Nilsson' referring to the fact, on which Drouzy placed a somewhat heavy Freudian burden, that Dreyer was the illegitimate issue of a Swedish nobleman and a Danish servant girl whom her seducer had promptly abandoned. The child was subsequently farmed out to Danish foster parents in Copenhagen after the unfortunate mother committed suicide.

The future director's adoptive parents were neither of them churchgoers. Carl senior was by profession a typesetter, traditionally one of the more radical trades in the nineteenth-century Danish capital. Sundays, the Day of Rest, were reserved for the activities of the cycling club of which he was branch president, rather than for any form of worship. The boy was baptised and confirmed, but these concessions

---

'When he got to the altar rail, he turned round and looked at his congregation with red-rimmed eyes. He was a thin, long-haired man, his trimmed beard scarcely covering his receding chin. He swung his arms like a skier and coughed, the hair on the crown of his head curly, and his forehead turning red. "I am sick," said the pastor. "I have a high fever and a chill." He sought sympathy in our eyes. "I have permission to give you a short service; there will be no communion. I'll preach as best I can, then we'll sing a hymn and that will have to do. I'll just go into the sacristy and put on my cassock." He bowed and for a few moments stood irresolutely as if waiting for applause or at least some sign of approval, but when no one reacted, he disappeared through a heavy door.

'Father rose from his seat in the pew. He was upset. "I must speak to that man. Let me pass." He got out of the pew and limped into the sacristy, leaning heavily on his stick. A short and agitated conversation followed. A few minutes later, the churchwarden appeared. He smiled and explained there would be a communion service after all, and an older colleague would assist the pastor.

'The introductory hymn was sung by the organist and us few churchgoers. At the end of the second verse, father came in, in white vestments, with his stick. When the hymn was over, he turned to us and spoke in his calm, free voice. "Holy, holy, holy, Lord of Hosts, heaven and earth are full of thy glory. Glory be to thee, O Lord most High." Thus it was [concludes Bergman] that I discovered the ending to *Winter Light* and at the same time a rule I was to follow from then on: *irrespective of anything that happens to you in life, you must hold your communion!*'

appear to have been mainly administrative – during his childhood he never set foot in a temple. When, as an adolescent, the future director occasionally did attend services in the French Reformed Church, it was primarily to improve his language skills; according to Drouzy, he enjoyed and profited from listening to the pastor Clément Nicolet preaching in French (during this formative period of his life Dreyer also learned to speak English and German fluently). The secondary school he attended for six years in Frederiksberg was Lutheran in origin, but under the charismatic direction of the writer and journalist Carl Ewald had moved in the direction of progressive secular liberalism; it is probably fair to say that the spirit of Georg Brandes more than that of N.F.S. Grundtvig reigned there. And so it went on; in the years following his graduation, when Dreyer worked as a journalist (specialising, eventually, in the field of aviation, of which he himself became a national pioneer), there were few signs of piety, and none at all of conversion. As far as we can see, the youth was a modern secular freethinker: clever, energetic, admired by his contemporaries and something of a rebel.

The move from journalism to script-writing was accomplished between the summers of 1912 and 1913. Established at Ole Olesen's Nordisk Film Kompagni, Dreyer went on to write 19 film scenarios before signing his first directed movie, *Præsidenten* (The President) in 1918. Crucial years – but until Tybjerg's long-in-the-making biography comes out, we have to say we know relatively little about them. Most of Dreyer's scripts were melodramas (rather than comedies), and by no means all of the finished films survive for examination. As far as religion comes into the matter, it is possible to point to the vital importance of the example of D.W. Griffith. Dreyer's second directed film, *Blade af Satans Bog* (Leaves from Satan's Book) (1919), follows the method of Griffith's great epic *Intolerance* (1916) in pinning much of the unhappiness of recorded history on the quarrels within established religion. Yet Griffith himself was a Christian, of course (as well as a racist, alas). At the centre of his film a distinction is made between what religion becomes in the hands of rulers and fanatics, and something else that one might call true religion, exemplified above all in the teachings and deeds of the Saviour. At some point, we can say (but when we have no precise idea), this distinction became established as Dreyer's own worldview. It penetrated deeply and became the intellectual and moral basis of a handful of his own finest masterpieces.

'A handful' of masterpieces – but not all. To repeat my earlier caution, that proviso needs to be borne in mind. A number of Dreyer's films, defined by subject matter, seem remote from the concerns of religion. Among these, we ought to include such idiosyncratic works as *Mikaël* (1924), from Herman Bang's bestselling novel; *Du skal ære din Hustru* (Master of the House) (1925) (a terrific comedy); *Vampyr* (1932) (a tale of horror, based on a text written by my ancestor, the Irish ghost-story writer Joseph Sheridan Le Fanu); *Två Människor* (Two People) (1944, a sort of filmed radio play made in Sweden); and finally *Gertrud* (1964), the already-mentioned spiritual-erotic melodrama which served as his swansong. All five of these possess spiritual power and authenticity without quite entering into the vocabulary of faith.

Yet three other films – *La Passion de Jeanne d'Arc* (1927), *Vredens Dag* (Day of Wrath) (1943) and *Ordet* (The Word) (1955) – do confront Christianity directly, and, for the remainder of this chapter, it is these movies that shall directly concern us.

*

The close-up of the human face filling the entire screen in front of us has been part of the vocabulary of cinema since its origins. In the early days it was not used consistently, and one might almost say it was not 'used' at all. The first film director consciously to grasp the expressive and artistic possibilities of the device was Griffith, closely followed by Eisenstein (his pupil in this matter). Their close-ups, in either case, have a marvellous vibrancy; while they last, the screen comes alive in a peculiar and indefinable way. The viewer seems to move onto a new plane, or else into a new time zone, abandoning temporarily the tired improbabilities of plot – the coincidences, the set-ups, the contrived happy endings – which intrude themselves into even the most intelligent early screen melodrama. Of course these close-ups are sporadic; it is part of their force that they surprise us. Dreyer, too, from his earliest films, had an exquisite sense of how to lay in a close-up in this manner, and the mood of added seriousness that could be engendered thereby. There are beautiful moments from films in the mid-twenties (such as *Mikäel* and *Master of the House*, mentioned above) which might be used as textbook examples of this discovery. One needs to remember, moreover, that this was silent cinema, so there was a special emphasis on the visual; perhaps it is exactly *because* film was silent that the impact of such moments is so memorable. Until the coming of the talkies the aesthetic forms of cinema were malleable; and the extraordinary – I would say unrepeatable – gamble that Dreyer took in 1926 when planning a new film whose long-cherished subject was to be the trial of Joan of Arc, was to ask himself what the effect on the audience would be if the whole of the film, and not merely part of it, were to be conceived of with this emphasis on the gravity and beauty of the human face.

Plainly, that could not be a merely formal research project; he needed to find the very special actress whose features and skin would respond to such unprecedented scrutiny. For it was one of his stipulations – one of his tests of authenticity, *spiritual* tests if you will – that the entire drama should be filmed without make-up. Renée Maria Falconetti was an important figure on the contemporary Parisian stage. The fact that this was to be her unique film role somehow reinforces the feeling that we are not really watching an 'actress' at work here; she belongs instead to some other category – I am not quite sure what we should call it. Yet whatever it is (or it isn't), there seems to be general agreement that her ensuing employment by Dreyer issued in one of the greatest and most iconic performances in film history.

We need to go back to silence at this point – the silence of silent cinema – not of course *strictly* silent ever; there was always music in the background to 'bring up' the plangency of the image and infuse it with powerful emotion. And there were words too, communicated through intertitles; the audience both sees and at the same time mentally 'hears' the dialogues. The depositions of Joan's questioning by her judges exist in the historical record, along with Joan's inspired answers, and the spoken/mimed dialogues of *La Passion de Jeanne d'Arc* (1928) are fashioned exclusively from these sources. Dreyer called this deposition 'the most beautiful document in our history'. The myth of Joan, notoriously, has been used over the centuries – above all by the French – for all sorts of dubious nationalist purposes ('glorious and patriotic memorialising' would be the other way of putting it). Yet the fact that, in this film, we are in the presence of the very words Joan delivered provides its own corrective to such excesses; the movie has an irreducible authenticity. What one can never get too much of is the simplicity and guilelessness of the future saint's answers to her judges. Even when she speaks of miraculous happenings (such as the provenance of the famous voices summoning her) it is, somehow, without superstition or sentimentality (following the lead of the Gospels in this matter). The purity of Joan's Christian allegiance means that she can never be tricked by her questioners – unless one counts it as being 'tricked' that, towards the end of the trial, and overcome by exhaustion and torture, she does indeed temporarily stumble. Joan's accession to the demand that she sign a recantation, followed by her torments of conscience and her decision to rescind the submission (opening up in turn the spectre of her inevitable execution) constitute perhaps the greatest, as they are certainly the most 'human', moments of her historical journey towards martyrdom. For without that Christ-like frailty would the audience not love her less? – granted that we love her at all.

Joan's accusers are properly characterised; in addition to being cruel they are dignified, and, however reluctantly, we are made to believe in their authority. The Church, in the medieval period, was a formidable entity. In a radio interview recorded in 1950, Dreyer maintained:

FIGURE 34 'Joan's accusers in the Church are properly characterised.' Eugène Silvain as Bishop Cauchon in Dreyer's *La Passion de Jeanne d'Arc* (1928).

'In both *Joan of Arc* and *Day of Wrath* I have consciously tried to remain impartial. The clergy did indeed condemn Joan [...] to the stake, but this was because they were caught up in the religious conceptions of the time and not because they were intrinsically evil.' To our modern ears, that may sound as if Dreyer is letting off these men rather too lightly. Yet on the other hand the fact that these accusers had something to say, and that they believed in it (however misguidedly), is precisely the requisite for there being any drama at all in the first place.

Indeed we can see the truth of this contention by looking at its opposite. In Lars von Trier's *Breaking the Waves* (1996), the puritanical Scottish clergy who combine to condemn the film's fey heroine for blasphemy are caricatured rather than characterised, so the subsequent conflict lacks 'ballast'. There is no loading of the dice in *La Passion de Jeanne d'Arc*, one of the greatest (and surely one of the most austere) movies that have come down to us from the heroic days of silent cinema.

No 'loading of the dice' either in *Vredens Dag* (Day of Wrath), the next film we need to consider. Here the other-worldly austerities embedded in the Christian hymn of death, *Dies Irae*, find themselves pitted against the sublime eroticism of the Song of Solomon, with an impartiality of outcome that (it seems to me) belongs only to the greatest art. The tablets of orthodoxy in this 1943 witch drama are upheld by the heroine Anne's buxom and opinionated mother-in-law Merete (played by Sigrid Neiiendam), and that woman is certainly 'formidable'. We are in rural Denmark in the early 1620s. Beautiful Anne (Lisbeth Movin) is married to Merete's by now elderly clergyman son Absalon (Thorkild Roose) as his second wife, and has the temerity to suggest that the keys of the household, carried loosely on an outsized ring, should by rights be under *her* charge. Conflict will follow from this impudent bid for independence, for the older woman holds the knowledge in reserve that Anne's birth mother, before our story began, had once been suspected of witchcraft, and had only escaped arraignment through the intervention of young Absalon, who already at that time had his eye on Anne.

There is yet further complication in the present ménage. Anne is young, while her clergyman husband is an old man now – it has never been a marriage of equals. Moreover, there was a son born from his previous union, and this boy, Martin (Preben Lerdorff Rye), grown now into a handsome youth, has returned from his studies in Copenhagen to take up residence in the household.

The adulterous love affair that subsequently arises between the two young people forms the substance of the movie's exposition. It will lead to renewed charges of witchcraft,[3] this time levelled against Anne herself, when Absalon conveniently puts himself out of the way by dying – perhaps from a cold (he has been called out to visit an ailing

---

[3] Among classic studies of the topic: H.R. Trevor-Roper, *The European Witch-Craze of the Sixteenth and Seventeenth Centuries* (Harper, 1967); Keith Thomas, *Religion and the Decline of Magic* (Weidenfield and Nicolson, 1971); Norman Cohen, *Europe's Inner Demons* (Chatto–Heinemann, 1975).

parishioner one rainy day), or perhaps, more sinisterly, as the result of a curse that issued unwittingly from Anne's lips in the midst of a fierce argument with him. Much more is now known about early-modern witch-hysteria than was known in Dreyer's day; indeed, from the late 1960s it has become something of a scholarly industry. Yet, Dreyer's drama (a good decade-or-so before Arthur Miller wrote *The Crucible*) gives among other things a really remarkably cogent account of the psychological tensions – the rivalries, the petty hatreds, the easy recourse to spitefulness – that enabled these kinds of accusations to flourish in the narrowly hierarchical environment of the time. Anne, at any event, is obdurate. An inner strength of character makes her a match for her formidable mother-in-law. One had better say now: the performance of Lisbeth Movin as the tender young bride in love with her stepson is one of the glories of classical Danish cinema. Without ever losing her virtue (as equally her modesty and demureness) Anne manages to maintain the sovereignty of the erotic. Her forthright espousal of sexual love for Martin gradually brings home to the audience the truth of the contention – it surely only adds to our admiration for her! – that in some way she really *is* a witch. How can this be? The loose or metaphorical meaning of the word contains the ambiguity, for in looks she is both 'bewitched' and 'bewitching'. The film concentrates on the eyes as the organ of entrapment, praised by Martin as 'deep and mysterious' and visible to us as burning and ardent. Are they, then – limpid and innocent – the window to her soul? Or are they, as her enemies maintain, the godless weapon of female destructiveness? In a quite wonderful way – Dreyer's lighting of Movin's close-ups miraculously confirms the ambivalence – they are *both*. Nothing is more beautiful in the film than the way Dreyer conveys the feeling that Anne's semi-supernatural powers are the source of as much fear and mystery to *her* as they are to everyone else. Because she is noble and forthright, the question, *did* she cause Absalon's death by that unguarded expostulation? becomes a growing burden on her conscience. Nor is she aided in her troubles by the fact that

Martin, her lover, slowly gives signs of ceasing to believe in her. Fearful of the ghost of his dead father, Martin lashes out: 'Can't you see? He stands before God, and accuses us'. To which Anne replies through her fears, magnificently: 'No, can't you see he is pleading for us; he sees how we suffer!'

We are ready for the momentous final confrontation that will take place at Absalon's funeral, when the mother-in-law Merete decides, at last, to make her accusations public.

The scene is set up beautifully. The camera follows a procession of singing boys, each with a candle in his hand, as they file towards the coffin past the gathered elders seated together in twos and threes in their black gowns and ruffs, like so many figures from an ancient Dutch group portrait. To the right of the catafalque looms the majestic ancient figure of Merete, resplendent in black; to the left, Martin, bowed in mourning, with Anne standing behind him dressed (remarkably to our eyes, I think) in widow's white, with a white cowl on her head. The service gets under way – a little nervously perhaps (it is awkward, if not plain provocative, for Martin to say: 'My father's death is not to be laid at anyone's door' – why, on the surface, should it be? – but the danger seems to pass). The priest is in the middle of the eulogy when Merete rises to her feet and, pointing towards her daughter-in-law, delivers her long-repressed indictment: 'Since no one tells the truth I am forced to do so myself: my son was murdered, and his murderer is sitting right here!'

We are near to the end even if the end hasn't quite come yet. At first Anne attempts to deny the charges by swearing on her husband's body; but at the last moment her hand falters, in tandem with her voice. So she comes to accept the inevitable: 'Yes, I have murdered you; you have got your revenge at last', she manages to whisper pitifully to the coffin. And with infinite poignancy she adds (speaking directly to her husband's corpse): 'I am seeing you through tears, and no one is coming to wipe them away.' The film closes with the camera focused on Anne, in visionary close-up, while on the soundtrack we hear in minor key the last

FIGURE 35 'Like so many figures [...] from an ancient Dutch group portrait.' Painting by light in Dreyer's *Day of Wrath* (1943).

verse of the *Dies Irae* whose previous verses (in major key, and with trumpet accompaniment) had opened the film so dramatically. The words speak, of course, of Christ's judgement, and with sardonic finality:

> Day of wrath, or day of mourning
> From the dust of earth returning
> Man for judgement must prepare him.
> Lord, all pitying, Jesu blest
> Grant them thine eternal rest!

What a movie!, we might still exclaim, 75 years after its appearance in the world. It was to be the last Dreyer made in his homeland for a decade. He had always had an uncomfortable relationship with the Nazi occupiers of his country, and the release of *Day of Wrath* seemed to act as a catalyst. The banning of this new Danish film – the censors having evidently found something allegorical and pointedly contemporary in its meditation on persecution and torture – led to Dreyer seeking refuge across the water in neutral Sweden, where he remained for the rest of the war.

*

When, back in Copenhagen in the early 1950s, Dreyer felt he was able to return to feature-length filmmaking, his choice fell upon a drama by one of Denmark's most important anti-Nazi resisters, the pastor–playwright Kaj Munk, murdered by the Germans in 1944 after a series of publicly dissident sermons. *Ordet* (The Word), written in 1925 and first staged in Denmark in 1932 in a performance which Dreyer attended, is a play dating from early on in the poet–priest's career (Munk was only 27 when he wrote it). It tells the story of two warring families in rural western Jutland who have been kept apart by sectarian differences. The Borgen family belong to the branch of reformed or liberal Lutheranism that came into being in the nineteenth century, largely under the influence of the philosopher N.F.S. Grundtvig (his bearded portrait, in Dreyer's film, hangs prominently in the family parlour); whereas the family of Peter Skraedder, Peter the Tailor, belong to the much more restrictive and puritanical Inner Mission (little beer or coffee on *their* table!). Neighbours, the families would in the ordinary course of events have kept their differences to themselves; except that Anders, Borgen's youngest son, has fallen in love with Peter Skraedder's daughter Anne, and wishes to gain permission to marry her. This is the premise the drama starts from.

A play and a movie are two separate things, and of course we are dealing with the movie here. Dreyer was an 'essentialist'. All his films are literary adaptations (fundamentally different in this respect from Ingmar Bergman); but in all of his films – and in none more than in this work perhaps – there is the feeling that, by paring it down and working it over, he is profoundly able to make the material his own. *Ordet* ends with perhaps one of the greatest single fictional sequences ever recorded on camera, and a question I have sometimes found myself asking is whether the impact of this ending (which we will discuss in detail in a moment) *could* ever have been as powerful in the original stage production. No writings I have come across specifically compare the two experiences. The key thing is that Dreyer himself had been struck by the potentiality of the play, and had given thought to what would be needed in terms of light, gesture, music (the score by Carl Nielsen's pupil, Poul Schierbeck, is marvellous) to turn it into a movie. 'My approach to working with Kaj Munk's *Ordet* has, therefore, been this: first to possess myself of Kaj Munk, and then to forget him!', Dreyer told a radio interviewer in 1954.

In *Ordet*, then, it seems to me it is the ending that particularly demands our attentiveness. At the same time, this ending can't be appreciated without taking into account the episodes that have led up to it. The film is all of a piece (like every great work of art, I suppose). Shot partly in the studio and partly on location in Jutland – in Vedersø, the very parish where Munk had practised his ministry – the film imposes from the start with its profoundly sustained level of realism. There is a seamless blending of outdoors and indoors. We don't see it, for example, as an 'effect', but, rather, as part of the film's documentary authenticity that every so often and at exactly the right moment, the cows can be heard mooing in the barnyard. Those who have seen the film won't forget either the sound of the horses' hooves over the cobbles as, towards the film's conclusion, the stately hearse enters the farm's courtyard: or, from earlier on in the film, the noise of the flapping linen on the washing-line as the Borgen family seek out among the sand dunes their lost mad prodigal son, Johannes.

Bearded Johannes (Preben Lerdorff Rye, the same actor who plays Martin in *Day of Wrath*) is a central figure in the narrative, though at first he seems marginal to the main thrust of the story (the dispute between Borgens and Skraedders). We are struck by his strange way of speaking, as also by his handsome distracted manner and the oddity, and informality, of his wardrobe (he wears an old seaman's sweater made of heavy oiled wool). One of old Borgen's three sons – the middle one, dedicated to the Church – he has lost his wits, we are led to believe, while studying theology in Copenhagen, and now fancies himself to be, in some strange way, an avatar of the risen Jesus Christ. The family put up with him, but only just. He disappears from the story, as mentioned above, only to reappear some time later in the midst of another fearful crisis, associated this time with Borgen's beloved daughter-in-law Inger (Birgitte Federspiel), who, pregnant from the beginning of the film, is going through the travails of childbirth.

In the long night that follows, periods of relative calm alternate with episodes of anguish. The summoned doctor, a calm and trustworthy fellow, seems to think all will be well. (Yet the beam from the headlights of his departing motor vehicle late on in the evening weaves a strangely ominous arc of light over the parlour's walls and ceiling.) Meanwhile Johannes has been occupying himself elsewhere in the house by comforting his little six- or seven-year-old niece Maren (daughter of Inger, who in turn is married to Borgen's eldest son Mikkel); she has seated herself on his lap to be closer to him. Yet Johannes's comfort includes words that seem to be stranger than ever; he speaks of the child's mother as being 'in heaven', and offers, even, the option of bringing her back from the dead...

Johannes it is, then, who rightly discerns, in his own mad way, that the crisis of childbirth is far from over, and indeed that it will shortly end in tragedy. Up until now, Mikkel has been busy attending to his wife in the bedroom with the doctor, while old Borgen and Johannes occupy the parlour. The bitterness of Mikkel's suffering as he reports back to old Borgen first the death of the infant ('Is it a boy or a girl?' asks Borgen, not yet aware of the extent of Inger's difficulties. 'A boy. He is lying in the tub in four pieces'), then the unexpected death of the mother, is unforgettably conveyed by the blond actor who plays him (Emil Hass Christensen), in episodes of overwhelming emotional might.

That mournful night, like all nights, comes to an end with Johannes quitting the farm by the window while the others are sleeping. He leaves behind a note with these words from the Gospel: 'Ye shall seek me and shall not find me. Whither I go, ye cannot come.' The following day, after fruitless searchings for the errant son, brings preparation for Inger's funeral (we see the announcement in the newspaper); and in due course, with neighbours gathered, the horse-drawn catafalque that has already been mentioned clatters nobly into the courtyard.

The sequence that follows has several stages, and it is in the combination of these different narrative elements, or rather, in their accretionary build-up, that its overwhelming force resides. First there is the reconciliation, on the human plane, between Borgens and Skraedders. Old Peter the Tailor has come to see that his behaviour has been harsh. He bethinks himself of the Gospel injunction to turn the other cheek and in a beautiful gesture of Christian generosity he publicly endorses, in front of Inger's coffin, the engagement of his daughter Anne to the young Anders Borgen. Next, there is the prayer of the priest; he is a handsome worldly man, whom we have met earlier in conversation with the doctor, swapping urbanities over a cigar. Nonetheless, the words that he now speaks at the head of the open coffin, with Inger's beautiful face in front of him, are appropriate and heartfelt. They are, as it were, the right Christian words, reminding his listeners that 'death is the gateway to eternity.' 'You two', he says, turning to Mikkel, 'will meet again and be united, never to part.' And Mikkel, casting aside his previous bitterness, shakes the priest's hand and thanks him for this conventional solace.

Now comes the moment when the lid will be placed on the coffin, prior to its being transported to the church; but before this can be done the door opens and the vanished Johannes reappears. He seems a

FIGURE 36 A scenario that takes its audience to the furthest limits of credulity and beyond: Inger's resurrection in Dreyer's sublime masterpiece *Ordet (The Word)* (1955).

changed man; his voice and his gait look normal again – a certain 'health' radiates from his features. Yet if there is hope among the assembled gathering that the erstwhile theology student has found his wits again, the words he speaks bring nothing but consternation. 'None of you has asked God to return her to you,' he tells the assembly, in all seriousness. Silence follows. 'Now you mock God!' expostulates old Borgen. Johannes: 'No, it is *you* who mock God with your half-heartedness!' And taking the child Maren's hand – she has quietly stolen up to her uncle, and looks at him with silent encouragement – he proceeds to utter the words (the prayer, the invocation to Christ) that will presently bring Inger back from the dead.

The 'resurrection' of Inger – registered first as a brief movement of the hands, then, seconds later, in the infinitely slow opening of the eyelids, along with a wisp of a smile as she turns to look up at her husband's face poised above her – is, to say it yet again, one of the most sublime moments in the whole of world cinema, leading on as it does to the couple's final embrace and some few incandescently noble fragments of dialogue. First, Skraedder, an old man himself, turning to Borgen, grasps him with rapture: 'He is still the God of old – the God of Elijah, eternal and the same!' 'Eternal and the same,' murmurs the farmer in agreement, accepting the embrace. The camera is now back on Inger, her face pressed closely to Mikkel's: 'And the child, is it alive?' she asks. 'It is alive, it lives with God.' 'With God?' 'Yes, Inger, I have found your faith. A new life is beginning for us.' 'Ah, life', she echoes contentedly, and repeats the word again. And then again, finally and softly.

*

I don't suppose there can be many viewers who are not overwhelmed with emotion by this time. If one doesn't weep here, when would cinema ever make one weep? Included within our hypothetical audience are people of all faiths and none, it makes not a shred of difference. Yet it is fascinating to try to work out why this should be so. We know – or at least we think we do – that physical resurrection is 'impossible', so what exactly is happening here, at the film's climax? Of course there is the *desire* for resurrection, when we love someone who is precipitately taken away from us; the scene we have just witnessed in this sense enacts a common fantasy. At the same time, it is a fact of life (though a rare one) that people do indeed come back from the dead; one thinks of the 'lucky ones' rescued from earthquakes and other natural perils, or even, on a lesser scale of miracle, those who recover from some deadly disease or survive an intricate hospital operation. On an absolutely naturalistic level, it happens that people have been pronounced dead and found, later, to be alive after all – they have pulled through, miraculously, even as they lie motionless in the depths of the morgue. So once we have adjusted our tears, and the lights have gone up, Dreyer's film allows itself, perhaps, to be rationalised in this manner.

Yet I don't think that, somehow, it works like this. *While it is happening, we believe it.* And afterwards too. That is the 'miracle' of Dreyer's *Ordet*. In its profound and idiosyncratic way, the film allows us truly to confront the meaning of resurrection. The Christian religion is, naturally, like all religions, full of paradoxes and mysteries; we needn't, at this stage, attempt to spell out the relevant contradictions, beyond venturing to observe that faith *is* extravagant, faith *is* impossible, and always must be. Few enough artists in history are able to dwell, like this, not in the realm of necessity and science (how can any modern person avoid respecting *science?*), but, grandly and boldly, within the pure realm of scripture and spirit. Dreyer, in the field of cinema, is surely one of them.

FIGURE 37 'You cannot imagine the richness of the mysteries of the Virgin Mary.' Edith Scob as the Queen of Heaven in Buñuel's *La Voie Lactée* (*The Milky Way*) (1969).

6

Spain: The Heresies of Don Luis

The Resurrection is one of the central mysteries of the Christian religion. In Luis Buñuel's film *La Voie Lactée* (The Milky Way) (1969), six further Christian mysteries are outlined and grappled with. In no particular order they may be expressed thus: (1) the simultaneously corporeal and divine nature of Christ; (2) the impossible arithmetic of the Trinity; (3) Mary's status as both Mother and Virgin; (4) the mystery of the ontology of the Eucharist; (5) the unsolvable problem of Evil; and (6) the coexistence, in Christian thinking, of grace, free will and predestination. It was one of the Spanish director's fundamental ethical tenets that mysteries were not to be solved, but contemplated and enjoyed – indeed, if one thinks that they *can* be solved, one doesn't understand what they are. In this he was like the English poet John Keats, who in a famous letter to his brothers George and Thomas (21 December 1817) urged them to consider 'the quality that Shakespeare possessed so enormously – I mean Negative Capability, that is, when a man is capable of being in uncertainties, mysteries, doubts, without any irritable searching after fact and reason.' Fact, reason and 'explanation' were bugbears of Buñuel. In his famous autobiography *My Last Sigh*, written in collaboration with scriptwriter Jean-Claude Carrière, he unpacks an anecdote about the reception of *La Voie Lactée* that is germane to this whole way of thinking. Apparently the film was having an opening in Copenhagen, and, every night for a week, a party of 30 gypsies showed up to see it – evidently, it enthralled them. At this point the cinema manager, feeling benevolent, said: 'Well, if they like it so much, let's show it to them free; we won't, from now on, charge them for entrance tickets.' The announcement was duly made. From then on, however, not a single gypsy appeared.

When Carrière told Buñuel this story for the first time (it was Carrière who had initially heard about it), the Spaniard asked him to repeat the tale. Buñuel then said: 'You must promise never again to mention this incident.' 'Alright – but why not?' 'Because', said Buñuel, 'a mystery is a mystery – and it is right to approach mysteries reverently.'

Commentary on art, of any kind, also needs to be open to mystery: to the ultimate mystery, and ambivalence, of the thing being contemplated. The critic or interpreter attempts of course to be as lucid as possible; what he or she offers is a reading, made in good faith. But that reading is powerful or persuasive only to the extent that it takes into account, at all stages of the process, possible contradictory readings. Criticism, in short (I hope it doesn't sound platitudinous to say so), needs to be dialectical and flexible, and to anticipate the counter-argument, in the very play of the critic's language, that the judgements that matter are usually suggestive and provisional.

We can apply this dictum very clearly to Buñuel's own oeuvre. The Spaniard, of course, is known for his atheism; he is, in the popular imagination, the nonpareil of atheistic directors. But it is equally a fact about the man – and one has to bring this out in the right way – that he was fascinated by faith and religion. Indeed, he wouldn't have been such a formidable atheist if he didn't (profoundly, and from the inside) know and admire what he was combatting.

There is, then, a 'religious text' across Buñuel's work, and we need to distinguish, as a matter of elementary lucidity, the place where this discourse is essentially satirical from those other places where something more complicated, ambivalent and serious seems to be operating. It's not my intention in this chapter to trawl through the surviving 35 movies of the Buñuel filmography; I take it for granted that some films are more interesting than others, and that a significant portion of the oeuvre, not being concerned with religion at all, will rule itself out of discussion.

Where then to start? We might do worse than begin with *Los Olvidados* (1950), Buñuel's Mexican-made 'comeback film' – the movie that put him back on the international map after 18 years of silence and exile (in France and America). Those years, as a matter of fact, were not as empty of practical filmmaking as is sometimes imagined; among other works, there were four unsigned Spanish comedies which did rather well at the box office in the final months before the outbreak of the Spanish Civil War (not many people have seen them – I include myself in that category).[1] And there was the day-to-day work he did in shaping and editing propaganda films for the American Government during World War II, and which – jejune as it was from an artistic point of view – served to teach him a lot about rhythm and structure. Yet whatever the educative power of these part-time and not wholly satisfactory activities, a new Buñuel can be seen to emerge on the far side of them.

We could look at it this way: *Un Chien Andalou* (1928) and *L'Age d'Or* (1930), great as they are, were dream films, pure works of surrealism. But with the arrival of *Los Olvidados* – out of the blue, so to speak (people thought Buñuel was dead, or in retirement) – we are confronted, for the first time, with a recognisable moral discourse: we are clearly in the world of people, not phantoms. Of course this new movie (which won the Prix de la Mise en Scène at the Cannes Film Festival in 1951) is one of the most terrifyingly bitter films about children ever made. Its principal moral vector – the character through whose eyes the main events of the movie are filtered – is 12-year-old Pedro, attached to a gang of street urchins from which he makes

---

[1] The films are *Don Quintín el aramgao* and *La Hija de Juan Simón* (both 1935), along with *¿Quién me quiere a mí?* and *!Centinela, Alerta!* (both 1936) – all four produced and scripted by Buñuel, if not officially directed by him. Francisco Aranda gives a detailed account of their making in his study *Luis Buñuel: A Critical Biography* (1969: English edition, Secker & Warburg, 1975), pp. 100–15.

various ineffectual attempts to escape. He is handsome, strong, innocent – an attractive personality – a boy who loves his mother and is for that very reason redeemable. But no redemption, in this tale, lies in store for him. He is slain in a knife fight with the gang leader Jaibo, after which his corpse is disposed of (by friends, misguidedly attempting to avoid police investigation) by being thrown from the back of a mule, at night-time, onto the municipal rubbish dump.

Brutal and severe as it is, *Los Olvidados* has no explicit anchorage in religion; there is not even the presence of the obligatory parish priest who, in films like this of American or Italian provenance, could be relied upon to represent the forces of civil and moral order. (As far as Italy is concerned, there are connections, of course, between *Los Olvidados* and neo-realism – one thinks of a movie like *Shoeshine*.[2]) Civil and moral order do indeed have a place in *Los Olvidados*, but it is not clerical – I am referring to the important figure of the enlightened youth leader who emerges in the course of Pedro's downward trajectory. The governor of a sort of 'home farm' where difficult children are given basic training in agriculture, this man sets up, through his kindness, an elementary bond of trust with the youngster. Yet affecting as these scenes are (they involve the governor's loan of 500 pesos, which Jaibo in turn steals from Pedro, making the loan effectively unreturnable), I wonder whether at a later date Buñuel might not have found them a trifle didactic.

Far more interesting and original, perhaps, are the sequences which dramatise Pedro's bond of love for his mother, a harassed and hard-working peasant woman who, it emerges, bore Pedro at the age of 14, and is now the parent of several other needy children by a series of different and non-present fathers. Part of a gang, Pedro is *ipso facto* an incipient troublemaker, and therefore rejected by this woman. But still he needs her desperately. A series of beautiful scenes

---

[2] De Sica's film of 1946 also ends with the violent death of its boy protagonist at the hands of his best friend, as the result of a fight that arises out of a tragic misunderstanding.

makes clear this heartbreaking dependency. In one, he clumsily seizes her hand while she is shelling beans and attempts to kiss it, succeeding only in upsetting the cooking pot. During another, in the midst of a fierce fight across the woman's double bed (on which is perched the bawling youngest member of the family), Pedro pauses, in a sweet fit of remorse, and lays down the stool that he was about to fling at her. (The look on his face is extraordinary.) Most notable of all is the devastating dream sequence in which Pedro imagines his mother arising from her bed in her nightgown to come over to comfort him. The temperature of the dream abruptly changes when the boy asks the now-retreating figure for food, at which point the mother returns to him bearing a sinister hunk of horse-flesh – only to be intercepted, in the dream, by Jaibo who emerges from a hiding-hole under Pedro's bed to grapple with and make off with the booty. Nothing 'didactic' about this sequence! It has the rawness and oddity that mark out authentic dreams in real life. It is visceral. As far as I can see, there is nothing explicitly autobiographical about the scenario of *Los Olvidados*; yet the viewer has the unmistakable feeling that, in making it, Buñuel is tapping extremely deep artistic wellsprings. Sentimentality is ruled out from the start; the premise, as I have said, is brutal, and terrifying. Nonetheless, in the little sub-gang that is constituted by Pedro, his Indian pal 'Little Eyes' and the 13-year-old *niña* Meche, there exists an affecting enclave of innocence – a corner of the world carved out by the director in which the audience is encouraged to believe in the existence of goodness. And this, in a way, is at the *centre* of the movie.

Thirteen films separate *Los Olvidados* from *Nazarín* (1958), the next film in the Buñuel filmography that demands attention. The Mexican period is immensely strong and prolific, and in another context it would give this writer nothing but pleasure to pause and expatiate. Films like *Él* (1952) and *Ensayo de un Crimen* (1955: known in English as *The Criminal Life of Archibaldo de la Cruz*) are perfect movies by any criterion, brimming with sophisticated irony.

(It goes without saying Buñuel had huge comic talent.) I even find myself liking those films from the period which he later repudiated such as *Una Mujer sin Amor* (1951) ('the worst film I ever made') or the ostensibly trashy *Susana* made the same year, whose melodramatic Spanish title (*Demonio y Carne*) gives little hint of its profound moral subtlety. *Robinson Crusoe* (1952), *Abismos de Pasión* (1953: Buñuel's version of *Wuthering Heights*), *El Río y la Muerte* (1954) and *La Mort en ce Jardin* (1956) are other landmarks from this period that may still be seen with enjoyment. Yet *Nazarín* beckons, not only on account of its intrinsic artistic quality but because it is one of the key films in the oeuvre where the question of an attitude towards Christianity – a reckoning, a 'verdict' – is most forcefully and beautifully encountered.

The tale is adapted from a novel by the Spanish writer Benito Pérez Galdós (1843–1920) and tells the story of a priest who loses his way (at least, seems to lose his way) by following too closely the Christian dictum that 'all of mine is yours'. Many, alas, are the wonderful exhortations of Jesus that depend for their effectiveness on not being taken too literally! A priest, in order to function effectively (that is, to be able to offer counsel and succour), would seem to need to establish a minimum distance between himself and his flock. For if he *is* his flock, what good is he? How can he offer leadership and guidance?

This is the dilemma of our man Nazarín (Francisco Rabal) – though perhaps not particularly *felt* as a dilemma. One of the most striking things about him is the calmness and fortitude with which he faces the successive predicaments that his too literal understanding of the Gospels keep throwing him. A prostitute seeks refuge in the little room he occupies? Well, he must *give* her refuge – even if the scandal this gives rise to means losing permission from his superiors to offer Mass in the church he has been attached to. Yet he is happy to forfeit class privilege, because class privilege means absolutely nothing to him. Shortly afterwards, the same woman burns down his room – not because she dislikes him, but accidentally, so to speak, out of misguided desire for revenge against the priest's sharp-tongued landlady. Homeless all of a sudden, and deprived of respectability, he now has the chance to become a mendicant (perhaps, anyway, this is what he has always wanted?). There is a complication, however, in that the prostitute, Andara (Rita Macedo), wants to accompany him – as indeed does another female lodger, Beatriz (Marga López), who has recently been having trouble with her lover. A lone priest on the road, surely, cannot be accompanied in this way? Nazarín profoundly knows the truth of this. He is not stupid – he can see the cost of losing caste. Yet *these* women, for their different reasons, will not allow themselves to be shaken off.

Francisco Rabal, the Spanish actor who plays Nazarín, possesses a vividly handsome and masculine presence, making it impossible to avoid encountering a sort of repressed field-force of sexuality in the interaction of the trio; realistically speaking, either the women will be attracted to him, or he will be attracted to *them*. Here would be an obvious chance for some deft anti-clerical satire, if Buñuel felt in the mood for it. In such a scenario, we could imagine the priest thinking he is above matters of the flesh; whereas the flesh in the end bears down on him. So he is revealed to be either a fool or a hypocrite. Yet this is not at all the way the story works out. Indeed, one could consider Buñuel's decision *not* to follow this beckoning path as one of the absolutely finest things about the movie. The whole issue of 'sexual attractiveness' (or its absence) is handled on the contrary, it seems to me, with the most consummate artistic delicacy. Thrown into the company of the women, as he is, Nazarín somehow never sets a foot wrong in the matter of sexual and moral conduct. Are we to think of him as 'sexless', then? No, for all the above reasons. We don't know what his temptations *are* – the story doesn't oblige us. What it does show us, instead, is his beautiful sense of responsibility. Thus he cares for his companions, exigent as they are; and on each occasion when he is able to, makes bold and brave decisions to ensure their welfare.

Both the women, in their different ways, are probably in love with him – if the love in question is allowed to contain a large admixture of hero worship. At an early stage of their journey together, for example, the little band stops off at relatives of Beatriz where there is a sick child under the roof, whom the priest succeeds in 'curing'. The child's recovery in fact is fortuitous. But in the eyes of the women the incident marks Nazarín down as being possessed of godly, miraculous powers. It all ought to be immensely embarrassing; but it is part of the greatness of this priest to be all but un-embarrassable.

I say above that the women are probably in love with Nazarín, but surely we can be more precise. The film is in one way an allegory of the Christian journey (we will come back to this), yet it derives its power and seriousness from what has to be called its psychological realism. So the women are properly differentiated; they are the opposite of mere stereotyped ciphers. Andara, the prostitute, is the simpler of the pair – I shall not spend time describing her, beyond noting, as anyone who enjoys the film must, her boldness and wit. While fanatically loyal to Nazarín, there is plenty in her character of the whore's traditional fickleness. (Marvellous, in this respect, are the scenes matching her up to the attentions of the lovelorn dwarf Ujo whom the party picks up, and reluctantly abandons, somewhere along the course of their pilgrimage.) Beatriz, on the other hand, the second of the pair, is a rather more complicated figure: a woman of the people, certainly, but not hailing from the ancient tribe of streetwalkers. When we first meet her, she is recovering from a love affair with the macho cowboy El Pinto (a brilliantly inserted dream sequence in which, in the midst of an embrace, she cruelly bites this man on the lip shows us how violently this episode has shaken her). Her reaction to withdrawal from 'carnal affection' is to put herself forward, in the priest's presence, as a sort of icon of probity and chastity. Of course this is not her real nature; she is a profoundly sensuous creature. Yet neither is she sly or conniving. So we are led to the fascinating situation of being able to see what she herself is blind to, namely, that her devotion to the priest is far more possessive and jealous than she is ever able to realise consciously. In due course, the veil will be torn from her eyes and she will go back to Pinto. (In Buñuel, to say it yet again, there is never any sentimentality about outcomes.) In the meantime, however, we are rewarded with one of the film's most truly beautiful sequences: the pause in the cave at night-time where, in front of a bonfire, she rests her head on the priest's shoulder, as a lover might, and puts her arms around him. There is no *clin d'œil* here on the filmmaker's part. The close-up of the actress's face has a genuinely extraordinary radiance and purity. As for Nazarín's reaction: his famous presence of mind defuses what is awkward about the situation, and renders it immune to all but the mildest of ironies. His forbearance at this point, you could say, is truly Christ-like – yet only in the delicate sense that it is wise and tender and human.

FIGURE 38 A serious moral tenderness: Beatriz (Marga López) and the priest (Francisco Rabal) solicit mutual comfort in *Nazarín* (1958).

Christ was surrounded by women – we know that. The loyal steadfastness of the three Marys, whether at the foot of the Cross, or in the face of the mystery of the Empty Tomb, has always seemed to me one of the single most moving aspects of the Christian story (as it is equally moving and beautiful that one of these Marys was a penitent prostitute). The little band in *Nazarín* are not meant to be read as substitutes for Christ and his sublime feminine entourage; but of course the parallel is present at *some* level. The artistic aim in these matters, I suppose, must have been to be clear without being too literal. As in the case of the record of the earthly pilgrimage of the curé of Ambricourt (in Bresson's masterpiece *Le Journal d'un Curé de Campagne*), Nazarín's pilgrimage both is, and is not, the pilgrimage of Jesus Christ. Push the parallel too far, and the fable descends into kitsch. In order for it to 'come off', the audience is required, as it were, to notice and to not notice at the same time – the thing has to be surmisable but not more. (An example of this comes later in the film when we slowly come to realise that Nazarín's companion in the prison cell – and the focus of some of the film's most recklessly brilliant dialogues – can be none other than the fabled Good Thief.)

The question, of course, is what Buñuel is doing with all these parallels – granted that we are not here in the realm of satire or parody. Buñuel, we have agreed, is not a believer – he never grew tired of saying so! So it is possible that one of the things that he is trying to show in this film is simply the misguidedness of faith. Faith 'exists' of course; but it is wrong; it doesn't meet the facts. It is tragically hopeful. I think of the beautiful episode in the movie where the party arrive at a plague town; the bells are tolling, bodies are in the street, infants are wandering around without mothers. Immediately Nazarín takes charge, issuing orders, and moving into households to give succour to the sick and the dying. In one house, however, his ministrations are clearly unwelcome: that of a beautiful young woman, Lucía, affianced to the mayor of the township. 'Not heaven!', she cries out to Nazarín on her deathbed, as the priest offers, or attempts to offer, the consolation of the Last Sacrament.

And sure enough, when shortly afterwards her fiancé strides into the room, his spurs jangling (he has been absent on errands of mercy), her last words to him before kissing him on the lips show contempt and weariness towards the ministrations of the little band: 'Tell them', she urges with her last breath, 'to go away!'

A priest, doubtless, needs to get used to having the gifts of Christ scorned like this; grievous as it is, it is part of his humility to bear such a burden. His vocation demands that he can witness such episodes without the seeds of his faith being shattered. Does there not come sometimes, however, in the lives of many such men of the cloth, *one* moment of irrevocable doubt? What if it were *not* true, after all? The issues invoked here find their ultimate expression in the film's famous ending, a tour de force of irony and ambivalence. If the reader remembers, Nazarín has been captured by the authorities under vagrancy laws and is being marched, alone, under police guard, to the neighbouring township. The camera keeps its gaze on his face which is beginning to show, almost for the first time, signs of sheer mortal weariness. Weariness, disappointment and a sense of human failure can only be compounded when he notices that the horse-drawn fly that has just overtaken him on the dusty road contains the receding figure of Beatriz, now reconciled to her lover El Pinto, the driver of the vehicle, on whose shoulder she is leaning ostentatiously (in just the same way she leant on *his* shoulder not so long ago). Shortly afterwards, the guard calls a rest pause, during which an old woman approaches Nazarín and offers him a pineapple to staunch his thirst. At first he refuses to take it; but then he hesitates and accepts the gift – yet without sign of thanks. A sort of numb despair has taken possession of his features as he stumbles forward, pineapple in hand, into who knows what desolate future. As the end credits roll up on the screen there is no music on the soundtrack, only the sound of the famous drumbeats of Calanda, stored up in memory from Buñuel's childhood, and relentless as destiny itself.

It might be tempting to see *Nazarín* as Buñuel's last word on the deceptiveness of religion. The priest has lost his faith, hasn't he? Or has he? Is despair (spoken of above) the same thing as anguish? And if it is not, which of the two is confronting us here? Practically speaking, the two states of mind belong at the same edge of the psychological spectrum and it might be difficult to say, at any given moment, which of the two is truly in possession of the field. Do we know which of the two *was* in possession of the field when Christ on the Cross uttered his famous lamentation: 'My God, my God, why hast thou forsaken me?'? Returning to our opening remarks about Negative Capability, it seems to me clear that for Buñuel it is just the presence of doubt that is responsible for making us human; without it, no interest or drama. By the same token, it is doubt itself which could be said to 'redeem' religious faith and give it dignity. I've spoken of the ending of *Nazarín* as a tour de force of irony and ambivalence, but surely there is nothing glib or frivolous in the irony invoked here. No, it is *tragic* irony we are confronted with in this film – and it makes its ending one of the most sober, beautiful and haunting in the whole of Buñuel's great oeuvre.

*

Nazarín was filmed in the Morelos region of south-central Mexico, 120 kilometres or so south of the capital city. In 2015, a documentary was released, *Tras Nazarín* (*Following Nazarín*) – directed by a Spaniard, Javier Espada – which had among other goals that of tracking down the various locations Buñuel had used in making his movie nearly 60 years previously. I find it a very intriguing movie, far more interesting than the usual run-of-the-mill 'making of' documentary; one feels that there is a real sensibility behind it, and that the enterprise of research has been properly financed and thought through. The richness of the film's visuals is immensely enhanced by its director having been able to access a collection of 900 or so high-quality 35-mm black-and-white photographs that were taken on location, back in 1958, by the film's official stills photographer, Manuel Álvarez Bravo. The glimpses we receive from this archive help to show just how technically ambitious *Nazarín* was; the extent to which it really can be called a grand, epic project. Buñuel sometimes gave the impression in interviews that the aesthetic aspect of his craft was not all that important to him, but these resonant still photographs demonstrate, I think, how wrong would be such an assumption. Though he was perfectly at home in the studio, Buñuel's work flourished on location: the ancient villages that Nazarín passes through (tracing their ancestry as far back as Aztec times, as their names make clear: Oaxtepec, Tlayacapan, Cocoyoc) are captured, in their individuality, with loving attention to the texture of decrepit alleys and old stone buildings. It is this concrete embeddedness in history and culture that finally lends *Nazarín*, I think, its gravity and seriousness, at the same time as rescuing the movie, all along the line, from the dangers of becoming a mere fable.[3]

I was struck again by the importance of 'detail' when looking recently at another 'making of' documentary about Buñuel's work, this one addressing itself to the slightly later Mexican film, *Simon of the Desert* (1965) (in fact the last film he made in that country before moving his operational base back to Europe). The movie is, or purports to be, about the fifth-century hermit St Simeon Stylites; and the detail I was struck by concerns the column in the desert that the ancient sage was reputed to have stood upon. It is useful to remember that this film was only a sketch in certain ways, planned as an episode in one of those portmanteau films that were popular in the 1960s but which have subsequently fallen out of fashion. So there was, perhaps, in the first

---

[3] Before leaving *Nazarín*, it might be interesting to double back for a moment to one of the master's previous films, the Franco-Mexican co-production *Le Mort en ce Jardin* (Death in the Garden) (1956), for this film too has a priest as one of its main characters: a missionary going under the name of Father Lizzardi, impeccably played by Michel Piccoli (the first of seven films this actor collaborated on with the director). One of a party of six Europeans who are hacking their way through the jungle to escape the corrupt pursuing military (we are somewhere on the borders of Brazil and Argentina), Lizzardi seems a ripe target for learning a lesson or two. Surely, in these atrocious circumstances, his Christian courage will falter? But no, Buñuel admirably allows this man to maintain his integrity, and even to continue practising his calling. Thus when the party comes across a crashed aeroplane in the thick of the jungle, it is Lizzardi who insists (and nobody mocks or discourages him) that all 50 bodies should be given a Christian burial.

place, no great pressure to make either the scenario or the execution more 'realistic' than they needed to be. Hence my surprise (and also, let's face it, my delight) in discovering, when viewing the 'making of' supplement on the film's DVD release, that the column had survived and was still lying, many years later, abandoned and immovable in the desert. So Buñuel, after all, *had* had it carved in stone, when he might easily have had it constructed from any number of lightweight, perishable materials (as undoubtedly he would have done if it was a play rather than a film that was in question). In the movie itself, in certain angles and close-up shots, we can actually see the incisions made by the sculptor on the surface of the column's capital. This material weight and solidity in the pillar's construction is no doubt registered by most viewers subliminally, but the fact that Buñuel went to the trouble of arranging it (bringing round his set designer, Edward Fitzgerald, to his point of view in the process) is, or was, typical of the director's subtle perfectionism.

Simon of the Desert is a comedy. It repeats in comic form many of the home truths that were suggested under a graver aspect in *Nazarín*. In particular, it delights in the Holy Man's disinterestedness, his asceticism and his scorn for material possessions. At one point, a monk mounts Simon's pillar on a ladder to engage with the sage in philosophical dispute. But his efforts at dialectic are defeated by the saint's cheerful literalism. Thus, attempting to dramatise the difference between 'owning' and 'not owning' as a metaphysical concept, his interlocutor gives as example: 'What if I was to say *your* food-bag was mine ...?' Alas, his expectation of dissent is frustrated when Simon replies immediately: 'Of course it is; please take it!' And hands it over.

The version of the saint's life that Buñuel made use of in constructing his script was based on a thirteenth-century compilation called *The Golden Legend* by the Frenchman Jacobus de Voragine. It was the poet Lorca, back in Spain in the thirties, who had pointed the text out to him, and told him how much he had enjoyed it. The emphasis on enjoyment is fundamental here – one can't get anywhere with *Simon of the Desert* without acknowledging its sweetness and charm – without understanding, that is, how much Buñuel *likes* Simon, and stands behind his rebarbative values. 'I am attracted to people who hold fixed ideas', he said mischievously, in an interview with Tomás Pérez Turrent, 'because, as you know, I am one of those people myself!' Later in the same interview he spells it out: '[Simon's] character really moves me. I enjoy his sincerity, his lack of interest, his innocence. Indeed he is even more innocent than a child, because a child clings to objects' (whereas Simon, as we have just seen, repudiates them).

So a certain kind of saintliness is being examined here, with indulgent affection. And because there is innocence contained in the sketch, there will also be its counterpart, temptation. Sometimes the temptations are *themselves* sweet and innocent, as when Simon, tired of standing on one leg on his pillar, owns up to the wish that, once again, he could feel the sensation of sand between his toes. There follows a lovely fantasy, where he imagines he is down on the desert floor – chasing his mother, of all people! When he catches up with her he clasps and embraces her, and together they tumble headlong in the sand dunes.

At other times – this epoch being the epoch of primitive Christianity – the temptations are more overtly sexual. So a young schoolgirl, playing with her hoop, runs up to the foot of the column and shows her breasts to him. Later, the same phantom reappears, disguised as a youthful bearded shepherd, and makes further lubricious overtures. In these two cases, he sees the vision off; but on a third and final occasion, when this same demon appears half-naked out of a moving coffin and insinuates herself behind him on the top of his column (she sticks her tongue suggestively into his earhole), he has to admit he is finally defeated. Subsequently a jet aeroplane transports the pair to the hell of modern New York, where Simon is next sighted, in a crowded nightclub, dressed morosely as a beatnik, and ostentatiously refusing to join the fun. (The demon, meanwhile, is vigorously disporting herself on the dance floor.) Of course it is an enigmatic ending, to put it mildly; and the truth is one can make what one likes of it. Personally, I love the deadpan sulky humour of this final sequence. Buñuel in old age was always lamenting the disappearance of silence and solitude; and here everything is noisy gregariousness. In the same interview I have quoted from earlier, he averred surprisingly, 'I would happily return to the Middle Ages [...] Holiness counts for very little now. But though we are not believers, we can surely feel the loss.'

In the end it seems to me the film works not because of the *thoughts* behind it, but because of its concrete realisation in movie terms – its dramaturgy, indeed. Not mentioned so far, but crucial to the viewer's sense of the film's poetry, is the wise and kindly physical appearance of the bearded actor Claudio Brook, playing Simon – along with the delightful mocking sexiness of Silvia Pinal, who plays the demon. The pair are truly splendidly cast.[4] Nor must we forget the extras in this instance – the crowd of ancient postulants gathered at the foot of the pillar, come to proclaim Simon's holiness, or to challenge it. How *exactly*, one feels, they correspond, in feature and gesture, to our vision of the prophets of the old days, when saints and giants walked the earth and made it interesting.

*

Between the making of the two Mexican films, *Nazarín* (1958) and *Simon of the Desert* (1965), Buñuel had been invited back to Spain and allowed to resume work there. One can speculate on the reasons why

---

[4] Pinal was married to the film's producer Gustavo Alatriste. According to the testimony she gives in a lively filmed interview included in the Criterion DVD, it was *her* fault that the movie (only 45 minutes long) never became a fully fledged feature film. As previously stated, *Simon* was originally planned to be one episode of a compilation picture made by a variety of directors – except that Pinal's skittish insistence on having the lion's share of screen time wrecked the enterprise. Thus Buñuel had asked her (as the wife of the producer) to take the proposal to Fellini. Fellini said: 'I'd love to do it, but Giulietta Masina has to be in my section.' Pinal: 'Sorry, all three episodes have to star me.' The same response from Jules Dassin: 'Of course I'll do it, but the actress has to be Melina Mercouri.' 'No deal.' And so on ... Such are the (charming) accidents by which movies come into being – or fail to do so.

FIGURE 39 Saintliness under pressure: Silvia Pinal as the demon and Claudio Brook as the holy anchorite in *Simon of the Desert* (1965).

the still-repressive Franco regime (it turned out to have 15 years yet to run) should have felt kindly disposed towards so public and inveterate an opponent of all that it stood for. Perhaps there was a feeling that *Nazarín*, after all, was not, on inspection, nearly as 'anti-Catholic' as some had feared it might be. Yet whatever the reasons, a shock was in store for the authorities. The screening of the completed film, *Viridiana*, at the 1961 Cannes Film Festival (where it won the Palme d'Or) caused the kind of scandal that Buñuel hadn't enjoyed since the days of *L'Age d'or*. *L'Osservatore Romano* (the Vatican newspaper) charged the enterprise with blasphemy in a strongly written denunciation. The film was promptly banned in Spain and only released there in 1977 – two years after the dictator's death, when the country was slowly beginning to reclaim its lost liberal heritage.

Even without the benefit of historical hindsight, it doesn't take too much imagination to see what the fuss was about. The film does indeed go 'rather far'. It's still a faintly shocking work, if the word means anything. (Some people of course are unshockable.) What do we have here on the surface? We have an innocent novice nun, Viridiana (Silvia Pinal), the target of seduction by her rich uncle before she can take her final vows. Actually, having met her, the man determines to marry her! Then, let down by her refusal, we have the same man's sudden suicide, a death by hanging, in the course of which he has made use of a skipping-rope belonging to a child we have earlier seen him ogling. There is further fetishism aplenty; before the uncle's death, Viridiana has interrupted him in his private apartment trying on his late wife's clothing – corset, shoes and wedding dress are given the full Freudian treatment by Buñuel. Later on in the film there is the incident that most likely must have triggered the 'blasphemy' charge: some beggars, to whom Viridiana has been offering charity, take over her mansion and stage a drunken party there (the mistress of the house being temporarily absent). In the course of their revels they group themselves into a cameo that parodies the poses of Leonardo's *Last Supper*, while a woman from their number 'photographs' the revellers by lifting her skirts towards them in a gesture of unambiguous obscenity.

One could go on – but perhaps we don't need to. The so-called blasphemy involved in the Leonardo incident is only shocking, perhaps, to people who want to be shocked. Rather more genuinely disturbing is the rape scene that follows on from this episode, when Viridiana, returning unexpectedly to interrupt the party, is manhandled by two ruffians into a back room and violated there. Buñuel doesn't overstep the bounds of what it is permissible to show in the course of such highly charged incidents – of course he is an artist, and a man of taste – but the scene is still, all things considered, remarkably frankly staged, and (if one wants to use such an expression) 'adult' in execution.

Even this episode isn't the final outrage to morals, however. The compelling cause for complaint, for those who wanted to complain, was that Viridiana finally joins the enemy. The movie's original conclusion was subject to pre-censorship by the licensing authorities, who happened to get their hands on the shooting script. Buñuel's getting round their objections has subsequently been held up – rightly, one has to agree – as a classic example of how to assuage the censor, while at the same time making sure that the message delivered is just as subversive (or possibly even more subversive) than the first time round. Thus, in the original script Viridiana comes crestfallen to the apartment of her cousin Don Jorge, the illegitimate son of her lately deceased uncle and (through this man's legacy) now part-owner, with Viridiana, of their inherited mansion. Jorge – played by Francisco Rabal, taking on a very different role here than the role he had undertaken in *Nazarín* – is an arrogant seducer: a positivist; a modern man without morals or scruple. Ever since arriving on the scene after his father's death, he has been pestering Viridiana to surrender her virtue to him. And here she is at last on his doorstep – defeated, broken, no longer demure in any way. As the film ends in the original script, the door shuts close on the pair of them. They have entered a 'sinful relationship'. The censors let it be known to Buñuel that it was mainly that 'shut door' (and the implications behind it) that was the cause of their worry.

What, then, if the director *didn't* shut the door? The ending that we know – the ending Buñuel finally came up with – is as sardonic as any, perhaps, in all of his work. First we see Viridiana, alone in her room, looking at her face in a broken vanity mirror that has been extracted from a nearby dresser. She examines a lock of her golden hair and wipes away a tear from a cheek that, as ever, faces the day without benefit of make-up. With a gesture of determination she gets up and exits her parlour.

When she arrives at Jorge's apartment (in the same house) he asks her why she has come; and when in turn she doesn't answer, he invites her in with an abrupt masculine gesture. Great is her surprise to discover that there is already another woman there – Ramona, her good-looking house servant, with whom Jorge has been flirting and playing cards, to a background of chirpy English pop music. Immediately her cousin sets her down on a cushion and invites her to join the game. 'You know, the first time I saw you I knew that some day we would end up shuffling the deck together', he remarks suavely. It is the last piece of dialogue in the movie. As the camera backs out of the room leaving the *ménage à trois* framed in the lamplight over the card table, the pop song is heard to repeat its banal chorus: 'Shake your cares away, oh shake your cares away.' 'Fin' flashes up on the movie screen.

Virtue defeated, then! Virtue will always be defeated. It is the way of the world. And yet virtue 'exists'. We needn't rejoice in its downfall, and neither does Buñuel. *Viridiana* shares some of the impulse of *Nazarín* in responding positively (at least, not negatively) to the tragic poignancy of Christian perfectionism – its sweetness, its earnestness, its definitional lack of worldliness. When Buñuel, in Mexico City, stumbled on a painting of the saint who subsequently lent her name to the heroine of the movie (from *viridium*, signifying 'a green place') what he was most struck by, he said, were the accoutrements of mortification present with her in her convent cell – the cross, the crown of thorns, the scattering of rusty nails. Later, he made sure that they appeared as symbolic objects in his scenario. We may imagine him smiling a Surrealist smile at his discovery of the painting – it must surely have been difficult for him to forbear doing so. Yet at the same time we are allowed to ask: was he not also moved, at a deeper level, by the passionate sincerity of the saint's primitive *mise en scène*? It is so difficult for us nowadays not to be satirical about such fantasies. And I repeat: Buñuel, at one level, *was* satirical about them. But he was not *only* satirical; he was also affectionate – he was (if one may use the word) indulgent towards their repressed sacred meaning. He responds, somewhere in his heart, to the pathos of the fantasy, and thus to its seriousness and asceticism.

Similar distinctions are germane to the other great theme that emerges from the movie, which might be called the limitations of the charitable endeavour. The provider of charity is always vulnerable to exploitation, and Viridiana is no exception. When her uncle dies and

Spain: The Heresies of Don Luis

FIGURE 40 'At some deep level ... a passionate sincerity.' Silvia Pinal as the much put-upon novice in Buñuel's *Viridiana* (1961).

the mansion passes into her possession (or part-possession, as we've seen above) she can't think of any more noble use for it than to open up its door as a refuge for the poor of the neighbourhood. Pretty soon they swarm in and take the place over. What an amazing collection they are too! – these rogues and beggars and drunken vagabonds. *Viridiana* is set in the twentieth century, but the *types* in Spain (more perhaps than in any other European country) go back to medieval times; we have seen these faces – and these gestures too – in old paintings in provincial museums as well as in the old masters at the Prado. Buñuel, at any event, knows the milieu intimately. He sees how cruel it can be; on the other hand he holds back from judgement. They are, after all, he says (in an interview with Tomás Pérez Turrent and José de la Colina attached to the Criterion DVD) 'believers'. 'Perhaps they have drunk too much and now they are taking liberties [...] That is very Spanish. They have no bad intentions.' He appears to like them, as he likes everybody in this film (even the old reprobate uncle).[5] Viridiana, of course, our heroine, comes close to being destroyed by the behaviour of these freeloaders. But the failure of charity in this particular case doesn't, or shouldn't, eradicate charity from the agenda of civilised human behaviour. Buñuel in the same interview supplies some of the appropriate nuances: 'The film' he says '[deals with] the counter-productiveness of Christian charity – because it produces catastrophes [...] Nevertheless, it's not an "anti-charity film", or, indeed anti anything. I don't think criticising Christian charity would be an important question in our times. It would surely be a little ridiculous.' And he himself admits to putting his hand in his pocket – when he feels like it. 'If I see a poor man who moves me, I give him five pesos. If he doesn't move me, if he seems disagreeable to me, I don't give him anything.' Viridiana's 'mistake' (but it is a wonderful mistake, at the very heart of Christian idealism) is to attempt to make her offer of charity unconditional. She is like Don Quixote, who freed the galley

---

[5] The uncle, Don Jaime, is played, I should have mentioned, by Fernando Rey, who went on to play memorable key roles in later Buñuel films, *Tristana* (1971), *Le Charme Discrèt de la Bourgeoisie* (1972) and *Cet Obscur Objet du Désir* (1977). Turrent and De la Colina put it to Buñuel that the character of this old hidalgo is very similar to the part Rey plays in *Tristana*, Buñuel's one remaining Spanish-based film (adapted – like *Nazarín* and *Viridiana* (though the latter only residually) – from a novel by Pérez Galdós). Buñuel, as always, is pedantic about distinctions: 'They are very different in fact', he says. 'Don Jaime is an old, good-natured soul, humble, capable of falling violently in love – a village nobleman. Though he is a selfish landowner, he kindles my affection . . . I identify with him a little bit.' Don Lope on the other hand 'is a playboy and skirt-chaser. Immensely vain. The only similarity is their ages.' I wish I had more space in this chapter to talk about *Tristana*, a film of great elegance and melancholy. Set in traditional Catholic Toledo at the beginning of the twentieth century, the movie stars Catherine Deneuve in one of her finest roles as the innocent ward of an outwardly respectable bourgeois (the film has that situation at least in common with *Viridiana*). She is seduced by Don Lope in due course, and grows up to exercise an implacable vengeance on him. Catholicism here, this being Spain, is still the integument of society – its outer covering, so to speak. But its rules are transgressed flagrantly and without recourse to conscience. The inner morality of the characters' motivations and behaviour has little to do, I think, with the tenets of religion. It is, in short, if the distinction makes any sense, a 'less religious' movie than *Viridiana*.

slaves, only to find them turning against him. 'In a certain sense', Buñuel suggested in the interview I've just quoted from, 'Viridiana is Don Quixote in skirts.'

*

The remarks made so far about religion in Buñuel's films have limited themselves to what might be called the moral side of the equation – to the sort of ethical dilemmas that, *mutatis mutandis*, could be faced by each and every one of us, whether or not we choose to call ourselves Christian. Yet surprisingly enough – though actually not so surprisingly – Buñuel was also interested in (and has interesting things to say about) the specifics of theology. As I remarked at the beginning of this chapter, one of his later films, *La Voie Lactée* (*The Milky Way*) (1969), has many sharp remarks on the subject. The narrative framework that encloses Buñuel's freewheeling speculations involves a couple of tramps (Laurent Tertzieff and Paul Frankeur: impeccable casting) who, starting in France, make their way southwards, as pilgrims, towards the shrine of St James at Santiago de Compostela. On their journey various incidents and personalities are encountered that bring out, in dramatic and/or comic form, one after another of those thorny paradoxes that have bedevilled Christian apologetics since the earliest days of disputation: the Virgin Birth, the mystery of the Trinity, the problem of Free Will and so on. Since it is Buñuel, as much time is taken with the heresies as with the dogmas, yet the balance I think is not tilted unfairly. For it is part of his vision of life that *both* parties to these kinds of conflict have merit, and that wisdom might consist, precisely, in holding back from over-hasty choosing. A philosopher (if not a believer) should be *au dessus de la mêlée*. In the words of the famous Keats letter that we quoted earlier, a man has to be capable 'of being in uncertainties, mysteries, doubts, without any irritable searching after fact and reason.' Certainty breeds dogmatism, as dogmatism in turn leads to violence. Mysteries, let us remember, are to be approached 'reverently'.

Yes, they *are* mysteries, and they are wonderfully expounded here. At least six different controversies are broached in the course of the movie, but I will limit myself to commenting on only two of them – perhaps the central two, at least in human terms. And these two mysteries are: what is, or was, the ontological nature of Jesus? Correspondingly, how are we to approach and make sense of the divinity of Mary his mother?

Mother and Son are characters in the movie; I mean by this that they make their appearance in a number of sequences – flashbacks, you could call them. Each of these cameos is enigmatic, with inflections of comedy (though not quite 'skits' in the Monty Python sense). When they first make their appearance we are in the holy dwelling in Nazareth, and Jesus is addressing his appearance in front of a mirror. 'Don't shave!' his mother commands him (she is played by the lovely French actress Edith Scob): 'I prefer you with your beard!' The son acquiesces without protest. Jesus is played by the well-known French actor Bernard Verley, and there is a distinct element of merriment and irony in his bearing; certainly he is very different from the ascetic Basque actor Enrique Irazoqui who incarnates Christ in Pasolini's *Gospel According to St Matthew*. That flavour of solemn militant piety (and the pathos that accompanies it) is foreign to Buñuel's intentions – and predilections.

The element of domesticity so incongruously introduced in the scene we have just glanced at ties up in due course with a wider theological question that the film comes back to, concerning the proportion of the divine and the human that makes up (or constitutes) the ontology of the historical Jesus. In the 'present-tense' section of the film, we first come across the controversy debated in the unlikely setting of the dining room of a smart country restaurant in Tours, into whose garden the tramps have found themselves trespassing. One of the waitresses puts her puzzlement frankly to the maître d'hôtel. 'What I don't get', she says, 'is how Christ can be both God *and* man.' 'It is difficult, I know', the butler replies smoothly as he polishes the silver, before launching into an erudite disquisition on the Monophysite heresies of the early Church fathers, Marcian and Nestorius. Some, in the past, said that Christ was 'only' divine; others that he was 'only' human. A third proposition (what in fact was proclaimed Christian orthodoxy at the fifth-century Council of Chalcedon) averred that, in some mysterious yet satisfying way, he was *both*.

Bernard Verley's performance, as I have just said, would seem to hint at a 'bubbly' and irreverent Jesus. Yet, without being militant (in the Pasolini sense), the characterisation of Christ Buñuel chooses to give us lays stress on the violent exclusiveness of his teachings. The speeches quoted from in the course of his appearances contain some of his thorniest commandments. Thus from the tenth chapter of Matthew (where Christ, having gathered his apostles, lets them know what he expects from them): 'I am come to set man against father, daughter against mother, daughter-in-law against mother-in-law. Verily, verily, man's foes shall be in his own household. He that loveth his parents more than me is not worthy of me.' And so on. (In the same passage, we find the famous declaration: 'Think not that I come to bring peace on earth. I come not to bring peace but the sword!')[6] And yet he is not exactly *terrible*, this Christ. At the marriage feast of Cana he is convivial and friendly; he is happy to perform the miracle of turning water into wine, telling a light-hearted parable as he does so. Later, he cures or seems to cure two men of their blindness, but, in the closing scenes of the movie, the gestures and hesitations of these beggars (they fumble with their sticks when they come to a ditch in their path) allows us to surmise that they may *not* have been cured. What are we to make of all this? What exactly is Buñuel hinting at

---

[6] The impenetrable harshness of Christ's words take us back to a previous enigmatic encounter in the movie, where the tramps meet on the road a tall caped figure (played by Alain Cuny) who may or may not be interpreted as Satan. He tells them sternly: 'Take a prostitute for a wife. Bear children. The first shall be called "Ye are not my people" and the second "No more mercy".' Some time later, on the outskirts of Santiago de Compostela, they do indeed meet such an ambiguous figure (the actress is Delphine Seyrig) and bargain with her for her favours. The quotation is taken from a later prophetic book of the Old Testament, Hosea. The context is obscure, but the command and the punishment seem chiefly to concern themselves with one of God's periodic bouts of displeasure with the people of Israel – in this case, for worshipping false idols.

FIGURE 41 'He that loveth his parents more than me is not worthy of me.' Bernard Verley as an enigmatic Jesus in *La Voie Lactée* (1969).

here? Let us withhold any final judgement on the matter until we have looked at the parallel way the director brings Mary into the story.

Before we do so I should probably say a word or two about the narrative pattern of the movie. In 'late' Buñuel we have moved on from conventional notions of plot (with its corresponding emphasis on, or predisposition towards, psychological consistency) into something much more fluid and dreamlike. There is still the outline of a story of course – in this case, the journey of the tramps to Compostela – but within this basic framework characters tend to come and go without leave or explanation, exactly as they do in dreams. Incident succeeds incident with few worries about 'follow-up'; characters turn into other characters, just as the present tense morphs silently into past historical epochs, before moving back again, with an invisible shift of gears, into the world of motorways and time-schedules. The latter part of *La Voie Lactée* brings us down towards the Spanish border and over it, and for whole sections of these concluding sequences, the tramps (supposed protagonists of the movie) are merely figures in the background. Indeed at times they seem to have disappeared from the tale altogether, though such is the hypnotism of Buñuel's story-telling we can't say that we really miss them – they have been taken over by other 'pairs' of characters, who substitute for them.

With these provisions in mind let us insert ourselves again into the narrative at the moment when two black-caped young free-thinkers endeavour to escape their pursuers after voicing a protest against the burning of the corpse of an anti-Trinitarian heretic in the cloister of an ancient monastery. (Costumes of their military pursuers indicate – not that it matters; anachronism is encountered cheerfully – that we are in the late seventeenth or early eighteenth century.) Soon the young men find themselves in a woodland glade next to a small lake; and here – another abrupt change in time-scale – they come across the clothes of two modern hunters who have abandoned their outfits to go for a dip. Nothing seems more natural for these escapees than to swap their own costumes for this happily found new apparel; in a trice they are modern huntsmen. And in the pocket of one of the hunting-jackets, one of the young men turns up – a rosary.

From all indications, we are deep in traditional Protestant (prior to this, Cathar) territory. So the young men are puzzled. What is this object they have come across? Doubtless some 'papistical' device. The shorter of the two companions throws the beads onto the branch of a nearby tree, and pulverises them with his shotgun. Later that night, however, in a sheep-pen where they have been sheltering, the Virgin Mary appears to them in a vision and gives the restored rosary back to the amazed young marksman.

We pick up the two young men again in a Spanish tavern south of the border where they have come to seek a room for the night. (The 'pairs' spoken of above are important here: as well as the two young men, the two tramps are present in this scene, enjoying their evening meal, along with two young workmen who have turned up in their tiny Fiat – and two Spanish policemen who arrive to check everyone's hunting permits.) By the side of the fireplace a portly yet intelligent-looking curé is reading his breviary, and it is he who first notices the intense sorrowful look of the young hunter who has seated himself silently near him, fingering the restored beads of the Virgin. Soon the story of their miraculous encounter comes out, and the priest takes it up with this answer: 'A miracle is always an amazing thing. But you musn't let yourself get in a state. The Virgin has appeared thousands of times all over the world. She has performed countless miracles. May I tell you one?' At which, in front of the assembled company, he launches into a marvellous tale about a Carmelite nun, the treasurer of her convent, who had the misfortune to be seduced by a passing admirer, and ran off to live with him, having first flung herself at the feet of a statue of the Virgin situated in the convent chapel, and begged for forgiveness. Years passed, the liaison ended, and the woman returned to the convent, astonished to discover her fellow-nuns going about their business as if nothing had happened. Nothing *had* happened because, during all that time (so it dawned upon the Carmelite), the Virgin had taken her place and silently performed all her duties.

The curé's anecdote over, he ups and bids his audience goodnight, leaving the landlord to usher the two young pseudo-huntsmen to their sleeping quarters. There follows one of the movie's strangest, most extended (and at the same time most beautiful) sequences. The passage in question starts with a mild contretemps between the landlord and his two guests, for as this man enters the bedroom he has disposed for them, he places the lamp, not where one would expect, on the bedside table, but inside the cabinet, whose door he closes. At this point the younger of the two companions (whose name is Rodolphe) corrects the error, telling the landlord, in quasi-biblical tones: 'One does not put a lantern under a bushel, but on a candlestick, to give light.' Yet this observation serves only to anger his elderly host, who promptly separates the men into two different bedrooms, ordering them to lock their respective doors, and on no account to open them if anyone knocks – even if it is he himself who is doing the knocking.

Two bedrooms, then; each with two beds. The men prepare separately to retire for the night. In Rodolphe's bedroom occurs the second miraculous revelation of the day; for as he looks up he sees that the second of the two beds in his room is occupied by a beautiful young woman sitting up against her pillow, who smiles at him sweetly, as the Madonna had. Shortly after this acquaintance is made, the knocking starts, with the landlord's voice demanding entrance. 'Go away!' replies Rodolphe calmly, winking at his companion. 'But the priest is here,' insists the voice; and now the priest is heard from outside the door explaining his return nocturnal visit. 'When I spoke about the Blessed Virgin I forgot several important points', he tells them. The camera angle switches to the outside corridor as the priest eases himself into a chair and continues his blind monologue: 'You cannot imagine the richness of the mysteries of the Virgin Mary', he expatiates. 'First, the Immaculate Conception. Then the birth of Christ, presided over by the Holy Spirit. And finally, her precious Virginity. Do you follow me?' ('Yes', replies the girl, from behind the door, eagerly.) 'Imagine', continues the priest, unfazed by the sound of this female voice answering him, 'that she remained a virgin before, during and after the birth of the Saviour!' Here tears of regret well up in his eyes as he adds: 'Though certain heretics [he names two] have denied this.' Perking up: 'Still, dogma must be believed: Christ was born without breaking her virginity. Do you understand this?' Entering into the spirit of things, the girl answers bravely from the other side of the door: '*Yes, as thought springs from the brain without breaking the skull.*' To which Rodolphe adds his own metaphorical gloss on the mystery: 'As a sunbeam traverses a pane of glass.'[7]

---

[7] Rodolphe's additional analogy reminds me of Buñuel's metaphysical recipe for a perfect cocktail, as outlined in *My Last Sigh*. 'Connoisseurs who like their martinis very dry suggest simply allowing a ray of sunshine to shine through a bottle of Noilly Prat before it hits the gin bottle.' (Naturally, both bottles should be chilled so as to avoid the use of ice cubes. 'Nothing is worse than a watery martini', Buñuel tells his readers.)

This midnight dialogue continues for several more minutes, with the priest addressing the young people (as in a dream) sometimes from behind the door, sometimes face to face with them, transported magically into their presence. We needn't resume the entire conversation – suffice to say that it takes in, as further topics of contemplation, the mystery and beauty of the Assumption; the Virgin's overwhelming aversion to impurity (even in marriage); and finally the possibility, broached by certain Church Fathers, that our Blessed Lady herself, though incapable of committing sin, may at times have shown 'faults', or at least weaknesses ('a little vanity perhaps; the desire to be esteemed; doubt in the presence of the Archangel; a weakening of faith at the foot of the Cross.') At last the priest leaves the couple (but not before pestering the other huntsman who, from inside the security of his bedroom, firmly tells the holy man to get lost). Rodolphe and the girl, meanwhile, in their separate beds, wish each other good-night and – the candle extinguished – turn over to compose themselves for sleep.

The figures of Mary and Jesus throughout *La Voie Lactée*, it is impossible to avoid concluding, are presented us in a lightly ironised dramaturgy. In particular, the continued harping on about the Mary's virginity, and on questions of purity and impurity, belongs to a tradition of scepticism – of outright satire – that, with its roots in the enlightenment and the anti-clerical left, it is not difficult to identify and engage with. And yet (in my judgement) it would be wholly wrong to call this film anti-clerical or 'atheistical' – its elaborations, and tergiversations, are far too affectionate and heartfelt. '*You cannot imagine the richness of the mysteries of the Virgin Mary*', the curé has said. And, in a way, Buñuel believes this. Religion, properly understood, is only partly a matter of dogma. Just as important are allegiance and settled habit. As a young man, Buñuel repudiated the Catholicism of his ancestors; but the powerful impressions imbued in his childhood and reinforced by his education proved harder to shrug off than he thought they would. Must we not believe him when he said, in his later years, that he could never see a statue of the Virgin without tears welling up in his eyes? (As we have seen, both the priest and the huntsman, substitutes for Buñuel, find themselves similarly affected.) We should give the director the last word. 'Culturally, I am a Christian', he said in the interview with Tomás Pérez Turrent that I've already quoted from. 'I've prayed two thousand rosaries and I've taken communion I don't know how many times. All this has marked my life. I understand religious emotion. There are certain experiences of my childhood that I would give anything to enjoy again: the May liturgy, the locust trees in full bloom, the image of the Virgin surrounded by lights. These are, for me, profound, unforgettable experiences.'

FIGURE 42 'A [...] powerful psycho-political study of the conditions of life in contemporary Russia': Andrey Zvyagintsev's *Leviathan* (2014).

7

Russia Again: Millennial Faith and Nihilism

It has been one of this book's governing contentions that, when it comes to matters of high art and meaning, religion, even in this post-religious age, is still everywhere; it is impossible to escape from its heritage. The memory of religion brushes everything that is deepest in life, even in atheist societies. Russia is – or at least was, for the bulk of the twentieth century – an atheist society, officially; and yet it is possible to argue that in no other country in Europe have culture and religion been historically more entwined with each other.

From the beginning indeed; it was Pushkin who famously remarked that culture and religion were the same thing. That was an aristocrat's paradox – a witticism, if you like – though if proof is to be sought for, there is the inescapable fact of the country's two greatest nineteenth-century novelists being, each in his own way, so God-driven. This was not the case, I think, anywhere else in Europe; one wouldn't – one *couldn't* – say the same thing of pairs like Balzac and Flaubert, for example, or Dickens and George Eliot, or Thomas Mann and Theodor Fontane. Naturally, in singling out Tolstoy and Dostoevsky (to whom of course I am referring), I don't seek to disparage the other great national geniuses: Gogol, Turgenev, Chekhov etc. What incredible resources, in the literary field, Russia has always been able to muster! Imagine going through life without Chekhov ... Yet it remains true that Tolstoy and Dostoevsky, somehow, bring the weight of Russian culture back to religious issues; their writings can't be understood outside these parameters. And the same is true of important modern writers – Blok, Akhmatova, Tsvetayeva, Pasternak and Mikhail Bulgakov were all profoundly influenced by Christianity.

What goes for literature goes for other modes of writing and social thought. Philosophy in Russia has always had a mystical tinge to it. One thinks of the major philosophers – Rozanov, Berdyaev, Shestov, Solovyov, Losev etc. – as *theologians*, first and foremost; often that is the metier they followed professionally. (One could perhaps add to this list the names of Father Pavel Florensky and Sergei Bulgakov, observed together deep in conversation in a moving double portrait painted by Mikhail Nesterov in the year of revolution 1917, recently exhibited at the Royal Academy.)[1] 'Theologians' by profession and temperament, but not necessarily wedded to Orthodoxy – far from it. The writers and thinkers of Russia have traditionally stood at a certain distance from the Church as an official organisation. Notoriously, Tolstoy was excommunicated, and there are several other famous instances (in 1913, for example, Berdyaev was arraigned for blasphemy). The Church has tended to come out of all this badly, being regarded in certain circles as a byword for reactionary intransigence. It is certainly

---

[1] What are they talking about, besides the momentous events of the time? Florensky (who was murdered on Stalin's orders in 1937) was a mathematician who also published works on electrodynamics. He was a friend of the symbolist poet Andrey Bely and a follower of the teachings of Solovyov. Bulgakov – like Florensky, this man took holy orders in middle age – moved from Marxism to Idealism in the early years of the century, and by the time our dual portrait was painted had rejected revolutionary doctrines. He was subsequently expelled from his country at the end of 1922, along with other intellectuals like Berdyaev, in the so-called Philosophers' Ship. In exile, he engaged in theological controversy, attracting charges of heresy (especially Nestorianism). Nicolette Misler, in an essay accompanying the centenary exhibition *Revolution: Russian Art 1917–1932* at the Royal Academy, writes: 'In the twilight of Symbolism, they were [among] the last representatives of the Russian Silver Age: adducing scientific criteria, they pleaded for the retention of Orthodox beliefs, and at a time of State nationalisation and confiscation of private and ecclesiastical property, they argued for the preservation of churches, of personnel serving the Christian faith, and even [*sic*] of the former nobility' (exhibition catalogue, p. 209).

not, and never has been, a liberal institution. And yet one cannot deny that its twentieth-century history has been tragic. Forced, like senior rabbis in Nazi Germany, into ever greater compromises just to keep their heads above water, the leading patriarchs – Tikhon, Sergius, Alexey – found themselves again and again, during the period of communist rule, faced with atrocious dilemmas: to co-operate or not to co-operate? In a way it was easier to be persecuted. The full story of the Church's martyrdom is probably still to be written; a provisional tally of casualties during the first five years of Bolshevik rule shows that 28 bishops and 1200 priests were executed, and one could cite other dismal statistics. (The final death toll was hugely larger than this.) Countless more priests and nuns lost their livelihoods. Churches were looted wholesale and their treasures dispersed. Religious education was outlawed. Swingeing taxes were introduced against those clergy whose lives had been spared. In the face of such fierce ideological opposition – such motivated malice – how the institution survived at all continues to be a mystery and a miracle. (The resilience however is measurable; we learn from the scholar George Kline that the official census completed in 1937 found that, after years of open religious persecution, 57 per cent of Soviet citizens – about 80 million people altogether – were still willing to declare themselves religious believers. This census was never published, for obvious reasons.)

The characteristic image of the priest in Soviet cinema shows him to be slovenly, ignorant and cunning. Few, having seen the film, which came out in 1925, will forget one such classic portrait of the clergy – the cowardly conniving naval chaplain imagined by Eisenstein stationed on 'Battleship Potemkin'. We see how he fawns on the officers while distancing himself from the mutineers. Crucifix in hand (he uses it as a kind of weapon), he is a slithery, sly sort of fellow whose one ambition, when the going gets hot, is to save his own skin by hiding himself. It is a superb piece of anti-clerical satire. Even as one deplores its malice (in the context of contemporary persecutions), one has to acknowledge – one always has to acknowledge – Eisenstein's genius for portraiture.

Now that the Church has been welcomed back into the fold for the second time (the first time was during the war, for 'nationalist' purposes), it is interesting to investigate whether such hostility persists or not. We have already mentioned, in the first chapter if this book, the sympathetic way Pavel Lungin treats his somewhat eccentric collection of Northern monks in *The Island* (2006); the director's humane and tolerant friendliness towards them is part of that movie's spiritual distinction, in my opinion. Elsewhere, in some widely seen films, a rather more critical stance prevails; quite as much as in past times, the clergy doesn't seem to be trusted. Kirill Serebrennikov's *The Disciple* (2016) is about a clever and odious schoolboy whose fascination with the Bible, coupled with oral mastery of some of its more bloodthirsty passages, allows him to assert a sort of spiritual domination over his fellow pupils that reaches into the furthest corners of the institution – ultimately into the staffroom itself, playing havoc with assorted secular orthodoxies.

The overwhelmed adults in the film are sketched with precise psychological accuracy. Among 'types' we come across: the timid female principal of the college, along with her elderly unreconstructed deputy (this latter acknowledges the Stalinist Terror, but avers that it might have been 'necessary'); an overweight gym teacher who ogles the girls, and can't hide his disappointment when an edict goes out that bikinis have been banned in the school's swimming baths; this man's girlfriend, a Darwinist biology teacher (heroine of the movie in so far as there is one); and finally a bumptious red-headed priest employed on the staff as spiritual counsellor, who is sent in to reason with the pupil who is causing the disruption, but who finds himself helpless, as they all are, in front of the boy's glib and ferocious antinomianism. No one comes well out of this brouhaha. Nor, in this fiercely anti-Christian film, are they meant to.

The Church and its representatives are treated no more kindly in Andrey Zvyagintsev's *Leviathan* (2014), one of the major Russian films of the past few years. On a picturesque isthmus of land in northern Russia where his is the only private dwelling, an irascible mechanic Kolya (Alexei Serebryakov) is holding out against the blandishments of

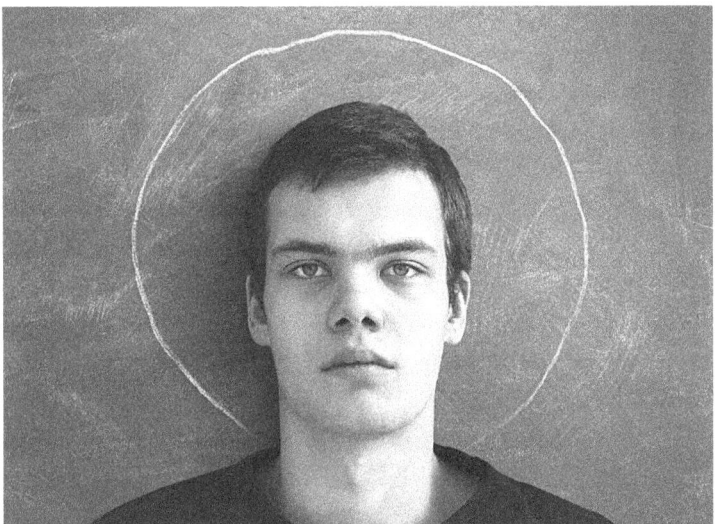

FIGURE 43   A glib and ferocious antinomianism... Pyotr Skvortsov as the sinister young fundamentalist Veniamin in Kirill Serebrennikov's *The Disciple* (2016).

local developers. Faced with the ruthlessness of the nearby township's bibulous mayor, Vadim (Roman Madyanov), our quirky individualistic protagonist — also a drinker — doesn't stand a chance, though you could say he puts up a good fight. Indeed he is one of nature's born fighters (his nature being compounded of heroism and blindness). When, eventually, his house is demolished by the bulldozers, it is to make way for a gleaming new basilica, a prestige project that has been held back from our attention, though in the course of the story we have had more than one chance to meet the local bishop, and to make a judgement about his imperturbable worldliness.

The Church and local government are in cahoots, in other words. It could be argued that the Erastian nature of Russian Orthodoxy — the way that it is, and has always been, legally subservient to the diktat of the State — makes its servants particularly vulnerable to pressures, if not of outright corruption, then of an ideological conformity that would not be so insistent under a more independent and protestant dispensation. I don't know if this is true, or if true how one would go about proving it. Certainly, the Church's servants do often seem to go out of their way, to 'push' the nationalist–governmental line; they do not always behave in a very tolerant or Christian manner. Lower down the hierarchy, however, the forces at play are less intractable (or so one would like to believe). At any event, that smooth and unpleasant bishop is not the only cleric in the movie; the viewer encounters also from time to time Father Vasily, a parish priest, and an interesting character. Outside the village store where he has been buying his groceries, he addresses the battered Kolya in a spirit of fierce comradely concern. Appropriately enough, his speech is proverbial, soaked in the language of the Bible. Poor Kolya (if we may call him that) is an atheist, so he won't know, or can't recognise, that the afflictions that are facing him are comparable to the afflictions of Job. About Job's sufferings there are many things a priest may say, but perhaps the most important thing is that the holy man 'came through' them. The trials were a test, and in the end the prophet triumphed. Ultimately, evil is unfathomable; but from past theodicies the poor contemporary muzhik (battered down by the oppressiveness of the State) draws what comfort he may.

One of the distinctions of this grand and thoughtful film is that Zvyagintsev is alert to religious meanings, without insisting that this is what the film stands for. Sometimes, perhaps, things *can* only be made sense of by recourse to the language of our ancestors. Zvyagintsev

FIGURE 44   'Church and local government [...] are in cahoots.' Contemporary Orthodoxy indicted in Andrey Zvyagintsev's *Leviathan* (2014).

himself has said (in a recent interview) that he believes the Bible contains 'the entire knowledge of humankind about itself'. I am reminded of a beautiful essay about funeral services by the Irish historian Eamon Duffy (he calls his text an 'Apology for Grief, Fear and Anger'; it can be found in his memoir *Faith of our Fathers*). Duffy's thesis is that the modern tidying-up of the traditional funeral liturgy, and in particular the suppression of the great Christian hymn *Dies Irae*, banishes important emotions that are essential to our coming to terms with grief and bereavement. The old service, he reminds us,

> was organised around a series of psalms which alternated between expressions of fear, anger and dismay in the face of death, and of comfort, reassurance and trust. These psalms were arranged in three groups, or 'nocturnes', and accompanied three sets of readings, nine in all, from the Book of Job. These passages from Job, put in the context of the funeral liturgy, were astonishing. They explored the whole gamut of human feeling in the face of death and suffering: fear, anger, self-justification, reproach, longing for relief, trust, affirmation.

And Duffy concludes by saying candidly: 'One of the most remarkable emphases in the readings is that of bitterness and complaint against God.'

So, God railed against – the Deity *needs to be* railed against, from time to time. Duffy quotes these words from the Book of Job:

> My soul is weary of life, I will speak of the bitterness of my soul
>   I will say to God, do not condemn me, let me know why you contend against me
>   Does it seem good to you to oppress me, to despise the work of your hands?
>   Your hands have made me, and fashioned me about, and yet now you destroy me
>   Are your years as the years of men, that you should seek my iniquity, and search out my sin?

None of this language comes into the film *as such*, needless to say; the message isn't spelled out. But it is present in the shadows, and part of the film's deeper meaning – chiming in with the title of the movie itself, and the implied comparison that is made there between the monolithic Russian State on the one hand, and the great sea beast named in the Bible (Leviathan is the oceanic equivalent of the land-dwelling monster Behemoth). While we are in a quoting mood, here is what the Book of Job says about *that* creature:

> Any hope of subduing him is false; the mere sight of him is overpowering.
> When he rises up the mighty are terrified.
> The sword that reaches him has no effect,
> He makes the depths churn like a boiling cauldron.

And so on. Yet the Bible also tells us, does it not, that, at the end of Time, Leviathan shall be slain, and its flesh served up to the righteous. There may or may not be some comfort in that, for those who are willing to listen.[2]

The grandeur of a given film, when it *is* grand, is made up of many different elements working harmoniously, including its visual palette and the way it treats landscape and nature. *Leviathan* is not, essentially, despite anything I may have implied inadvertently, a 'thesis film', or even perhaps a film 'about religion'. No, the film is a plea against injustice – a profoundly powerful psycho-political study of the conditions of life in contemporary Russia, mounted with care and precision. As such it pays as much attention to minor characters as it does to the film's major players – there isn't a distinction between levels here. I haven't mentioned the figure of Kolya's wife Lilya (Elena Lyadova), but she too has an important part to play in the overall story, and before leaving the film we might think about her for a moment – the handling of her fate shows a tender

---

[2] Father Vasily's diatribe (at the grocery store) is delivered in the authentic cadences of the Old Testament. His counsels have richness and 'heft'. Elsewhere, the language of the film is full of modern slang and obscenity. The coarseness of some of the dialogues was singled out for criticism in official circles when it dawned on the same authorities (who of course had partly paid for the movie) that the vision of Russia communicated here was far from friendly to the current power structure.

sober seriousness on the director's part that seems to me representative of his general seamless humanism. Thus, in the midst of the crisis about their house being possessed, Lilya takes a lover, Dmitri (Vladimir Vdovichenkov), a handsome lawyer who happens to be Kolya's best friend. Despite sexual chemistry, the relationship doesn't work out. He is a rationalist and cynic, calm in a crisis. She on the other hand is wracked by feelings of guilt and inadequacy. The episode ends tragically. After being subjected to a violent verbal attack by her teenage stepson Romka (who has found out about the affair), Lilya commits suicide by drowning.

Kolya, we have said, is an atheist. But we can sense that his wife Lilya has, or had, religious feelings; they are part of her depth and her delicacy. It is hard to say whether conditions in Russia are objectively more terrible than they are anywhere else in Europe, and if so how properly to respond to them. Common sense would say that it partly depends on what position you occupy in the pecking order. Nonetheless, I am sure there is a sense in which it could be argued that the history of that country in the twentieth century *has been* uniquely sad and benighted. In no other country in Europe was the citizenry oppressed for such a long time; no other country suffered over such a long period the curtailment of basic human freedoms (including freedom of worship). The end of communism, in 1991, was meant to bring an end to all that, but of course we know that it didn't. The experiment with imported market capitalism brought in its wake fresh horrors and iniquities, which ought to have been foreseen but weren't, as rival forces in society battled for the control of hitherto monolithic state assets. Criminality and assassination emerged from the shadows into the broad light of day; while life expectancy (for men particularly) declined markedly. Horrendous wars in the Caucusus followed on, almost seamlessly, from the ill-judged fiasco of the invasion of Afghanistan. To those in the habit of reflection, these abrupt and on the whole unasked-for changes amounted to a profound spiritual crisis – with different phases, naturally, ranging from anarchy to autarky (from 'Yeltsin to Putin', if you like), but held together by an underlying continuity. We have mentioned in the course of this book some of the cinematic chroniclers of the new post-communist dispensation – Balabanov and Lungin in a previous chapter; Zvyagintsev and Serebrennikov above[3] – without attempting to draw far-reaching conclusions. Unless one is a specialist, the films in question are sometimes hard to see; it is hard to get a firm grasp on the wider picture. Here, then, I propose, in the final pages of our study, to look at three last filmmakers who I believe are worthy of scrutiny. They are absolutely *not* Christian artists, but in some way they are indeed profound witnesses. All three are experimentalists in the formal sense, with the vices and

---

[3] Serebrennikov is under house arrest as I write these lines, on charges of embezzling 68 million roubles (about £900,000) donated by the State to subsidise the Moscow Theatre of which he is (or was) artistic director. The affair is as judicially murky as such affairs always are in Russia, but it seems that behind these evidently trumped-up charges (the money was demonstrably spent on the eight or nine plays staged in the season before his arrest) lie the manoeuvrings of the Orthodox Church and its current *éminence grise* Father Tikhon, outraged, so it is said, by *The Disciple*'s overt anti-clericalism. It certainly shows that, whatever has been the past persecution of Orthodoxy, the the Church as an institution is once more a power in the land. (This same Father Tikhon allegedly spoke to Putin himself to launch the complaint.) The affair has echoes of the Pussy Riot scandal of 2012, as indeed of another ongoing controversy, concerning the release of a trashy melodrama called *Matilda* (2017: director Alexey Uchitel), a multi-million-rouble bagatelle about the supposed adulterous love affair between Tsar Nicholas II and the Mariinsky ballet dancer Mathilde Kschessinska.

Tsar Nicholas himself, it will be recalled, has rather recently (2010) been beatified, and it seems that the secular fringe group Christian State-Holy Rus had been going round threatening to fire-bomb cinemas where the movie was scheduled to play (so far as I know, the threat was not carried out). Obviously the Church itself, qua institution, distances itself as far as it can from such 'activist' hooliganism, but there is no hint, I think, that it is unhappy to see its cultural influence increased generally; the new-found alliance of Church and State is part of the government's overall strategy to reassert the importance of Russia as it was perceived in the days of the empire (a similar obsession with 'strength' and 'prestige' underlies the – on the surface paradoxical – current rehabilitation of Stalin). Nor, ideally, do these manifestations of nineteenth- and early twentieth-century pride stop at Russia's borders: a vigorous attempt is currently being made to reclaim the Russian churches in exile for the Moscow Patriarchate. Meanwhile descendants of Russians from the 1917 diaspora – aristocratic families included (perhaps even especially) – are being wooed back to the motherland with the promise of special 'compatriot' status on their passports. As far as one can judge, these culture wars are unlikely to relinquish any time soon.

affectations that can accompany this (prolixity, repetition, narrative obscurity). Their works are difficult to interpret; but at the same time they are original – and beautiful. The combined oeuvre of the three filmmakers represents perhaps the most important contribution to Russian cinema since Tarkovsky's death. Indeed they are his heirs and his rivals. Perhaps the reader will have guessed by now that I am referring to the trio of filmmakers made up of Kira Muratova (1934– 2018), Aleksey German (1938–2013) and Aleksandr Sokurov (b.1951).

*

Muratova, to take her first, was born of a Romanian mother and Russian father who was killed in the Great Patriotic War behind enemy lines, carrying out important intelligence work. Her childhood and youth were passed in Romania in what might be termed privileged surroundings; among other occupations, her highly placed mother sat on the board that dealt with the import of foreign films, and so from an early age Muratova was able to see and discuss movies from the West that would have been harder for her contemporaries to access. In due course, she moved to Moscow and enrolled in VGIK, the national film school, where her tutor was the veteran Leningrad actor and director Sergei Gerasimov. Her time there was successful; she was popular and apparently looked up to. On graduation, she married the son of a Ukrainian writer and moved to Odessa, the city that became her permanent base (the marriage, we hear, didn't last).

In Ukraine during the 1960s there were two directors of note working at the height of their powers by whom she could scarcely escape being affected: Marlen Khutsiev and Sergei Parajanov. It seems that the latter's example was especially important to Muratova both formally, as an artist, and also as a symbol of independence and free-thinking. (Paradjanov, it will be remembered, is or was – he has been dead now for some time – the director of the path-breaking films *Shadows of Our Forgotten Ancestors* (1964) and *The Colour of Pomegranates* (1968), discussed briefly in the first chapter; already at this time he was beginning to experience the hostile attention of the authorities that would lead to lengthy periods of imprisonment in the 1970s.)

Muratova's first two films as an independent director, *Brief Encounters* (1967) and *A Long Farewell* (1971), ran into difficulties with the censors; the release of the first was limited to 'lowest-category' status (i.e. shown, if at all, only in film clubs), while the latter was banned outright, only surfacing during glasnost, at the end of the 1980s, when shelved films were allowed out of the closet. It is rather difficult to guess *why* these films of Muratova were treated so harshly at the time; they are not in any obvious way anti-Soviet. They are certainly dazzlingly put together. *Brief Encounters* explores the unspoken rivalry between an educated Russian housing official (played by Muratova herself) and her 'maid', a simple country girl, over the charms of a handsome wandering geologist (he in turn is played by the legendary poet and balladeer Vladimir Vysotsky). *A Long Farewell* shares, one would have thought, an equally unexceptionable premise, in this case the difficult personal relationship between a sensitive 15-year-old boy and his highly strung extrovert mother (the father has exited the household). In the light of Muratova's future experimental obscurity (let's call it that for the moment), what's important, I think, to stress about both these films is the deftness, and I would even say the wisdom, of their psychological insight. The *telling* of the tales is elliptical and sophisticated – that is very much part of their formal pleasure (Muratova was a simply brilliant editor) – but the actual human situations dramatised in each case are recognisably 'sane' and naturalistic.

Years of struggle followed for Muratova, succinctly summarised by the American academic Jane Taubman in her excellent short book on the director. Few Western viewers have seen *Getting to Know the Big, Wide World* (1978), *Among the Grey Stones* (1983) and *A Change of Fate* (1987), so we will quietly pass them by. But evidently something interesting was going on that allowed Muratova's voice to emerge, just

Russia Again: Millennial Faith and Nihilism 221

FIGURE 45 A sombre psychological realism: the boy Sasha in Kira Muratova's 'shelved' movie *A Long Farewell* (1971).

as communism was ending, with a renewed authority and energy; and a new outlook also – an altogether idiosyncratic view of the modern world that henceforth mingled humour and blackness in fantastically odd and perverse combinations. The key film here is probably *The Asthenic Syndrome* (1990), where the view of contemporary society, in its brittle dyspepsia, couldn't be more at odds with the humanism, openness and intellectual optimism that characterised art in the brief flowering of the Gorbachev epoch. It is the blackest of black comedies – if indeed it is a comedy at all. ('Asthenic', in the title, seems to be a neologism; in so far as the viewer can pin down a meaning to the word, it refers to the narcolepsy, or 'sleeping sickness', that afflicts one of the film's key characters, a schoolteacher, whose unfortunate propensity to lose consciousness in the middle of tasks or meetings is contemplated by the filmmaker with sardonic objectivity.) Other films followed – by now Muratova was becoming a prolific artist – of an equally sombre hue: *Passions* (1994, about horse-racing), *Three Stories* (1997), *Letter to America* (2000, a short), *Chekhov's Motifs* (2002),

The Piano Tuner (2004), *Two in One* (2007) and, her final film, *The Eternal Return* (2013). I use the phrase 'sombre' as an umbrella characterisation of her work, but I can see that it is not quite the right word. It fails to account for another aspect of Muratova's art, what I would call her satirical glee – her *méchanceté*, or perversity. It may become a bit clearer if I attempt to describe one of her works in more detail. So let us look at the portmanteau movie *Three Stories*, a film I know fairly well, having seen it several times, and even taught it to students.

Three tales, then – unconnected. In the first episode a middle-aged man lugs a coffin-like box into the cavernous boiler room of an extensive if old-fashioned apartment building, where he engages in a baroque conversation with the janitor, apparently an old schoolfriend of his, who also seems to be a poet of sorts. A poet of sorts (he recites a long poem), but also an 'underground man' in another sense – he runs a gay sauna club, hosted by a semi-naked opera singer, who now appears on the scene with two companions, before heading off to indulge in some unseen antics in the shower room.

Meanwhile, the gist of the conversation between the janitor and his visitor hinges on the question of what he should do with his tiresome female flatmate who constantly annoys him, he says, by walking around their shared apartment nude. 'I would smash her on the head with an axe, or slit her throat', says the poet-janitor eagerly. 'Well, that's just what I have done', replies the visitor imperturbably, opening his box to reveal the body of a naked young woman with her throat cut. Mild consternation on the janitor's part, but not really moral shock, I think. The episode ends with the men sitting round wondering what to do next; disposal of the corpse in the roaring furnace of this underground purgatory would seem to be the obvious solution.

Episode two introduces us to a beautiful hospital nurse named Ophelia. She is played by the actress Renata Litvinova who appears in many of Muratova's films and is something of a personality in her own right, writing scripts and plays (including the scenario of this current episode) and is, or was in the 1990s, a prominent glamorous figure in Moscow's artistic circles. So here she is playing a nurse in a maternity hospital, with glistening make-up and polished red nails, but otherwise not very encouraging to the patients under her care – she advises one healthy young mother, Tania, to abandon her newly born infant. Shortly afterwards – the advice apparently taken – the two women accompany each other on a walk through some ruined buildings in the neighbourhood, behind the walls of which each in turn squat down to urinate. It will be Tania's last human act, for Ophelia, having stealthily removed her stockings, proceeds to strangle the other woman when she isn't looking. The crime is accompanied – perhaps one could say 'finished off' by – an illicit orgasm.

We are not yet through, however, with this tranche of the film, which proposes to dramatise not one but two grisly murders. Ophelia has been rummaging in the hospital archives and has found the name and address of her own mother who abandoned her years ago and whom she now proceeds to track down. She follows this woman as she leaves her apartment and walks down to a neighbouring wharf: evidently it is a habit of hers to sit on the quayside, reading. At any event, the older woman pays no attention at all to her daughter (whom she may or may not recognise – their clothes however are oddly similar), who has sat down beside her, attempting to engage her in conversation. Annoyed by this apparent show of indifference on her mother's part, Ophelia snatches the book from her hands and tosses it into the water. Seconds later, she pushes in her mother too, and watches her drown with satisfaction.

That was episode two. In episode three we are once more in new surroundings: the walled terrace of a bourgeois-artistic apartment where an old professor in a rocking chair has been left in charge of a five-year-old girl while her parents are out on some errand. The child is lively, pretty and precocious and the pair of them engage at first in some rather wonderful banter (the spontaneity of the child's acting throughout the episode is a marvel to behold; it is as if she is completely undirected, just doing and saying what occurs to her – though viewers of course know this can't be true). Now the child rushes off and shortly afterwards reappears naked. There follow more word games and witty banter, in the course of which the old man insinuates the thought (playfully or seriously, it's hard to tell) that the girl's mother is a thief, who steals bread and pastry. Annoyed by this suggestion, or possibly not (again, it's hard to tell), the child disappears into the depths of the flat and proceeds carefully to scoop up the poisons that have been lying around in the apartment's many mousetraps. This powder she mixes into a freshly made mug of tea and presents the drink to the professor. Sipping the concoction, he remarks on its bitterness ('it must be my gall bladder') but continues to imbibe nonetheless. Shortly afterwards, in the course of a lengthy telephone conversation to an unidentified third party, he topples forward and dies. The girl comes out to look at the body. After jumping around with glee, she settles down to enjoy a game of spinning tops.

A black comedy is a black comedy (three black comedies in one, in this case). There is not much use wasting ink in speculating whether we think (or whether we think Muratova thought) that Russia is really like this, in its lower reaches – in other words, that it is genuinely so beastly and heartless. Perhaps we may agree that the vision of society offered here and in some other of Muratova's films is a shade or two more stylised than that offered by Balabanov in *Cargo 200* (see Chapter 1 for my discussion of *that* ferocious movie). We needn't remind ourselves that terrible things do happen every day – one only has to read the papers, or watch the news, to be swamped by stories of crime. But a difference between *Three Stories* and *Cargo 200* is that the latter film (like *Leviathan*, indeed) seems to possess a residual regret somewhere in the depths of its narrative that religion and morality are no longer part of the common discourse of society. Then one could make sense of – if not of course cure – those inexplicable acts of individual wickedness that one reads about. Muratova, if I haven't said it yet, was

Russia Again: Millennial Faith and Nihilism

FIGURE 46 Professor and imp in Kira Muratova's godless black comedy *Three Stories* (1997).

an immensely cultivated person, and *Three Stories* is not alone in her work in being full of clever literary references to past masters of dark subject matter: Chekhov, Shakespeare, Gogol, Dostoevsky, etc. Yet she refused to moralise her storytelling. Morality was absolutely not her 'game', even if 'play' and pleasure are vital to the vitality of her art. 'A cat plays with a mouse before eating it. What is that play?', she asked rhetorically. 'It's theatre!' And that aestheticism seemed to be enough for her – more than enough. 'The gloomiest thing, if it is well done', she wrote, 'leaves an impression of joy.' She claimed to be an optimist. 'Biologically, I'm a healthy organism, with an optimist's nature', she wrote in 1997, the same year that *Three Stories* was released, and, perversely, one can see what she meant. She stands in this chapter, perhaps, as a counterweight to the lure of Christian earnestness – a counterweight indeed to the very plea of this book's argument, that religion still vitally 'matters' in art. Muratova disposed of her intellectual enemies succinctly – perhaps one ought to say aristocratically: 'I don't believe in God. I don't believe in anything supernatural. *Art* is my religion!'

*

Aleksey German (the G in his name is pronounced hard) is, or was (he died in 2013), a rather different kind of filmmaker, but he and Muratova share at least three characteristics that draw them into the same spiritual territory, and allow them to be compared coherently for the purposes of our current discussion. In the first place, he is a completely independent artist; we will discuss in a moment the interesting, complex ambiguity of his relationship with communism, but it is important to note at the outset that no matter what he was saying, in whatever context, he was absolutely fearless – he didn't mind what anyone thought of him. Such total honesty is rare perhaps, anywhere and at any time, and it is surely right to honour it in passing.

Then he is also like Muratova in that the more his career progressed, the more experimental and anti-mainstream his art became – one would have to say therefore (from the perspective of the ordinary viewer) the more difficult to understand. The prestige of late films like *Khrustalyov, My Car!* (1998) and *Hard to be a God* (2013) is curiously tied up with their obscurity – their narrative opacity, their 'intellectualism'; we will come back to this too. Lastly, German shares with Muratova a more or less black vision of society that at times, especially latterly, seems to be taken to outrageous extremes. He is a portraitist of Russia as a living hell. The rhetoric of redemption doesn't interest him.

German's courage, noted above as a constant feature of his life, is visible in the treatment of the subject matter of the first film he made as a solo director, *Road Check* (1971), or as it is sometimes called *Trial on the Road*, in that it dares to look at a taboo subject – that of Russian soldiers who fought for, or collaborated with, the Nazis in World War II. Normally such men wouldn't stand a chance: captured, as traitors, they would be mercilessly disposed of. (This carried on long after the war was over.) One such ex-collaborator, Lazarev (Vladislav Zamansky), makes contact with a Russian partisan division whose captain (warmly played by Rolan Bykov) chooses for some reason to trust him – against the advice of his own superior officer, a cynical and unsentimental major played by Anatoli Solonitsyn. There will be tests, of course, to prove the turncoat's sincerity – immensely suspenseful action sequences behind the enemy lines that are thrillingly filmed by German: all his work has a staggeringly detailed 'texture' to it (inherited perhaps from the realism of his first teacher Kozintsev, but observable also in the fluent black-and-white widescreen photography of contemporaries like Larissa Shepitko and Andrey Smirnov. Tarkovsky too – the battle scenes in *Andrei Roublev* are clearly related to this aesthetic). Lazarev will eventually die in one final heroic test of his bona fides, taking on an enemy troop train. One could say, therefore, that, at this stage of his career, redemption *is* a relevant desideratum for German; at least it makes sense, in the moral economy of the narrative. But then Lazarev isn't really the 'hero' of the movie. That position is reserved for the shrewd captain played by Bykov. And, in this man's relationship with his superior, the Major, the film seems to broach another theme fraught with ideological danger, which one could call the independence and integrity of military orders, especially when, as was often the case, the field commander and the political commissar in a given regiment (in theory they were equals) disagreed about policy or action.

Readers who have patiently stayed with me so far may recall that this is a subject that is brilliantly explored by Vasily Grossman in his great novel *Life and Fate* (finished in 1960 but not published until the 1980s). I am thinking of the episode in which the brave tank commander Novikov at the beginning of a vital forward thrust in the Stalingrad region holds back his troops for a full nine minutes in order to avoid senseless casualties from an enemy barrage – knowing perfectly well that his action will be interpreted and reported back to headquarters as cowardice by his particular enemy and nemesis, the opportunistic political commissar

Getmanov. In early Soviet fiction and movies, commissars were presented as positive heroes, whereas in real life, as often as not, they were cowards, bullies and hypocrites. The Major, in German's film, is not a coward; but he is a dangerous and odious ideologue, contemptuous of his fellow countrymen's lives, as we see in the powerful flashback sequence where the Captain is berated for not blowing up a bridge when an enemy train was crossing it, whereas we know (and the Major knows) that beneath the bridge lay a barge of captured Russian soldiers who would have perished as a result of this action.

Here, in short, were more than enough reasons – though some of them subtle enough – for German's film to find itself, on completion, banned from release (just as, in the same year, 1971, *Long Farewells*, by Muratova, had been banned). We learn that the the authorities were so incensed by German's outspokenness that Lenfilm Studios were actually made to pay compensation to the State for the money that had been 'misspent' on the project – an unprecedented penalty, and surely a humiliation for German. After that, the road to being allowed to make films again must have been long and arduous; one might wonder that it happened at all. When he did eventually re-emerge as director, it was of another film set in World War II. *20 Days without War* (1977) has a somewhat more conventional storyline than *Road Check*, perhaps for obvious reasons; there would have to have been especial care taken that toes were not trodden on. So we will pass over this second film (though it is not without interest – no film by German is, I think), and move on another eight years to his next movie, *My Friend Ivan Lapshin*, which came out in the middle of the eighties, just as perestroika was getting under way.

Here is a work that speaks with immediate cinematic authority. Its originality was, and is, plain for everyone to see. Its subject matter is fascinating (especially perhaps to foreign audiences) – nothing less than the activities of the NKVD, or secret police, in a provincial city in the 1930s, in fighting the forces of local crime. Local crime – not political crime – a vital distinction. The film is not an indictment of the

Terror. The evident depravity of the underground hoodlums (magnificently sketched, in a series of wonderful character parts; German's textural realism, evident in all of his films, surpasses itself here) has the effect of putting the audience on the side of the *chekists* – in so far as 'sides' *are* taken, or offered, in a film which concentrates on accuracy of locale and gesture, while seeming to take an almost perverse pride in not explaining itself.

What does need explaining perhaps (the viewer may feel) is German's equanimity vis-à-vis the ruthlessness and sometimes the outright cruelty of this group of men and women he is sketching – members after all, or associates, of a secret police combine, shown for the most part as 'exemplary citizens', taking their share in the ordinary pleasures of life: parties and love affairs, theatrical outings, parades extolling Stalin's leadership and so on. Maybe we can guess what German is driving at; communism *was* like that, he wants to say. There was a sort of day-to-day brutality that can't not be acknowledged, but also an exaltation, a democratic confidence, a feeling, for some, that life was 'going places'. That this phenomenology of daily life verged on hysteria and unreason is probably not lost on the filmmaker – at one point Lapshin, our fearless detective, gives the game away. 'Without Stalin', he exclaims, 'there'd be no reason to live!' Many people did indeed think this – perhaps including German's own parents. (There is evidence from interviews that he saw his film as being a portrait of their generation – a homage, indeed.)[4] Once again, as with Muratova's stance, there seems to be a sort of anti-Tarkovskian bravura at play here. Culturally speaking, and in terms of family ethos, the film stands at the opposite pole to the portrait of family life offered by Tarkovsky in *The Mirror*. It is not that Tarkovsky's family was in any way 'godly', in the churchgoing sense; but Christianity was present in another way: it underwrote the values that in turn informed his family's self-definition as part of the noble tradition of the intelligentsia. None

---

[4] Aleksey was the son of a notable Soviet writer, Yuri German (1910–67). *My Friend Ivan Lapshin* was based on one of his stories, as was *Road Check*.

FIGURE 47 An ambiguously warm regard towards the NKVD: Andrei Boltnev and Andrei Mironov in Alexei German's *My Friend Ivan Lapshin* (1985).

of that cultivation is present – it is ruthlessly *not* present! – in the characters we meet in *My Friend Ivan Lapshin*. The world we encounter there is bleakly godless, as in all of German's movies.

My Friend Ivan Lapshin is set in the early to mid-1930s. It starts with an allusion to the murder of Kirov in 1934, the event (in all probability stage-managed by Stalin himself) that is widely understood to have triggered first the purges and show trials of the Old Bolsheviks, and in due course the Great Terror itself (1937–9). In an interview that he granted to *Variety* magazine at the time of the film's release, German called the film 'a premonition of some horrible things that were going to happen in the future'. So we are asked to understand, I think, that the pursuit of the common criminal subculture that is shown in the movie in such fascinating detail is in some sense symbolic of, or substitutable for, the round-ups and persecutions of ordinary non-criminal citizens that so infamously characterised the later stages of the decade, in its headlong descent into madness. If one were to ask, then, why not *show* Stalin and the NKVD's persecution of the innocent as well as the 'guilty', German could reasonably answer that that is for another film, not this one. But his method is certainly elliptical, and was to become even more so. In *My Friend Ivan Lapshin* the story, you could say, just about holds together: omissions, allusions and insinuations can be supplied by the audience, who know how to read between the lines. The problem is that in German's next film, *Khrustalyov, My Car!* (1998), and even more in his swansong *Hard to be a God* (2013), these basic courtesies of storytelling – plot, suspense, recognisable characters, distinction (at some level) between good and bad – seem to slip away without regret. Detail itself, in its most material incarnation – how things look, feel, touch, crumble, liquefy, impact on the body – becomes everything, at the expense of any political, moral or humanistic considerations. There are critics who have argued that these two final films are justified in their own aesthetic terms – a triumph of avant-garde cinema. Yet what vision of Man are we faced with here?

The slightly odd title of German's fourth and penultimate movie – exclamation mark included – refers to the order that was reputedly given to his chauffeur by the NKVD chief Beria the moment Stalin expired: he wanted to get a head start on his rivals. *Khrustalyov, My Car!* presents a minutely detailed reconstruction of Russia in the last years of the tyrant's life in the early 1950s, focusing (in so far as there is a focus – more of this in a moment) on two individuals: a lowly stoker in the palaces of the great whose voiceover gets the tale going; and a burly commander-general who is also a surgeon, and whose destiny it is to be the last doctor to examine Stalin alive.

The examination in question is filmed by German with typically grim realism – the once all-powerful dictator has soiled himself on his sickbed and, as the surgeon's hand presses down on his stomach, the comatose body is made to emit a deep fart. (One could think of this as Stalin's 'last sign of life'.) Meanwhile German's mobile camera has explored the living quarters of the film's large cast of characters with a sense of vivid sordid detail that has perhaps never been seen before on screen. 'In 1950', Francis Spufford writes in his essay 'The Soviet Moment', 'you could be director of a major Moscow hospital and live behind a curtain in one-seventeenth of a tsarist ballroom.' Never before has the viewer been offered such a vividly concrete picture of the way that in communist Russia people were squashed up against each other without privacy in a maze of ingenious and improvised habitats – corridors that have become living rooms, cupboards that reveal entire sleeping quarters, kitchens that double as bathrooms and so on. In such circumstances, petty quarrels about territorial 'ownership' could scarcely not be the order of the day (people even laying claim to their own lavatory seats!). All this is brilliantly done – no commentator will want to gainsay that.

But the film itself, it is time to say now, is tedious and prolix. Surely, there are diminishing returns to be had from such categorical miserabilism. The critical reception of *Khrustalyov, My Car!*, which took four years for the filmmaker to make, was relentlessly negative both in Russia and abroad (the author of these lines was present at the Cannes premiere, when large numbers of journalists walked out. Not that that means anything – a number of the greatest movies in film history began their lives under ostracism). It certainly says something for German's courage, determination and yes, his stature and integrity as an artist, that he returned to the fray just a few years afterwards with a film that was, if anything, even *more* extreme. *Hard to Be a God* (2013), based on a novel by the Strugatsky Brothers (who also wrote the novel that Tarkovsky's *Stalker* is adapted from), took twelve years to make and, perhaps unsurprisingly, turned out to be German's final movie; he didn't live to see it released. (After his death in 2013 at the age of 75, his wife and filmmaker son completed the sound recording. Meanwhile the director's fame, or notoriety, ensured the film's relatively wide distribution). The tale is set on a foreign planet called Arkanar, similar to Earth, except 'about eight hundred years behind in its history', with the consequence that the Renaissance and (it follows) the Enlightenment have not yet taken place. Thus to all intents and purposes we are plunged into a medieval landscape – as detailed and specific, on the surface, as that imagined by Tarkovsky and Konchalovsky for *Andrei Roublev* (and quite as magnificently muddy and rain-sodden; like all of German's films, this one too is shot in black and white, with fine attention paid to long shot and depth of field). Through this landscape strolls a certain Don Rumata (Leonid Yarmolnik), a handsome and dandyish warrior prince, whom at first we can't help being attracted to. He has a pleasant smile and some interesting accomplishments. For example, he is by no means a bad musician (oddly, the notes emanating from his breakfast-time horn solo have a strangely modern jazz flavour!). With his open countenance and apparent benevolence of gesture, he will surely help bring justice and enlightenment wherever his path takes him. The whole film – of monumental length: it lasts for three hours – is constructed to give the impression of a sort of seamless quasi-royal progress undertaken by Rumata, as if we were constantly in his company in the present tense, and there were no camera cuts (though in fact there are several). So it is with a genuine sense of revelation and dismay that the audience gradually comes to realise that, far from being benevolent, Don Rumata is as devious, cruel and morally deformed as any of the other bent characters we meet on this pilgrimage. One could say that over the course of the film, slowly and in front of our eyes, Rumata's embrace of bonhomie turns into the suffocating grip of the executioner. That surely is the film's central puzzle, if there is one – that the person we *thought* was a hero isn't a hero at all, but a monster.

There is obvious irony at work here – the irony of the title: 'hard to be a god', indeed. Much more clearly than in German's previous films, with this work we enter the realm of allegory. And as always with allegory, there follows ambiguity of interpretation. Which of the movie's copious details do we attach ourselves to, in order to arrive at what the film really 'means'? How important is it to know, for example, that Rumata was never in fact an indigenous inhabitant of Arkanar, but a human, one of a party of scientists sent out from Earth to observe living conditions on this planet with instructions not to become involved (and above all, not to take part in any killing)? Since this is the case, then Rumata has plainly gone rogue; but his motives for doing so (and how 'gradually' it happens; and with what, if any, resistance) remain mired in impenetrable obscurity. It stands to reason that, somewhere in the scheme of the film, there *must* be an allusion to Russia, we think. But if so, what is German saying about his country? He is entitled to maintain – his whole career has done nothing *but* maintain, with bravery and distinction – that Russia's twentieth-century history was bloody and tragic. So he needs no permission, as I have been arguing all along, to paint the picture very, very black: as black as a canvas by Bosch. Still I think that, were we to compare 'late' German to the very greatest witnesses – to Solzhenitsyn, for example, or to Grossman, or to Svetlana Alexievich, or to Nadezhda Mandelstam – we can only be struck by a vital missing ingredient to his vision, simply the absence of hope, at any level. Grossman's great novel *Life and Fate* (since we have already mentioned this epic work in passing) is implacably clear-sighted about the iniquities of the system, and about how the false rhetoric that sustained the communist ideology allowed individual acts of evil to flourish. But crucially, he also saw the obverse of the picture: that there will always be pockets of resistance, pockets of refusal, because (fortunately for all of us) the human spirit is indomitable. These nuances and discriminations about our fellow men and women are why we read Grossman; they are the essence of his wisdom, humanity and religion. In contrast to this, the *lack of shade* renders the late films of German hysterical – perhaps even stupid – for all their great energy and inventiveness.

*

Finally we arrive at Aleksandr Sokurov, the youngest of my three 'exemplary witnesses'. The son of an army officer, he was born in the

Siberian village of Podorvikha (Irkutsk oblast) in 1951, and spent much of his childhood travelling round Russia following his family's military postings. (The army background, which comes up in a number of his films, is an important element of his patriotism.) Graduating from the department of history at Nizhny Novgorod (ex-Gorki) University in 1974, he enrolled at VGIK the following year, where he came under the influence of Tarkovsky's films. His formal studies ended in 1979. By this time he had already made his debut film, *The Lonely Voice of Man* (1978), which, like Muratova's *A Long Farewell* and German's *Road Check*, had the distinction of being immediately shelved; as well as a number of mainly local television documentaries. Documentary shorts and features have continued to be a vital part of his output throughout a career notable for its intense productivity. Sokurov's current (2019) filmography gives a tally of 59 films, of which 37 are listed as documentaries – although, since he has always been a self-consciously experimental film artist, the distinction between the two genres is in his case sometimes difficult to maintain.

'Experimentalism', in Sokurov's case, seems to me to be an absolutely essential aspect of his identity as a filmmaker. As far as I can

FIGURE 48   Hero or monster? Leonid Yarmolnik as Don Rumata in Aleksey German's *Hard to Be a God* (2013).

see, he has never solicited box-office approval. Which doesn't mean that a number of his films aren't extremely suave and beautiful; and, indeed, in certain cases (these judgements are always personal and relative) easy enough for the general viewer to follow. Yet it means that, just like Muratova and German, he is not frightened of being thought difficult. Often enough, the obstacles to understanding seem to operate at the simplest plot level. Can anyone say, for example, what is *really* going on in a film like *Second Circle* (1990), ostensibly about a boy's struggle to remove from his house a coffin bearing his father remains? Or in *Whispering Pages* (1993), beyond the fact that its atmosphere is so plainly grim and 'Dostoevskian'? Or in *Father and Son* (2003), where for some inexplicable reason the paterfamilias of the title seems to weigh in at the same age as his offspring? These are films (I might have substituted others) that seem, like all avant-garde works, to cry out for third-party exegesis before viewers can properly assimilate them.[5]

At other times (especially in the case of the documentaries), the experimental element lies in the challenge of their extraordinary length. Thus, *Spiritual Voices* (1995) invites the viewer to spend five-and-a-half hours in the company of soldiers stationed in remote corners of the ex-Soviet empire. Soldiers who are on the whole engaged in... not very much! *Confession: From the Diary of a Naval Commander* (1997) (scarcely shorter: 'only' 260 minutes) engages in a similar scrutiny of the Russian merchant marine, caught sailing off the icy shores of Vladivostok. With so little going on, over such lengthy running times, how can the audience not be bored, we wonder? Unless it is that in the very activity of *waiting*, some mysterious source of spiritual solace is being opened up to us: hard to define, but cognate with melancholy, with contemplation, with prayer itself perhaps ...

---

[5] I shouldn't want to exaggerate their obscurity. The films in question may be no more difficult to read than the typical video installations that we sit through (patiently or impatiently) in certain modern art exhibitions, wondering what on earth the artist is up to. In their favour, we might add that Sokurov's soundtracks are always remarkable; half the power of these rather abstract movies derives from their imaginative sound design.

Sokurov's espousal of experiment, as I have said, has been wholesale, and extends not just to form but to the very content of his cinema (if, indeed, the two can ever be genuinely disentangled). I am thinking here of his extraordinary trio of films about twentieth-century dictators: *Moloch* (1999), about Hitler; *Taurus* (2000), about Lenin; and *The Sun* (2005), about the wartime Japanese emperor Hirohito. What is 'experimental' here is their political stance – or rather their ostensible lack of it. For there can't be much doubt that Sokurov, as a responsible modern citizen, disapproves of the deeds that these men's collective policies gave rise to. But about the men themselves, as individual human beings, he appears to be astonishingly non-judgemental. With the partial exception of the film about Hirohito (where General MacArthur is given a prominent role), the movies manage to avoid any of the usual references to historical facts and personalities that viewers would naturally expect to find in a more conventional 'biopic'. They focus instead on the day-to-day conversations of the protagonists with their close associates, often on the most trivial of topics, and yet somehow – filtered through the imagination of the director and of his long-time co-scenarist Yuri Arabov – given a turn, a sense of wit and even humanity which, under the circumstances, the viewer may be forgiven for finding dismaying. What strange species of revisionism is being practised here, we wonder. Alas, there is not much point in asking Sokurov himself; in interviews, he avoids straight answers, merely pointing, in an airy fashion, to the distance between 'Shakespeare's time', when men were apparently *in charge of their actions*, and our own dismal epoch, characterised by 'inertia and irresponsibility'. Such formulations are too vague to be helpful, I think. (Especially when directly followed up by a second thought: 'Inertia is sometimes an energy!') No, we are on our own here...

At the time of writing, Sokurov's best-known film is *Russian Ark* (2002), a work of magisterial authority. Compared to some of the films we have been talking about, it is a film that feels pleasant to navigate in — it welcomes us with its relative lucidity! Set in the palace of the Hermitage (St Petersburg), the movie offers a wonderfully idiosyncratic guided tour of the building's pictorial treasures, conducted (supposedly, the whole episode is entirely invented, in fact) by a French nobleman, the Marquis de Custine (Sergei Dreiden) — a real-life historical personage who visited Russia in the middle of the nineteenth century and wrote extensively, and controversially, about his experiences there.[6] Nor is he our sole guide on this eccentric expedition: Sokurov and his scriptwriter have arranged for the Marquis to be accompanied by an unseen Russian companion, acting as the film's narrator; throughout the film the two men converse and frequently disagree with one another, with amusing results. The film is first and foremost a meditation about cultural politics, then; it partakes of the old debate about the rival value systems of Russia and the West, seen through the prism of their different interpretations of Christendom. As a Frenchman and a Catholic, Custine shows himself to be slyly complacent about the West's superiority to what he considers to be his backward and barbarous host country. It is certainly indisputable that the great canvases we are looking at — by artists such as Rembrandt, Van Dyke and El Greco — belong, in the main, to the Western tradition, just as, inescapably, does the architecture of the palace itself, of course; conceived of by Peter the Great, the entire city pays homage to Western notions of classicism and order. ('This loggia's a bit like Raphael', Custine remarks superciliously at one point. 'Are we in Russia or the Vatican?') Famously, the movie was shot by Sokurov in a single take lasting 99 minutes, and the way that this is done, following Custine as he proceeds at a civilised walking pace, gliding up to the paintings, glancing at them, pausing perhaps for a sly remark or witticism before

---

[6] George Kennan's classic study *The Marquis of Custine and His Russia in 1839* (Princeton University Press, 1971) sees Custine's account of Nicolas I's tyranny as 'a prophetic parallel to the despotism of Stalin' (Robert Darnton). There is a good modern biography of this homosexual aristocrat by Anka Muhlstein: *A Taste for Freedom: The Life of Astolphe de Custine*, trans. Teresa Waugh (New York, Helen Marx Books, 1999).

moving off again – all this slowly and subliminally takes on in its accumulation, it seems to me, the very rhythm and respiration of the history painter's elegant brush-strokes, so that finally (this is surely one of the things that is most wonderful about the film) it is as if a work of art *about* painting were somehow, in front of our eyes, to turn into a painting itself.[7]

Nothing, meanwhile, forces the audience, whether Russian or foreign, to agree with Custine's ideological critique – or to disagree with it, either. It is provocative, but at the same time sophisticated, mysterious, hermetic, and always nicely balanced, so to speak, by the scepticism of his invisible companion. Here, then, we need to confront the second strand of the movie's meditation – what might be called its politics, or its attitude towards Russia's pre-Revolutionary history. Thus, as we journey on through the Hermitage under Custine's guidance, from time to time we meet up with parties of the palace's former guests and residents – historical figures such as Pushkin, Catherine the Great, poor Tsar Nicholas and his doomed family: ghosts of the past, dressed in appropriate costume, and arranged, at first, in the form of picturesque tableaux vivants. Unobtrusively these aristocratic cadres join the onward procession, swelling it in numbers as they go, until the whole throng arrives at a magnificent ballroom where musical celebrations are in progress. The court orchestra is playing a mazurka, and in no time at all the gallant Custine (camera behind him) is mingling with the swirling dancers – the women in fabulous white ball-gowns, their partners in stunning military uniform. Meanwhile, expensively dressed dowagers and elderly privy councillors stand about on the sidelines commenting on the spectacle, their stray remarks picked up as the camera passes them.

---

[7] The German Steadicam operator Tilman Büttner had previously shot Tom Tykwer's *Run Lola Run* (1998) – at a frenetic pace. Sokurov, who had hired this technical whizz-kid for his unique skills, spent half of his energy in the shooting of *Russian Ark* trying to get him to slow down. Against all the pressures that must have existed to hurry things up (daylight running out etc.) the rhythm of the finished film remains, triumphantly, one of calmness and contemplation.

Eventually the dance comes to its lively end, and the party (amounting by now, one would imagine, to fully a thousand guests) begins to disperse itself, taking its stately exit down the palace's grand staircase, and on through a seemingly endless underground corridor. Yes, we are on a ship – we have gathered that. The Hermitage is an ark or a refuge. And now the mood is changing, becoming subtly more sombre and elegiac. Gliding over the guests' heads, the autonomous camera, at a certain point, veers off at a right angle. Leaving the convivial throng, it heads out of doors into the dark and icy winter landscape. On the soundtrack are overheard the following words, gravely spoken by the invisible narrator: 'The sea is all around', he tells us. 'We are destined to sail for ever. To live forever!'

The whole sequence, of course, in its marvellous portentousness, amounts to an unbelievably bravura feat of choreography: a climax, or grand finale, such as one has rarely encountered in any spectacle. But what is perhaps even more striking – original, counter-intuitive, 'experimental' in the way I have been using the word – is the clarity of Sokurov's endorsement of aristocratic values. If there is gaiety, there is little satire in these scenes which I have been describing which dare to show regret for the passing of Russia's *ancien régime*. The whole film then is a homage to a vanished class – a vanished, or extinguished, way of doing things. That, I suppose, must be the real meaning of the closing voiceover: 'we', or they – the people being looked at here – are destined to live forever *in memory*. In reality, this ark is a *Titanic*; the melancholy fall of the film's final cadences surely tells us this. The posture is reactionary by definition, and anti-revolutionary, but perhaps there is no harm in that, unless you think (which many people do, I know) that the past is to be explained merely as a chronicle of the brutal exploitation of the poor. Sokurov has little time for socialist sentimentality, even if he recognises well enough, I think, that good things as well as bad came out of the Bolshevik upheaval (including his country's educational system, of which he himself was and is a beneficiary). His stance is patriotic, without being nationalist, for it is evident that he likes Germany, Japan and France as much as he loves and admires his native Russia – he is nothing if not cosmopolitan. If this, then, amounts to a *political* position, it might be harder to gauge his metaphysical and religious predilections – though of course we need to try to do so. One wonders whether he would admit to being Christian, for example. In an impressive filmed conversation recorded (over the space of many hours) with the author of *The Gulag Archipelago* back in 1998, Sokurov broaches Christianity on two occasions, firstly to agree with Solzhenitsyn that one of the values of religion lies in the 'encouragement it gives to repentance' (we remember how Eisenstein agreed about this); and then, in a later section of the film, to praise the piety of the typical Russian peasant's approach to death, the ease and tranquillity with which, traditionally, such men and women, he thinks, are able to 'deliver themselves into the hands of the Lord.'

Might there be in these words, we wonder, a hidden regret that what comes naturally to 'them' (the old peasant survivors) is no longer available to 'us' (the modern bourgeoisie)? Has the modern world forgotten how to die properly? Might it be one of art's tasks to remind us? Such thoughts inform the meditation of one of Sokurov's

FIGURE 49   'Destined to sail forever. To live forever!' A group of the insouciant party guests assembled by Aleksandr Sokurov in *Russian Ark* (2002).

profoundest and most beautiful works, *Mother and Son* (1997). In this movie, a handsome young man bears his dying mother in his arms through an extraordinary Romantic landscape of trees, sand dunes and distant romantic vistas. Formally, this is more or less all the film amounts to. Seventy-one minutes of intimate pilgrimage, shot in burnished autumn colours through slanted anamorphic lenses that push the image out of its normal vertical axis (as if we were viewing the screen in close-up, only at an extreme oblique angle, giving rise to the effect, perhaps, of glimpsing the screen through a veil of tears). And the first thing we notice, when we have oriented ourselves, is the tenderness of the young man's carrying technique. He is strong, patient and thoughtful towards his precious burden. The journey is punctuated by pauses of rest that allow the conversation of the pair to emerge in tones of the richest love and intimacy. 'Be patient, dear Mother, we will meet again', he urges her on the cusp of her departure from the world. 'We will meet again', he says – the sublime Christian hope! And instead of asking how this can be *literally* true, we go along with it, in the context it is being given us in the movie.

Yet how consistent is this affecting piety, is surely the interesting question. As stated above, Sokurov has made 59 films, and across that vast oeuvre there will naturally be differences of emphasis; even, at times, of philosophy. If a film like *Mother and Son* seems clearly to speak up for the possibility and beauty of redemption, what are we to make of Sokurov's 'Icelandic' version of *Faust* (2011) that ends, so shockingly, with the film refusing to allow the intercession of Gretchen (her ghost, I mean, the maiden herself long dead of course)? Here Goethe's traditional tale of sacrifice is seemingly turned on its head. Physically, the movie is one of Sukurov's most ambitious and beautiful, shot in the richest of hues by a French cameraman, Bruno Delbonnel. It begins with a descent through the clouds onto a walled township nestling on the side of a mountain – one of those beautiful aerial model shots that

Murnau did so well (see, for example, the silent version of *Faust*, from 1925); reminiscent also perhaps of the opening of *Triumph of the Will*, with the audience sharing Hitler's godlike view of the earth as the dictator's plane descends through the clouds over Nuremberg. Here, at any event, the location itself is a typical German village with gabled houses and twisting cobbled streets – unchanged in essence since the Middle Ages. Within one of these houses is Faust's atelier, and as the film starts the scientist is dissecting a cadaver – a close-up of the corpse's damaged, mottled penis momentarily filling the screen space. Faust, as incarnated by the German actor Johannes Zeiler (the film is written and spoken in German), is a handsome saturnine fellow whose glance doesn't give much away. In conversation with his assistant he enquires where the soul is located – is it in the head or the heart, or even possibly the soles of the feet?

The matter is left unresolved as master and apprentice take themselves off to the hospital where Faust's father (one of those strange, Sokurovian figures who look physically as young as their offspring) is resident professor of medicine. Though father and son

FIGURE 50   'A glimpse [...] of the Christian paradise'. Alexei Ananishov and Gudrun Geyer in Sokurov's *Mother and Son* (1997).

appear to dislike each other, they share, it emerges, a similarly instrumental attitude towards their chosen professions; there is to be no limit – either of tradition, or piety or even of common sense – to the pursuit of material scientific knowledge.

Throughout these scenes – the prologue is long and I have left out several details – there is a pervasive emphasis on poverty and hunger, what one might call the stench of life at street level. The decor is crammed with realistic Gothic detail. Though the costumes of the characters indicate a setting sometime in the early nineteenth century, when Germany was on the path to nationhood and prosperity, the references to dirt and decay and snatched meals of scraps take us back to an earlier time of want, and serve to remind us, subliminally, of the tale's medieval origins. Some such neediness, at any event, now pushes Faust to make a visit to the pawnbroker, Mauricius (Anton Adasinsky); there is a golden ring in his possession ('no ordinary ring: a philosopher's ring') that he hopes he may get money for. But though Mauricius initially accepts the pledge, the following day he changes his mind and brings the item back to Faust's apartment.

There follow a series of peripatetic conversations between the pair in the course of which the pawnbroker slowly takes advantage of Faust's melancholia in order to insinuate himself into his service. He is certainly a strange fellow, this pawnbroker, with his old-fashioned smoking cap, straw-coloured hair and peculiar lolling gait – not quite human indeed? That seems to be one conclusion we may be invited to draw when, in the course of their wanderings, the pair of them visit the local bathhouse, and find it full of women, young and old, stripped down to their shifts, gaily going about their business. Uninhibited always, Mauricius takes off his clothes to join them, revealing peculiarities in his nether regions that shock and amuse his audience in equal measure. Is that a tail we have glimpsed on his back? Or what? One of the amused girls, Margarete (Isolda Dychauk), is exceptionally pretty; she catches Faust's eye on the sidelines – but not before

Mauricius has gone up to her and smelled her skin lasciviously. She smacks the devilish phantom playfully: 'Such impudence', she remarks. 'I'm not a rose garden!'

The 'tropes' of the traditional Faust story, and the characters associated with it, are beginning to fall into place. Next we have the unprovoked murder of Margarete's brother Valentin, in the drinking den. It happens in a flash. Somehow a bloody sword finds itself in Faust's hand. How had it got there? The protection from the authorities offered by Mauricius at this point (though of course it is he who set up the whole encounter) leads Faust slowly and inevitably back into the mesmerising orbit of Margarete. First there is the paying-off of Frau Emmerich, Margarete's mother; the pawnbroker just happens to have gold for the purpose. Then at Valentin's funeral – strangely interrupted by the intrusion of yapping hounds from a hunting party – Mauricius engineers it so that Faust is able to rub his hands up against the mittens of the grieving maiden. In the long post-funeral walk back through the forest, more wooing takes place and, despite the opposition of Frau Emmerich (who calls her black-clad daughter a witch), it doesn't take much to set up a further meeting, this time in a deserted church, where Faust, in the confessional box, impersonates a priest, the better to press his designs on her.

It is only after this last encounter, really quite far on into the film, and following numerous leisurely episodes which I haven't itemised, that we come to the business of the contract signed in blood, in the course of which Mauricius-Mephistopheles guarantees his companion possession of the beloved's body in exchange for… In exchange for what? It isn't spelled out. But of course we who know the story may fill in for ourselves that the price of the bargain is nothing less than the surrender of his immortal soul.

From here on matters become largely surreal. True to his promise, Mauricius disposes of the inconvenient mother Frau Emmerich, by poisoning her. This leaves Faust free to act. Surprising Margarete standing alone beside a lake, he sinks with her ecstatically into the turquoise depths (an amazing image, I should say in passing, in a film that simply brims with extravagant imagery). Next morning he awakes in a ruined room to find the naked girl beside him; asleep or dead, it is difficult to make out. Yet he will leave her in any case. Mauricius, grumpy as usual, has arrived on the scene, apparently to lead his protégé to safety. (Weird disfigured wraiths have been haunting the premises.) Buckling on protective armour, the pair leave the village and head off up into the mountains. What a strange landscape it is that they now encounter! Raging torrents, volcanic rocks and churning geysers mark their itinerary, symbolically attesting to the turbulence of their feelings. A reckoning of accounts is in the offing, but on which side, we wonder, will victory fall? One has the feeling that Mephistopheles is teasing Faust, humbling himself in his service the better to spring a trap on him. But Faust for his part will have none of it. In his delirium he claims there are still fresh fields of knowledge to

FIGURE 51   'He is certainly a [...] strange fellow, this moneylender.' Adam Adasinsky as Mephistopheles in Sokurov's puzzling retelling of the Faust legend: *Faust* (2011).

be conquered! Turning on his tormentor, therefore, he stones him to death, before striding on upwards towards snow-covered peaks. From the sky Margarete's voice can be heard crying plaintively, 'Where are you going?' 'Farther and farther' is Faust's icy, proud and (by now) indubitably mad reply.

This final section of the film was evidently shot in Iceland, whereas the earlier parts are authentically 'German' in character (though shot, we are told, in the Czech Republic). Once again taking his cue from the master painters of the Romantic era, Sokurov proves himself here as elsewhere to be one of our great contemporary landscape pictorialists – I think an equal in this matter to painters like Richter or Kiefer. Plainly this isn't the place to argue in any detail the rival claims of cinema and painting; yet since the comparison has raised its head I can't help mentioning a further distinction attaching to Sokurov's canvas, and that is the intricacy of the soundtrack, crafted as it is with extraordinary density, so that when one is in the forest, for example, listening to the dialogue between Faust and Margarete as they walk back together from Valentin's funeral, one hears not just their voices but the crackle of the twigs, the sound of the birds singing, and something beyond all this that one can only describe as atmosphere, a dense invisible 'vibration' that communicates, as elsewhere in the movie, a mysterious sense of poetic exaltation.

So there is indeed an aspect of the sublime in the film, to balance its distinct strands of satire and malice. Somehow the two moods don't contradict each other. The tone of the film is equally conveyed by the extraordinary acting style that Sokurov managed to impose on his performers – far more mannered and theatrical than we are used to in most contemporary cinema, and a possible barrier, one might have thought, to those viewers (most of us, probably) who go to the movies expecting naturalism. All of the performances are conceived of in this heightened and exaggerated modality, but above all that of Adasinsky as Mauricius-Mephistopheles who dominates the film in much the same way that Sergei Dreiden (playing the Marquis de Custine) dominated *Russian Ark* a decade previously. Yet in both these films, the quality of the acting, in all its mannered brilliance, is bound up with the quality of the script, by which I mean both the structured unfolding of episodes and the dialogues that accompany them. It may seem an odd attribute to claim about an artist as puzzling and portentous as Sokurov, but one of the most striking things about this late version of *Faust* is how witty it is.

*

And yet the film *is* a puzzle. Perhaps that is why I have taken so long (too long, the reader may well think) to describe it. If I say there is everything here except human kindness, it acknowledges my feeling, and perhaps also my disappointment, that this great contemporary artist who has shown himself in the past so open to life's wonder should have turned his back – at least temporarily – on the message of Christian forgiveness. As I remarked earlier, we don't expect Sokurov to be edifying, and maybe we should leave it at that. With all the qualifications I have just made, Sokurov's hermetic, elegiac worldview (the word 'elegy' appears in no fewer than ten of his 59 film titles) emerges as much more open than those of Murotova and German to spiritual values, and to the faithfulness of the human heart. Perhaps it puts the matter succinctly enough to say that he is closer to Tarkovsky than they are. Tarkovsky's name, often cited in the course of this chapter, should bring us back to the question which set this book going, of whether and how it is possible for a modern artist to be, in the old-fashioned and uncomplicated sense, a 'believer'. It was the sense that Tarkovsky *was* one of the rare believers in the ranks of film directors that intrigued me so much when I first came across him, half-a-century ago. With hindsight I acknowledge the naivety (perhaps I should say the ingenuousness) of my discovery of that master's possession of 'faith'. The intervening years

Russia Again: Millennial Faith and Nihilism   249

FIGURE 52 'Everything at last [...] in some way fits together.' Margarita Terekhova and Oleg Yankosvky in Tarkovsky's *The Mirror* (1974).

have given me plenty of time to think about the matter. Certainly, Tarkovsky's Christianity can be odd at times, but at least it is never shallow. It expresses itself best, I think, when it is least dogmatic – least wrapped up, so to speak, in the 'mantle of the prophet'. It is a bit late in the day to be discussing *The Mirror* at this point, but readers will perhaps remember the wonderful scene towards the end of the film where we glimpse the director's fictional parents (played by Oleg Yankovsky and Margarita Terekhova) lying together next to a stream running close to the family dacha. Their relationship hasn't been easy (Tarkovsky's father left his mother for another woman at the beginning of the war), and they each appear to be lost in their own self-communing universe. Quietly we notice: almost invisible tears are streaming down the mother's cheek. Yet somehow one knows, paradoxically, that she is weeping with happiness! Yes, everything, in some strange way, is 'all right'. The misery of war, poverty, future family break-up, isn't *separate from* this feeling of acceptance, but bound up into it, part of the overwhelming significance of life, and what one might call its sublimity.

'Love exists', or, even perhaps, 'God exists.' That is what comes over in this sequence, one of the most beautiful in Tarkovsky's work, and a fitting place, I hope, to take leave of our enquiry.

Afterword

I have just been reading the travel diary of an ancestor of mine. Lucie Moore was married to an Anglo-Irish clergyman, and was the mother of five children aged from teenage years to young twenties when she invited them to accompany her on a continental tour in the summer of 1843. The journey was to start in Antwerp, move across to Cologne via Brussels, then up the river Rhine by steamboat, taking in Wiesbaden, Frankfurt, Mannheim, Strasbourg and so on, till they reached Freiburg and the Swiss border; then on by coach through Switzerland and down into Italy via the Simplon Pass, ending the outward leg of their expedition in Florence. Though her clergyman husband was slated to have joined the trip, he seems for some reason not to have done so, so the burden of organising the quite complex travel arrangements, and seeing to it that their hotel rooms and *table d'hôte* were as they should be, fell on the uncomplaining Lucie's competent shoulders. The diary is amusing to read among other reasons because, though her observation of the sights encountered tends to be fierce and single-minded, her temperament, on the whole, is un-neurotic and even cheerful.

Yet her deeper thoughts are often gloomy and gathered round the subject of salvation. Unremittingly Protestant as she was by conviction, the art of Catholic Europe set a perpetual challenge to her sensibility and was frequently the cause of almost physical distress. Here she is visiting Brussels cathedral:

The tinkling of bells, the sound of the priest's voice as he monotonously reads out the Latin text, the walking about of the numbers assembled, the crossing of the holy water, the variety of genuflexions, the apparent blind devotion to those baneful errors where Mary is all, and God and Christ, our ALL, scarcely noticed much less honoured – all this made me pained and melancholy. The very scent of the incense reminded me of the smoke of the bottomless pit.

Yet her response to Christian art – even the art of a Catholic painter like Rubens – can at the same time be impressive in its seriousness and simplicity. Here is a typical entry describing a Deposition of Christ by the great Flemish artist, hanging in Antwerp cathedral: 'The helpless frame of the Holy Jesus – given up to be tortured and dislocated and pierced. What a joy to think that he had long since entered into *his* Joy, and that the lifeless and bruised body was now radiating with glory.' *Radiating with glory* – she really seems to feel the power of it. By the end of the trip, in Florence, art trumps confessional allegiance, as when we observe this stern critic of Mariolatry dissolve her prejudices in front of the beauty of Raphael's Madonna della Seggiola, hanging in the Palazzo Pitti: 'Quite the most wonderful [...] the most *exquisite* expression of maternal and filial love I have come across', she exclaims. By the time we have reached this stage in her journal, there is no reason to doubt her sincerity.

Confronted with a document like Lucie Moore's diary, the modern reader can't but be aware of its narrowness in certain ways: the very fact of its author refracting all experience through the optic of religion being the *essential* narrowness in the first place, perhaps. Unless one were to turn the thing around ... What if her faith on the contrary was a gift and a privilege? What if its possession illumined the experience of life and made it meaningful, and then wonderful? I myself, as I hinted earlier in this study, was brought up in a Catholic household; my education was in Christian establishments. But I can't remember being particularly pious as a child, and I think I can say the same things about my siblings. The monastic boarding school in Yorkshire in which I and my brothers spent four years of our adolescence was, rightly, compunctious in its demands that we attend Mass on Sundays and holidays of obligation, but otherwise we were allowed to roam freely. The forum at which we debated the events of the day and under whose aegis we made our first philosophical forays was named, oddly enough, the Athenian Society, in defiance, as it seemed, of more saintly patronage. Theology, at any event, was not part of the curriculum; indeed we would have found its presence in our lives forced and outlandish. It was the same at university where I read English at Dr Leavis's old college. The magnificent poems of our forebears from Chaucer onwards were expounded to us by teachers (marvellous teachers all of them – I owe them the deepest gratitude) without it ever being thought necessary to connect these works' unique expressiveness to the body of religious thought in which, in so many cases, it had been nurtured and marinated. Shakespeare was taught, but not the Bible or the Book of Common Prayer – I had to discover these for myself, over the years, in private reading. If I wanted to summarise my attitude towards matters of religion during a large part of my youth and early adulthood, it would be something along the lines of: religion is for *them*, the unenlightened! The enlightened person, surely, would wish to pledge his allegiance to literature or philosophy.

The foregoing pages of this book, of course, could not have been written by someone who still cleaved to that mentality. How I came to alter my opinions over the years on crucial metaphysical questions would take too long to chronicle here; I am not sure how interesting it would be to readers anyway. Curiously, the writer most responsible for inculcating the sceptical attitude in me as a matter of habit, George Santayana (it was he who famously remarked that scepticism is the chastity of the intellect), was also, at a later date, crucial in allowing me to have second thoughts. I remember at a certain point in my life coming across an impressive passage in his collected letters in which he tells his correspondent – Lewis Mumford I think it was – that all his philosophical opinions are foreign and heretical and transitory from the point of view of the great stern tradition of Spanish Catholicism that he was brought up in, and to which he still owed his ultimate allegiance. Well, I am not a conservative Spanish gentleman and I never will be. But I feel I can see what he was getting at.

Other influences played their part in what I will always be reluctant to call my 'conversion', the discovery of Ruskin, for example, being an important milestone (once again I have to say discovery – he was never on the Cambridge English syllabus; though in retrospect I'm pleased that he wasn't). It was through Ruskin's eyes, through his incomparable prose I should say, that I came really to understand how unavoidable it is that thinking about Western art and architecture – the architecture of the great cathedrals, for example – meant thinking about (that is, confronting, conjecturing, being open to) the latent and still-living truths of Christianity. After that I was even ready to broach theology! It was good to discover that there *were* theologians, like Ian Robinson and David Bentley Hart, who wrote with clarity, wit and absence of sentimentality – often indeed even with sharp waspishness; just as it was simultaneously a joy to discover (almost accidentally as it were) that during my adult lifetime we have been living through one of the great ages of English-language ecclesiastical historiography. Diarmaid MacCullough, through his exposition of the Protestant tradition, and Eamon Duffy (allied as he is to Catholicism) have between them marked out an interpretation of early-modern Europe that constantly manages to put us in mind of the faith and spirituality of our ancestors, who are still attached to us by invisible but unbreakable filaments.

Secularism, of course, is a fact of our epoch: *the* fact. We are all – even believers – secular, more or less. From the time of the Enlightenment, the great thinkers of the age have been busy recasting morality to fit in with the laws of psychology. The eighteenth century is full of ingenious treatises that attempt to redefine human nature from first principles, free from the clutter of religion and superstition. I am not in a position to pass judgement, in this sphere, on the achievement of a Hume or a Kant (or even a Rousseau or Voltaire) – beyond stating the obvious, that each of these thinkers, in their different ways, was possessed of titanic intellect and energy. Nearer our own day we have Nietzsche and his genealogy of morals – his presumption to take his readers to limits 'beyond good and evil'. I always enjoyed reading Nietzsche; I read most of his major works in my twenties. But the truth is, I never believed in his morality; I never believed (though perhaps at one stage I wanted to) that his 're-valuation of all values' was *more* intelligent than the values already to be found secure in the Bible.

Naturally the scriptures have to be read properly, it goes without saying. The one way *not* to read them is literally. I have nothing to say to fundamentalists except to excuse myself politely from their company – and from the burden of listening to their arguments (there are many things life is too short for). Yet otherwise, surely, the Bible is the book that contains everything – everything for 'us', I mean – everything we need to make us more sentient thinkers, and better human beings. It really is where we come from – even if we behave most of the time as if we don't recognise this. That intuition, anyway, has been my constant inspiration in writing and now finishing this book: that cinema itself, most secular of artforms, offspring of modernity, mirror of contemporary obsessions, is *still* inflected by our past in ways that we ought to be conscious of. And that (following from this) a significant number of the great European film directors, often against their will even, have been brushed by this profound knowledge – and responded to it with full tact and artistry.

Acknowledgements

Books are or should be written in solitude, but sustained by friendship and conversation. A number of people helped in the production of this work by reading and commenting on individual chapters, or else by communicating their thoughts on related aspects of the topic in useful and challenging ways. I would like to extend my thanks to the following: Ariane Bankes, Teresa Cherfas, Adrian Dannatt, Eva Hoffman, James Le Fanu, Jill Nicholls, Dominic Power, Richard Raskin, Christopher Silvester, David Thompson and Casper Tybjerg. They have given me sustenance and inspiration, often in impalpable ways, over the years. I am not a great conference-goer, but the 'Protestantism and Film' symposium organised by Erik Redling at Wittenberg in 2015 (at which I presented a version of my chapter on Scandinavia) gave me plenty to think about. Anne-Marie Salleo very kindly lent me her flat in Paris at a moment when I needed to get away from it all; the last chapter of the book was written there, and downstairs at the Café de l'Université. I am exceptionally grateful to Christian Viviani at the *Positif* archive for permission to use the stills that illustrate this work; Luke Neima and Sam Goff gave invaluable assistance on the technical side of this operation. Since I have mentioned *Positif*, it would be fitting to pay a more general homage to this monthly publication and its regular writers (Michel Ciment, Jean-Loup Bourget, Lorenzo Codelli, Hubert Niogret and Viviani himself among them) – they know how to write lucidly about cinema! Thanks are equally due to my editors Alex Wright and Rebecca Barden, production editors Sara Magness and Angelique Neumann and to the staff at I.B.Tauris and Bloomsbury Academic for their determination to make this book into a handsome and user-friendly volume. One person above all gave me unstinting support over the years of composition (suitably enough – the book is about belief after all); her name is to be found on the dedication page.

List of Illustrations

Chapter 1 Russia: Tarkovsky, Eisenstein and Christianity

Figure 1 A modern Christian epic: Tarkovsky's *Andrei Roublev*. 12

Figure 2 'Among the most beautiful works of art of this period, in any medium'. Sergei Parajanov's *The Colour of Pomegranates* (1968). 15

Figure 3 'Finding [...] the moral strength to face what is going to happen to him.' Boris Plotnikov as the Christ-like partisan Sotnikov in Larissa Shepitko's *The Ascent* (1977). 16

Figure 4 An unintended flavour of paganism? Domenico (Erland Josephson) in Tarkovsky's *Nostalghia* (1983). 19

Figure 5 'A film that [...] delivers a definitive judgement'. Nikolai Cherkassov as the tormented tsar in Eisenstein's *Ivan the Terrible*. 31

Figure 6 'So you don't believe human beings have immortal souls, do you?' Denizens of a sinister hooch-making cabal in Alexei Balabanov's *Cargo 200* (2007). 33

Figure 7 'Faith that can accomplish miracles'. Monks set sail with Father Anatoly's coffin in Pavel Lungin's *The Island* (2006). 37

List of Illustrations   259

Chapter 2   Poland: A Trio of Catholics

Figure 8 'Premonitions of fate [...] and mortality'. Zbigniew Zapasiewicz and Piotr Garlicki in Zanussi's mordant portrait of pre-Solidarity Poland, *Camouflage* (1977).   38

Figure 9 Polish Romanticism's debt to Christianity: Zbigniew Cybulski and Ewa Krzyżewska in Andrzej Wajda's *Ashes and Diamonds* (1958).   43

Figure 10 A domestic affirmation of paradise? Ambassador Wiktor reunited with his departed wife in Zanussi's *Persona Non Grata* (2005).   51

Figure 11 A formidable presence on the Polish cultural scene during the 1970s and 1980s: Krzysztof Kieślowski directing Philippe Volter in *The Double Life of Véronique* (1991).   53

Figure 12 'A commandment we all know about.' The execution of the young murderer in *A Short Film about Killing* (1988).   58

Figure 13 Following the path of whim or of providence? Exemplary student Witek (Boguslaw Linda) in Kieślowski's *Blind Chance* (1981).   63

Chapter 3   France: The Apostasy of Robert Bresson

Figure 14 'One of the bleakest films in existence': Robert Bresson's *Lancelot du Lac* (1974).   66

Figure 15 'A typically riven member of the species.' Jean-Louis (Jean-Louis Trintignant) stumped for excuses in Rohmer's *My Night at Maud's* (1969).   71

Figure 16 An underground subplot of melodrama? Night-time Paris imagined by Bresson in *Les Anges du Péché* (1943).   75

Figure 17 'Every shot is as true as a handful of earth.' Claude Laydu as the cure d'Ambricourt in *The Diary of a Country Priest* (1951). 80

Figure 18 'Measuring, sawing and fitting [...] the whole film is caught up in a subtly religious atmosphere.' François Leterrier in *Un Condamné à mort s'est échappé* (1956). 90

Figure 19 'In rural France of that epoch [...] the bottle is everywhere in evidence'. Typical bar scene in Robert Bresson's *Au Hasard, Balthazar* (1966). 94

Figure 20 'Whatever happened to the parable of the Good Samaritan?' Marie (Anne Wiazemsky) beaten and humiliated by a gang of rural voyous in *Au Hasard, Balthazar* (1966). 96

Figure 21 'A real child, rather than a saint from a nineteenth-century oleograph.' Nadine Nortier in Bresson's *Mouchette* (1967). 99

Chapter 4 Italy: Christianity and Neo-Realism

Figure 22 The meek shall inherit the earth. François Périer and Giulietta Masina in Federico Fellini's *The Nights of Cabiria* (1956). 104

Figure 23 Everyday Christianity in *The Nights of Cabiria* (1956). 110

Figure 24 'A shaky marriage ...' Ingrid Bergman and George Sanders in *Viaggio in Italia* (1953). 114

Figure 25 The origins of the Franciscan order reimagined with documentary simplicity: Roberto Rossellini's *The Flowers of St Francis* (1950). 118

Figure 26 The loneliness of a Northerner among Southern peoples. Ingrid Bergman as Karin in Rossellini's *Stromboli – Terra di Dio* (1950). 121

Figure 27 'A master-finder of [...] beautiful faces.'
The Angel of the Lord outside the Empty Tomb in
Pasolini's *Gospel According to St Matthew* (1964).   125

Figure 28 The trials of faithfulness. Anna Canzi as the lonely
fiancée in Olmi's *I Fidanzati* (1963).   127

Figure 29 A psycho-metaphysical thriller with God at its
centre. Curzio Malaparte's *Il Cristo Proibito* (1950).   138

Chapter 5   Scandinavia: Lutheran Interludes

Figure 30 'Artistic options continue to be envisaged
[...] within the traditional language of religion.'
Medieval Dance of Death in Ingmar Bergman's
Seventh Seal (1956).   140

Figure 31 'Where is the Friend I seek where'er I'm going?'
The meal on the terrace from *Wild Strawberries* (1957).   146

Figure 32 'I shall bear this memory between my hands, as
carefully as this bowl of fresh milk.' Max von Sydow as the
Knight in Bergman's *Seventh Seal* (1956).   149

Figure 33 A face-off between Christianity and paganism?
Birgitta Pettersson and Gunnel Lindblom in Bergman's
The Virgin Spring (1959).   152

Figure 34 'Joan's accusers in the Church are properly
characterised.' Eugène Silvain as Bishop Cauchon in
Dreyer's *La Passion de Jeanne d'Arc* (1928).   164

Figure 35 'Like so many figures [...] from an ancient Dutch
group portrait.' Painting by light in Dreyer's *Day of
Wrath* (1943).   168

Figure 36 A scenario that takes its audience to the furthest limits of credulity and beyond: Inger's resurrection in Dreyer's sublime masterpiece *Ordet (The Word)* (1955). 173

Chapter 6   Spain: The Heresies of Don Luis

Figure 37 'You cannot imagine the richness of the mysteries of the Virgin Mary.' Edith Scob as the Queen of Heaven in Buñuel's *La Voie Lactée (The Milky Way)* (1969). 176

Figure 38 A serious moral tenderness: Beatriz (Marga López) and the priest (Francisco Rabal) solicit mutual comfort in *Nazarín* (1958). 185

Figure 39 Saintliness under pressure: Silvia Pinal as the demon and Claudio Brook as the holy anchorite in *Simon of the Desert* (1965). 193

Figure 40 'At some deep level … a passionate sincerity.' Silvia Pinal as the much put-upon novice in Buñuel's *Viridiana* (1961). 197

Figure 41 'He that loveth his parents more than me is not worthy of me.' Bernard Verley as an enigmatic Jesus in *La Voie Lactée* (1969). 202

Chapter 7   Russia Again: Millennial Faith and Nihilism

Figure 42 'A […] powerful psycho-political study of the conditions of life in contemporary Russia': Andrey Zvyagintsev's *Leviathan* (2014). 208

Figure 43 A glib and ferocious antinomianism … Pyotr Skvortsov as the sinister young fundamentalist Veniamin in Kirill Serebrennikov's *The Disciple* (2016). 213

List of Illustrations

Figure 44 'Church and local government [...] are in cahoots.' Contemporary Orthodoxy indicted in Andrey Zvyagintsev's *Leviathan* (2014). 214

Figure 45 A sombre psychological realism: the boy Sasha in Kira Muratova's 'shelved' movie *A Long Farewell* (1971). 221

Figure 46 Professor and imp in Kira Muratova's godless black comedy *Three Stories* (1997). 225

Figure 47 An ambiguously warm regard towards the NKVD: Andrei Boltnev and Andrei Mironov in Alexei German's *My Friend Ivan Lapshin* (1985). 230

Figure 48 Hero or monster? Leonid Yarmolnik as Don Rumata in *Hard to Be a God* (2013). 235

Figure 49 'Destined to sail forever. To live forever!' A group of the insouciant party guests assembled by Aleksandr Sokurov in *Russian Ark* (2002). 241

Figure 50 'A glimpse [...] of the Christian paradise'. Alexei Ananishov and Gudrun Geyer in Sokurov's *Mother and Son* (1997). 243

Figure 51 'He is certainly a [...] strange fellow, this moneylender.' Adam Adasinsky as Mephistopheles in Sokurov's puzzling retelling of the Faust legend: *Faust* (2011). 246

Figure 52 'Everything at last [...] in some way fits together.' Margarita Terekhova and Oleg Yankosvky in Tarkovsky's *The Mirror* (1974). 249

Bibliography

Aranda, Francisco, *Luis Buñuel: A Critical Biography*, trans. David Robinson (Secker & Warburg, London, 1975).
Baecque, Antoine de and Herpe, Noël, *Eric Rohmer: A Biography*, trans. Steven Rendell and Lisa Neal (Columbia University Press, New York, 2016).
Barthes, Roland, 'On Robert Bresson's film *Les anges du péché*', in James Quandt (ed.), *Robert Bresson* (Cinémathèque Ontario Monographs) (Toronto International Film Festival Group, Toronto, 1998).
Baxter, John, *Buñuel* (Fourth Estate, London, 1994).
Bazin, André, '*Le Journal d'un curé de campagne* and the stylistics of Robert Bresson', in *What is Cinema?*, Vol. 1, trans. Hugh Gray (University of California Press, Berkeley, 1967).
——— The following essays: '*Bicycle Thieves*', 'Vittorio De Sica: *metteur en scène*', 'A saint becomes a saint only after the fact: *Heaven Over the Marshes*', 'Neorealism, opera, and propaganda (*Forbidden Christ*)', '*Umberto D.* A Great Work', 'De Sica and Rossellini' and '*Cabiria*: voyage to the end of neorealism', collected in *André Bazin and Italian Neorealism*, ed. and trans. Bert Cardullo (Continuum, New York, 2011).
Bergman, Ingmar, *Images: My Life in Film*, trans. Marianne Ruuth (Faber & Faber, London, 1994).
Beumers, Birgit and Condee, Nancy (eds), *The Cinema of Alexander Sokurov* (I.B.Tauris, London, 2011).
Bondanella, Peter, *A History of Italian Cinema* (Continuum, New York, 2009).
Bresson, Robert, *Bresson on Bresson: Interviews 1943–1983*, trans. Anna Moschovakis (NYRB Books, New York, 2016).
Buñuel, Luis, *My Last Sigh: An Autobiography*, trans. Abigail Israel (Vintage Books, London, 1984).
——— *Objects of Desire: Conversations with Luis Buñuel*, conducted by Tomás Pérez Turrent and José de la Colina, trans. Paul Lenti (Marsilio Publications, New York, 1992).
Burbank, Jane, *Intelligentsia and Revolution: Russian Views of Bolshevism 1917–1922* (Oxford University Press, Oxford, 1986).
Cardullo, Bert, *Vittorio De Sica: Director, Actor, Screenwriter* (McFarland, Jefferson, North Carolina, 2002).

Cawkwell, Tim, *The New Filmgoer's Guide to God* (Matador, Kibworth Beauchamp, Market Harborough, 2014).
Coutarel, Philippe, *Alexeï Guerman* (Éditions du Revif, Paris, 2016).
Cowie, Peter, *Scandinavian Cinema* (The Tantivy Press, London, 1992).
Curtiss, John Shelton, *The Russian Church and the Soviet State 1917–1950* (Little, Brown & Co., Boston, 1953).
Dreyer, Carl Th., *Dreyer in Double Reflection: Essays and Interviews*, ed. and trans. Donald Skoller (E.P. Dutton & Co., New York, 1973).
Drouzy, Maurice, *Carl Th. Dreyer né Nilsson* (Éditions du Cerf, Paris, 1982).
Duffy, Eamon, *Faith of Our Fathers: Reflections on Catholic Tradition* [2004] (Bloomsbury, London, 2013).
────── *The Stripping of the Altars: Traditional Religion in England 1400–1580* (Yale University Press, New Haven, Connecticut and London, 1992).
Dyer, Geoff, *Zona: A Book about a Film about a Journey to a Room* [on Tarkovsky's film *Stalker*] (Canongate, Edinburgh and London, 2012).
Eliot, T.S., 'Shakespeare and the Stoicism of Seneca' [1927], in *Selected Essays* (Faber & Faber, London, 1951).
Fellini, Federico, *Fellini on Fellini*, trans. Isabel Quigley (Da Capo Press, Cambridge, Massachusetts, 1996).
Figes, Orlando, *Natasha's Dance: A Cultural History of Russia* (Allen Lane, The Penguin Press, London, 2002).
Fletcher, William C., *A Study in Survival: The Church in Russia, 1927–1943* (SPCK, London, 1965).
Fraser, Peter, *Images of the Passion: The Sacramental Mode in Film* (Praeger, Santa Barbara, California, 1998).
Gaisman, Jonathan, 'The devout sceptic: Hope for those of little faith', *Standpoint*. (September 2018, Issue 104).
Gallagher, Tag, *The Adventures of Roberto Rossellini: His Life and His Films* (Da Capo Press, New York, 1998).
Gregory, Tobias, 'Lecherous goates' (review of *John Donne* by Janel Mueller), *London Review of Books*, 20 October 2016.
Hart, David Bentley, *Atheist Delusions: The Christian Revolution and Its Fashionable Enemies* (Yale University Press, New Haven, Connecticut and London, 2009).
────── *In the Aftermath: Provocations and Laments* (William B. Eerdmans Publishing, Grand Rapids, Michigan, 2009).
Kastan, David Scott, *A Will to Believe: Shakespeare and Religion* (Oxford University Press, Oxford, 2014).
Kieślowski, Krzysztof, *Kieślowski on Kieślowski*, ed. Danusia Stok (Faber & Faber, London, 1993).
Kline, George L., *Religious and Anti-Religious Thought in Russia* (University of Chicago Press, Chicago and London, 1968).
Kozliv, Leonid, 'The artist and the shadow of Ivan', in Richard Taylor and Derek Spring (eds), *Stalinism and Soviet Cinema* (Routledge, London, 1993).
Krajewski, Stanisław, *Poland and the Jews: Reflections of a Polish Jew* (Wydawnictwo Austeria, Kraków, 2005).
Le Fanu, Mark, *The Cinema of Andrei Tarkovsky* (BFI Books, London, 1987).
Leprohon, Pierre, *The Italian Cinema*, trans. Robert Greaves and Oliver Stallybrass (Secker & Warburg, London, 1972).

Levi, Primo, *The Drowned and the Saved* (Michael Joseph, London, 1988).
Leyda, Jay, *Eisenstein at Work* (Methuen, London, 1987).
Luxmoore, Jonathan, *The God of the Gulag*, Vol. 1: *Martyrs in the Age of Revolution* (Greenwing, Leominster, 2015).
MacCullough, Diarmaid, *All Things Made New: Writings on the Reformation* (Allen Lane, London, 2016).
Macdonald, Dwight, *On Movies* (Prentice-Hall, Englewood Cliffs, New Jersey, 1969).
Marshall, Herbert, *Masters of the Soviet Cinema: Crippled Creative Biographies* (Routledge & Kegan Paul, London, 1983).
Proust, Marcel, 'Preface to *La Bible d'Amiens*' [1910], in *On Reading Ruskin*, trans. and ed. Jean Autret, William Burford and Phillip J. Wolfe (Yale University Press, New Haven, Connecticut and London (1987).
Robinson, Ian, *Prayers for the New Babel* (Brynmill, Corbridge, 1982).
—— *Who Killed the Bible? Last Words on Translating the Holy Scriptures* (Brynmill, Corbridge, 2006).
—— *Cranmer's Sentences* (Edgeways/Brynmill, Corbridge, 2003).
Santayana, George, 'The absence of religion in Shakespeare' [1896], in *Selected Critical Writings of George Santayana*, Vol. 1, edited by Norman Henfrey (Cambridge University Press, Cambridge, 1968).
—— *Reason in Religion* [1905] (Charles Scribner's Sons, New York, 1933).
—— *The Idea of Christ in the Gospels* (Charles Scribner's Sons, New York, 1946).
Scruton, Roger, *Our Church: A Personal History of the Church of England* (Atlantic Books, London, 2012).
—— *The Face of God* (Continuum, London, 2012).
Seton, Marie, *Sergei M. Eisenstein* (Grove Press, New York, 1960).
Shapiro, James, *1606: William Shakespeare and the Year of Lear* (Faber & Faber, London, 2015).
Snyder, Timothy, 'God Is a Russian', *New York Review of Books*, vol. LXV, no, 6. 5 April 2018.
Sorokin, Vladimir, *Day of the Oprichnik*, trans. Jamey Gambrell (Farrar, Strauss and Giroux, New York, 2012).
Spufford, Francis, *Unapologetic: Why, Despite Everything, Christianity Can Still Make Surprising Emotional Sense* (Faber & Faber, London, 2012).
—— *True Stories and Other Essays* (Yale University Press, New Haven, Connecticut and London, 2017).
Swift, Daniel, *Shakespeare's Common Prayers: The Book of Common Prayer and the Elizabethan Age* (Oxford University Press, Oxford, 2013).
Tarkovsky, Andrei, *Time within Time: The Diaries 1970–1986*, trans. Kitty Hunter-Blair (Seagull Books, Calcutta, 1991).
Taubman, Jane, *Kira Muratova* (I.B.Tauris, London, 2005).
Truffaut, François, 'A certain tendency of the French cinema' [1954], in Bill Nichols (ed.), *Movies and Methods*, Vol. 1 (Berkeley, University of California Press, 1974).
—— *The Films in My Life*, trans. Leonard Mayhew (Allen Lane, London, 1978).
Tsivian, Yuri, *Ivan the Terrible* (BFI Film Classics, London, 1992).

Tybjerg, Casper, 'The sense of *The Word*', in Lennard Højbjerg and Peter Schepelern (eds), *Film Style and Story: A Tribute to Torben Grodal* (Museum Tusculanum Press, Copenhagen, 2003).

Warshow, Robert, 'Reviewing the Russian Movies' [1955], in *The Immediate Experience* (Harvard University Press, Cambridge, Massachusetts and London, 2001).

Werner, Mateusz (ed.), *Polish Cinema Now!* (Adam Mickiewicz Institute, Warsaw, 2010).

Wiazemsky, Anne, *Jeune Fille* [on working with Bresson] (Gallimard, Paris, 2007).

Wood, Robin, *Ingmar Bergman* (Movie Magazine/Studio Vista, London, 1969).

Wright, Alex, *Exploring Doubt: Landscapes of Loss and Longing* (Darton, Longman and Todd, London, 2016).

Zygar, Mikhail, *All The Kremlin's Men: Inside the Court of Vladimir Putin* (PublicAffairs, New York, 2016).

Index

Films are noted under their English-language release title except in cases (for example, *La Dolce Vita*) where the original-language title tends to be the one in general use.

Adasinsky, Anton, 244, 247
Akhmatova, Anna, 210
Alatriste, Gustavo, 192n
Alexievich, Svetlana, 234
Almodóvar, Pedro, 7, 36
Amidei, Sergio, 119
Andersson, Bibi, 145, 148
Andersson, Harriet, 155
Andreotti, Giulio, 132n
Antonioni, Michelangelo, 108, 113, 126
Arabov, Yuri, 237
Augustine of Hippo, 123n
Aurenche, Jean (& Bost, Pierre), 68
Axel, Gabriel, 8
Ayfre, Amédée, 67

Bach, Johann Sebastian, 9, 18
Balabanov, Alexei, 29
  Cargo, 200, 29–33, 218, 224
Balthus, 95
Balzac, Honoré de, 209
Bang, Herman, 161
Barthes, Roland, 77–78
Bazin, André, 67, 80, 85, 114, 130–32, 135–36

Beauvois, Xavier, 68
Bely, Andrey, 210n
Berdyaev, Nikolai, 210
Bergman, Ingmar, 6, 36, 142, 169
  Cries and Whispers, 143, 154
  Fanny and Alexander, 143
  Persona, 143, 154
  The Seventh Seal, 148–150
  The Silence, 153–54
  Through a Glass Darkly, 153–56
  The Virgin Spring, 150–53
  Wild Strawberries, 143–48
  Winter Light, 153, 156–158, 158n
Bergman, Ingrid, 113, 118–123, 123n
Beria, Lavrenti, 28, 231
Bernanos, Georges, 78, 80, 93
Bertolucci, Bernardo, 108
  Novecento, 130n
Björnstrand, Gunnar, 149, 155, 156
Blok, Alexander, 210
Borowczyk, Walerian, 41
Borzage, Frank, 7
Bosch, Hieronymus, 234
Brandes, Georg, 160

Bramante, Donato, 107
Bravo, Manuel Álvarez, 188
Bresson, Robert, 8, 72–103, 142
   Les Anges du péché/Angels of Sin, 73–78, 102
   L'Argent, 100, 102
   Au Hasard, Balthazar, 93–97
   Un Condamné à mort s'est échappé/ A Man Escaped, 87–90
   Les Dames du Bois de Boulogne, 78
   Le Diable, Probablement, 100
   Une Femme Douce, 100
   Le Journal d'un curé de campagne/ Diary of a Country Priest, 78–86, 102, 186
   Lancelot du Lac, 100
   Mouchette, 97–99
   Pickpocket, 91–92
   Le Procès de Jeanne d'Arc/ The Trial of Joan of Arc, 92–93
   Quatre nuits d'un rêveur/Four Nights of a Dreamer, 100
Brüggemann, Dietrich, 7n,
Bulgakov, Mikhail, 210
Bulgakov, Sergei, 210
Buñuel, Luis, 6–7, 177
   Mexican-period films between *Los Olvidados* and *Nazarín*, 181–82
   Spanish-made films of the 1930s, 179n
   recipe for the perfect dry martini, 205n
   L'Age d'Or, 179, 193
   Un Chien Andalou, 179
   Le Mort en ce Jardin, 188n
   Nazarín, 181–189
   Los Olvidados, 179–181
   Simon of the Desert, 189–192
   Tristana, 198n
   Viridiana, 192–99
   La Voie Lactée/The Milky Way, 177, 199–207

Büttner, Tilman, 239n
Bykov, Vassily, 16

Catherine the Great, 239
Caravaggio, 3
Cardullo, Bert, 107, 132n
Carraro, Don Andrea, 124
Carrière, Jean-Claude, 177, 178
Castellani, Renato, 108
Chabrol, Claude, 68
Chaplin, Charles, 131
Chaucer, Geoffrey, 253
Chekhov, Anton, 5, 209
Christianity
   author's childhood experiences of, 30, 144, 252–53
   Book of Common Prayer, 1–2, 253
   Erastian nature of Russian Orthodoxy, 212–14
   and eternal life, 50–52, 174–75
   intransigence of the demands of faith, 9, 156–58, 188, 196, 201
   and Mariolatry, 203–07, 251–52
   and miracles, 36–37, 108, 110–111, 113
   mysteries, 177, 199–200
   poetic sublimity of, 10, 157, 165, 173–74
   rivalry with paganism, 3, 105, 151–52
   survival under communism, 33, 39
Ciment, Michel, 102
Cohen, Norman, 165n
Craig, Edward Gordon, 10
Cranmer, Archbishop, 1
Cuny, Alain, 201n
Custine, Marquis Astolphe de, 238

Daniel, Marco, 7n
D'Annunzio, Gabriele, 135
Dante, 1
Darnton, Robert, 238n
Dassin, Jules, 192n
Delacroix, Eugène, 3–4

Delbonnel, Bruno, 242
De Mille, Cecil, B., 7
Deneuve, Catherine, 198n
De Sica, Vittorio, 106, 110
   Bicycle Thieves, 130–32
   Miracle in Milan, 131
   La Porta del Cielo/The Gate of Heaven, 106–108
   Shoeshine/Sciuscia, 180n
   Umberto D, 130
Dickens, Charles, 209
Donne, John, 2–3
Dostoevsky, Fyodor, 209, 236
Dovzhenko, Alexander, 19
Dreiden, Sergei, 238, 248
Dreyer, Carl Th., 6, 36, 79, 92, 142, 158
   Day of Wrath/Vredens Dag, 165–68
   Gertrud, 142, 161
   Master of the House, 161, 162
   Mikaël, 161, 162
   Ordet/The Word, 142, 169–75
   La Passion de Jeanne d'Arc, 161–64
   Two People, 161
   Vampyr, 161
Drouzy, Maurice, 159
Duffy, Eamon, 215, 254
Dumont, Bruno, 8
Dychauk, Isolda, 244

Edwall, Alan, 151, 157
Eisenstein, Sergei, 6, 19, 124, 161, 211
   Battleship Potemkin, 211
   The General Line, 23
   Ivan the Terrible, 24–30
   Mexican Fantasy, 23–24
   October, 22
   Que Viva Mexico!, 23
Eliot, George, 209
Eliot, T.S, 1–3
Erice, Victor, 88
Espada, Javier, 188

Fabian, Françoise, 69
Fabrizi, Aldo, 115
Falconetti, Renée Maria, 79, 162
Federspiel, Birgitte, 171
Fellini, Federico, 6, 108, 112, 116, 124, 192n
   La Dolce Vita, 108–09
   The Nights of Cabiria, 109–112, 130
   La Strada, 130
Figes, Orlando, 25
Fischer, J.C.F., 91
Fitzgerald, Edward, 190
Flaubert, Gustave, 209
Florensky, Pavel, 210
Fontane, Theodor, 209
Forman, Miloš, 126
Frankeur, Paul, 199
Frears, Stephen, 7n
Friedenberg, Olga, 25
Freud, Sigmund, 5, 194

Galdós, Benito Pérez, 182, 198n
Gallagher, Tag, 115, 123
Garibaldi, Giuseppe, 105
Genina, Augusto
   Cielo Sulla Paluda/Heaven Over the Marshes, 131–35
Gerardi, Nazario, 118
Gerasimov, Sergei, 219
German, Aleksey, 219, 226–34, 235
   Hard to Be a God, 231, 232–34
   Khrustalyov, My Car!, 231–32
   My Friend Ivan Lapshin, 228–31
   Road Check, 226–28
German, Yuri, 229n
Godard, Jean-Luc, 68
Goethe, Johann Wolfgang, 242
Gogol, Nikolai, 209
Goldmann, Lucien, 154n
Goya, Francisco, 3
Gregory, Tobias, 3

Griffith, D.W., 7, 160, 161
Grossman, Vasily, 227
  Life and Fate, 227, 234
Grundtvig, N.F.S., 160, 169

Handel, G.F., 10n
Haneke, Michael, 7, 50
Hart, David Bentley, 254
Has, Jerzy, 41
Havel, Václav, 39
Herzog, Werner, 8
Hitchcock, Alfred, 68
Holland, Agnieszka, 40–41, 87
Hume, David, 36, 255

Ibsen Henrik, 5, 141
Irazoqui, Enrique, 200
Isaksson, Ulla, 151
Ivan the Terrible, Tsar, 25–30

James, Henry, 4
Jaruzelski, Wojciech, 39

Kant, Immanuel, 255
Kastan, David Scott, 2
Kaufman, Mikhail, 20
Kawalerowicz, Jerzy, 46
Keats, John, 177
Kennan, George, 238n
Khrushchev, Nikita, 14
Khutsiev, Marlen, 16, 219
Kieślowski, Kzrysztof, 6, 41, 52–65
  Blind Chance, 62–65
  Blue, *White* and *Red* trilogy, 54
  Decalogue, 54–61
  The Double Life of Veronique, 54
  No End, 61
Kiefer, Anton, 247
Klimov, Elem, 16
Kline, George, 211
Klossowski, Pierre, 95
Kokotajlo, Daniel, 7n
Konchalovsky, Andrei, 14
Kozlov, Leonid, 26

Krajewski, Stanisław, 89n
Kurosawa, Akira, 151

Lanzmann, Claude, 40
Laydu, Claude, 79–80
Leavis, F.R., 253
Le Fanu, Sheridan, 161
Lenica, Jan, 41
Leonardo da Vinci, 18, 194
Leprohon, Pierre, 117
Levi, Primo, 89n
Lindblom, Gunnel, 151, 154
Lindström, Pia, 123
Litvinova, Renata, 222
Lorca, Federico Garcia, 190
Losev, Aleksei, 210
Łoziński, Paweł, 40
Lungin, Pavel
  The Island, 33–37, 212, 218
Lully, Jean-Baptiste, 91

MacArthur, General Douglas, 237
MacCullough, Diarmaid, 254
MacDonagh, John Michael, 7n
Macdonald, Dwight, 154–55
Machiavelli Nicolo, 1
Machulski, Juliusz, 41
Maciejewski, Wojciech, 41
Magnani, Anna, 112, 122
Malaparte, Curzio, 132, 139
  Il Cristo Proibito/Forbidden Christ, 135–39
Mamonov, Pyotr, 34
Mandelstam, Nadezhda, 234
Mann, Thomas, 209
Masina, Giulietta, 109–112, 192n
Melville, Jean-Pierre, 8
Menzel, Jiří, 126
Mercouri, Melina, 192n
Mikhalkov, Nikita, 16
Miller, Arthur, 166
Mizoguchi, Kenji, 151
Monicelli, Mario, 108
Montaigne, Michel de, 1

Monteverdi, Claudio, 101
Moore, Lucie, 251–52
Morgenstern, Janusz, 46
Movin, Lisbeth, 165–66
Mozart, Wolfgang Amadeus, 90
Muhlstein, Anka, 238n
Mullen, Peter, 7n
Mumford, Lewis, 253
Munk, Kaj, 169, 170
Muratova, Kira, 7, 219–26, 228, 235
   The Asthenic Syndrome, 221
   Brief Encounters, 220
   A Long Farewell, 220
   Three Stories, 222–25
Murnau, Friedrich Wilhelm, 243
Musorgsky, Modeste, 25

Nesterov, Mikhail, 210
Nicholas II, Tsar, 238, 239
Nielsen, Carl, 170
Nietzsche, Friedrich, 5, 255
Norwid, Cyprian, 44
Nowell-Smith, Geoffrey, 111

Olesen, Ole, 160
Olmi, Ermanno, 108
   I Fidanzati, 126–27
   Il Posto, 126
   The Tree of Wooden Clogs, 128–130

Pagliero, Marcello, 115
Panfilov, Gleb, 16
Parajanov, Sergei
   The Colour of Pomegranates, 15, 219
   Shadows of Our Forgotten Ancestors, 14, 219
Pascal, Blaise, 69, 123n
Pasolini, Pier Paolo, 108, 123
   Accatone, 123
   Arabian Nights, 125
   The Canterbury Tales, 125
   The Decameron, 125
   The Gospel According to St Matthew, 124–25, 200

   Salò, 126
   Scouting in Palestine, 124
   Teorema, 123
Pasternak, Boris, 25, 210
Pawlikowski, Pawel, 7n, 40
   Ida, 40n
Peter the Great, 25, 238
Pialat, Maurice, 8
Piccoli, Michel, 189n
Piesiewicz, Krzysztof, 54
Pinal, Silvia, 192, 192n, 194–99
Platonov, Andrei, 21–22
Polanski, Roman, 41
Pudovkin, Vsevolod, 19
Pushkin, Alexander, 18, 25
Putin, Vladimir, 217–18, 218n

Rabal, Francisco, 182–83, 195
Raphael, 238, 252
Reinhardt, Max, 10
Reitz, Edgar, 8
Rey, Fernando, 198n
Richter, Gerhardt, 247
Robinson, Ian, 1, 254
Rohmer, Eric, 8, 68–72
   Ma Nuit Chez Maud/My Night at Maud's, 69–72
Rohrwacher, Alice, 7n
Romm, Mikhail, 27–28
Rossellini, Renzo, 122
Rossellini, Roberto, 36, 108–123, 123n
   Europe, 51, 123n
   The Flowers of St Francis, 116–17
   Germany Year Zero, 123n
   Journey in Italy/Viaggio in Italia, 113–14,
   Il Miracolo, 112
   Paisà, 115–16
   Rome Open City, 115
   Stromboli – Terra di Dio, 118–122
Rousseau, Jean-Jacques, 255
Rozanov, Vasily, 210

Rubens, Peter Paul, 3, 252
Ruskin, John, 254
Rye, Preben Lerdorff, 170

Sanders, George, 113
Seneca, 1
Santayana, George, 1–2, 253–54
Schierbeck, Poul, 170
Schrader, Paul, 7
Schubert, Franz, 101
Scob, Edith, 200
Scorsese, Martin, 7, 152
Serebrennikov, Kirill
  The Disciple/The Student, 212, 218, 218n
Seton, Marie, 29–30
Seyrig, Delphine, 201n
Shakespeare, William, 1–2, 177, 237, 253
  Hamlet, 24
Shapiro, James, 2
Shepitko, Larissa, 16–17, 227
  The Ascent, 16
Shestov, Lev, 210
Shostakovich, Dmitri, 25
Shukshin, Vassily, 16
Sjöström, Victor, 145
Skolimowski, Jerzy, 41
Smirnov, Andrey, 227
Sokurov, Alexander, 7, 219, 234–48
  Confession: From the Diary of a Naval Commander, 236
  Father and Son, 236
  Faust, 242–48
  Moloch, 237
  Mother and Son, 242
  Russian Ark, 237–40
  Second Circle, 236
  Spiritual Voices, 236
  The Sun, 237
  Taurus, 237
  Whispering Pages, 236

Solonitsyn, Anatoly, 17, 227
Solovyov, Vladimir, 210
Solzhenitsyn, Alexander, 241
Spellman, Cardinal, 113
Spinoza, Baruch, 36
Spufford, Francis, 232
Stalin, Josef, 24, 229, 231, 238n
Stok, Danusia, 56
Strindberg, August, 141–42
Strugatsky Brothers, 18, 232
Swift, Daniel, 1
Sydow, Max von, 148, 150

Tarkovsky, Andrei, 6, 17–19, 103, 219, 227, 229, 235, 24–49
  Andrei Roublev, 13–14, 34, 152
  The Mirror, 17, 249–50
  Nostalghia, 18
  The Sacrifice, 18
  Stalker, 18
Taubman, Jane, 220
Terekhova, Margarita, 249
Tertzieff, Laurent, 199
Thomas, Keith, 165n
Thulin, Ingrid, 144, 154, 156
Tikhon, Father, 218n
Tolstoy, Alexei, 25
Tolstoy, Leo, 100, 102, 209
Trevor-Roper, H.R., 165n
Trier, Joachim, 7n
Trier, Lars von, 7, 36, 164
  Breaking the Waves, 164
Trintignant, Jean-Louis, 69–72
Truffaut, François, 68
Tsivian, Yuri, 29
Tsvetayeva, Marina, 210
Turgenev, Ivan, 209
Turrent, Tomás Pérez, 191, 197, 207
Tybjerg, Casper, 159–60
Tykwer, Tom, 239n

Uchitel, Alexey, 218n

Van Gogh, Vincent, 4,
Verdi, Giuseppe, 4, 130n
Verley, Bernard, 200–02
Vertov, Dziga, 19–22
   The Eleventh Year, 21
   Man With a Movie Camera, 20
Vidor, King, 7
Visconti, Luchino, 108
Voltaire, 255

Wagner, Richard, 4, 10–11
Wajda, Andrzej, 41
   Ashes and Diamonds, 41–45
Wallin, Johan Olof, 146
Weil, Simone, 123n
Welles, Orson, 29
Wenders, Wim, 8
Wojtyła, Karol Jósef
   (Pope John Paul II), 39, 46
Wood, Robin, 155

Yankovsky, Oleg, 249
Yeltsin, Boris, 217
Yusovsky, Iosif, 25

Zanussi, Krzysztof, 41–52, 61
   Camouflage, 49
   From a Far Country, 46
   Illumination, 47–48
   Life as a Fatal Sexually-transmitted Disease, 49–52
   Persona Non Grata, 50–52
   Spiralia, 49–52
   The Structure of Crystal, 47
Zaorski. Janusz, 46
Zavattini, Cesare, 106, 131
Zeiler, Johannes, 243
Zhdanov, Andrei, 24
Żuławski, Andrzej, 41
Zvyagintsev, Andrey
   Leviathan, 212–17